Tales from the Tailgate:

From the Fan who's seen 'em all!

Stephen J. Koreivo

www.collegefootballfan.com

authorHOUSE®

AuthorHouse™
1663 Liberty Drive
Bloomington, IN 47403
www.authorhouse.com
Phone: 1-800-839-8640

First published by AuthorHouse 8/10/2011

ISBN: 978-1-4634-1685-0 (hc)
ISBN: 978-1-4634-1686-7 (sc)
ISBN: 978-1-4634-1687-4 (e)

Library of Congress Control Number: 2011909339

Printed in the United States of America

This book is printed on acid-free paper.

I dedicate this book to my wife Laurie, my daughter Alex and my son Eric for the times they joined me at some of these games over the years and for those times when I ventured out on some weekends without them. I also thank them for tolerating the amount of time I spend on the computer to update my website and to write this book.

I couldn't have done this without their patience, love, and support.

Contents

Tailgate party at the Meadowlands in Lot 17B: an unidentified tailgater and Tommy Bednar of Boonton, NJ partake of a van full of beer balls before the Notre Dame – Navy game of 1980.

Acknowledgments

This adventure and this book could not have been done without the help and support of a lot of friends and family who helped me enjoy these many years of traveling and attending 402 college football games since I started doing this in 1979. Many of them have joined me at games to be quoted in my weekly Game Reviews on www.collegefootballfan.com as my Guest Game Analysts (GGA's). I got to stay at their homes and tailgate with them when I went out of town to visit while attending games. Many helped with input, editing, and proofreading of my drafts to help finalize my manuscript for publication. Special thanks go out to my long-time friends since the beginning: my Auburn connection, Charlie and Lynda Murren, and to my Penn State connection, John and Kelle Massimilla. I've attended games with them longer and more often with them than with anyone else.

Also among the many are Steve Ciesla, (Juniata/Montclair) who's traveled many beaten paths with me; Bob "Polecat" Marcello and Kenny Gallagher who attended most of the games at The Meadowlands; Mary Kay and Gunther Neumann (this started with them at the URI vs. Delaware game in 1979); Charlie and Laura Roberts (Lehigh and PSU); Seton Fred and Emilie Bacchetta; the Emmy-award winner James Lewis III and his wife Judy, a Cincinnati Bearcat; fence-climbing Amy and Frank Lorito, my Fresno connection; Nancy and Bruce Wylie, parents of GGA's Matt and Ben; my Brother Knights of Columbus from Boonton's Walter J. Barrett Council 1954; all the friends and friends of friends that showed up at many tailgate parties in Lot # 17B at the Meadowlands over the years; Les Di Vite, Boonton Bomber and proud Seton Hall grad; my late father Allen who took us kids to the Army-Navy game in 1973; Terry and Sue Rubritz who took care of our big bar bill somewhere in College Park; Tommy, Linda, Staff

Sgt. Brian, and Scott Bramhall; Tracy and Dave Headden, avid tailgaters; Florida Gator Andy Jacobson; Mike and Pam Morgan of South Carolina; Bernie Olszyk and his daughter Heather who dwelled at 708 Comstock at Syracuse U.; Rich and Laurie (the other Saint Laurie) Williams; my late mother Kathleen and late step-father Bill Hefferle who made even Rutgers-Colgate interesting (in a future book maybe); Bob " I don't wanna go home" McKenna; The Brigade of Midshipman (1974-1975); Jack Hessler of Michigan State and Long Beach St; Stash "Stanley" Greshko and Ken "Kippy" Carroll, Boonton Bombers to the end; Chris of Penn and Jill of UCLA and their kids Emily and Nick; fellow Juniatians Pat and Joan Daly; Tim Potopa of Kutztown State; Roger Arnold (Juniata) and family from Bedford, PA; Tony Lagratta (Juniata) and Dane Taylor (Notre Dame) and all the tailgaters from Allegany (Maryland) Community College; unnamed dates to protect the innocent; PSU's Mark Massimilla and Diane Turchetta; former Richmond Spider T.J. Nelligan; Bob Jones, "The Rock" of Slippery Rock and family; the Krajewski's of Secaucus; the Fiore family of Altoona whose mobile home got us to and from Iowa City; Alpha Wire drinking buddy Greg Hardman; Ned Ehrlich, Juniata trainer and van driver; Jim Buckley, Cal alum, who also helped me with ideas to develop this book; the bus driver from the Boston Transit Authority who got us to the BC-Stanford game on time after our train cancellation; Rutgers fan Frank and Jessie Scarpa; UT Longhorn via Juniata - Todd Kulp; the Esoda family of NC State; Joe and Kelly Massimilla, Nittany Lions; Tennessee Vols Mary Jean and Bruce Shannon; Daryl, Kim, and Whitney Reigel (Juniata, Pitt, and Maryland); Ms. Auburn Megan Murren and siblings Charlie IV, Laura, and Danny; Penn State fans Jimmy and the late Elizabeth "Biffy" Malayter; the late Gary Smith, Georgia Bulldog fan; Mizzou's Tom Richardson; my Juniata friends Toni Anne Svetkovich and Cheryl Ondrejek; Nittany Lions Kirsten, Brian, and Sarah Massimilla; Cousin Aimee, Villanova; Al Warwick, my first NC State host; Boilermaker Barbara Glazar and husband Denny; Ohio State connection and swimming champ Greg Masica; Gil Schlerf, Beth Griffin, and Steve Smith – business associates in Delaware; Cousin Mike and Maureen (Rutgers and Delaware); W.H. "Bud"Griest, 1996 Chairman of the Rose Bowl Committee; *Kermit the Frog*; Don Di Vite; Tony and Brenda, tailgaters; the nuts in the middle out in Fresno – Frankie, Sam, and Marie Chimienti; the Rafferty's, Bonnefond's, Costa's, McDonald's, Leyden's, Groome's, Sullivan's, and other families of Byram Twp; Megan Ward, who brings what everyone looks forward to at our big tailgate parties; Cousin Vickie; Mr. San Diego State, Tom Ables and his wife Nancy; Dave Plati, SID, University of Colorado; my Tulsa connection, Joe and Tyler Pistoia from Long Beach, California; John Martens, brought cold weather from Oswego State to West Point; the SMU Pony Club; the Keyes and Graper families of TCNJ; Aunt Connie and Uncle Tony Cavalli in Orlando; Paul Chambers and friends of the Nevada Wolfpack; former Michigan cheerleader Dave Imrick; the Kalmbach family, MSU Spartans; fellow Juniata alum and Penn State fans John and Carol Van Horn; Alex Nagler, Stony Brook Press; Phil Hess, Director of Athletic Communications at Stony Brook U; Carol and Mike Barish of LSU along with family and friends of "Stinky"; Spencer Jacobson of UNC and her sister Bailey; WVU fan John Kuhn; "War Eagle" to Rick Selleck and his family in Memphis; and to Al Grant, no shrinking Violet from NYU, Tina Webb, a Penn Quaker, and Professor of Journalism Jeff Seglin of Emerson U. originally from Boonton, all for proofreading. Thanks to Mike Lester and Bill Garner who allowed me to use their artwork from some of my favorite game program covers from my extensive collection. Also, thanks to many other unnamed friends and acquaintances met over the years at various games where we got to enjoy some fun times together.

Introduction

"College football—what better way to spend an autumn afternoon?" That catch-phrase of ABC's Chris Schenkel always stirs memories of growing up watching NCAA football on television every fall Saturday afternoon. As a kid, I would tune into the games to not only witness the exciting action on the field, but to experience emotions from the sights and sounds surrounding the games - horns, drumbeats, school colors, cheerleaders, card sections, chants, feisty mascots, and passionate crowds – and I wanted to experience it all in person some day.

After graduation from Juniata College in 1979, I had made myself part of it, practically every fall weekend since. Without an actual plan in place, I'd eventually see half of the big-time teams play. Graduate school forced me to cut back on my favorite pastime from 1987-1992, but by then I began to look for a quality instead of quantity -- in life as well as in football. In the late 1980s, my marriage to a beautiful, forgiving woman (eventually referred to as the self-proclaimed, "St. Laurie") changed life as I had known it. We settled into a typical but happy, home life. Two wonderful kids were born and changed life even more during the 1990s. Through all of the typical, ongoing, lifestyle changes, I still managed, more often than not, to join up with friends or to bring the family along on a fall Saturday for "what better way to spend an autumn afternoon?"

Before the 2000 college football season began, I typically perused team schedules to check out what games I wanted to attend. I realized that I could possibly see nine teams that year that I hadn't seen before. That's when the idea hit me. Just how many D-1 teams had I seen? I charted my personal history and found that I had already seen more than half of the 117 Division 1A teams play. Add the nine new teams in 2000 and less than 50 Division

1A teams remained to see them all in person. Could such an unimagined goal be possible? Could I actually get to see every 1A team play in person at least once in my lifetime? Had anyone else ever done it? I didn't care. This was something that I'd *love* to do. It wouldn't be easy based on time, some extra travel, growing responsibilities, and of course, money.

I'd read about baseball fans making trips across the United States and Canada to see as many Major and Minor League teams play in as many venues as possible. Why couldn't I try something similar with my own great sports infatuation -- college football? What was stopping me from seeing every one of the 117 Division 1-A college football teams play at least once? Of course, I couldn't do it in one season. Though it might take years, I knew it would be an experience to savor. Also with a wife and two kids, I'd have to figure out how I could get them to buy into my plan cutting into quality, family time and the household budget. Realize my endeavor wasn't to make it to every stadium. That would be divorce by now no matter how saintly my wife may be. Someday maybe I'll consider it, but for now I'm glad I took one team (and sometimes two) at a time. This would be difficult enough.

I started to put together plans looking at future schedules - where I could drive to, where I'd possibly have to fly to, who I could stay with, etc, etc. I set out to get this done. Some close to me had doubts. Of course, I couldn't have continued my Goal, or maybe I should say "habit", over the years without the blessings of the aforementioned St. Laurie, patron saint of *college* football widows.

For more than thirty years now, attending college football games in person has provided me with memorable, fun-filled, rewarding experiences. I've witnessed great games, visited new places, made great, new friends, enjoyed some memorable travel experiences, and shared a lot of good laughs along the way. I will always cherish both the historical and personal memories, but being able to share these "adventures" with other college football fans makes it all even more fun. This book takes you back with me through over thirty years on this surreal trip, my ultimate tailgate tour to see 'em all!

So buckle up your chinstrap, or crack open a few cold ones, or both if you can fit the cans through your facemask. I hope you will enjoy reading about this as much as I've enjoyed doing it.

Note: The numbers you will see listed with each school, for example, "(1) Army" *are based on the chronological order toward The Goal. The numbers aren't rankings, but the order in which I checked off each team during my march to get to see every team. Keep in mind I've seen many several times as*

I've attended 402 games from 1979 to January 2011. Each story is basically about the first time I watched a particular team play. In the meantime, South Alabama, Texas State, and UT San Antonio recently announced they will join the Division-1A (sorry, the Football Bowl Subdivision) fray in 2011. As I'm editing my final draft, the University of Massachusetts announced they would join the Mid American Conference in 2012 and play home games at Gillette Stadium. That will be an easy weekend trip to New England. Strike asterisks now for team numbers 121-124. I intend to see 'em all - eventually! You can track all this on my website, www.collegefootballfan.com.*

America's Teams

(1) Army vs. (2) Navy
December 2, 1972

Philadelphia - My introduction to this classic rivalry and to "big-time" college football started on a low, wooden, end zone bleacher seat on an unseasonably warm December afternoon at John F. Kennedy Stadium in Philadelphia. My father said he "wrangled" four tickets somehow to the sellout between 5-4 Army and 4-6 Navy. We drove three hours to Philly from north Jersey with extra warm clothes and bundles of blankets. We watched caped, gray-clad Cadets and Midshipmen in woolen, navy blue overcoats march along the cinder track and onto the plush, green field before us as we shed layers of jackets and sweatshirts on that unbearably hot, December Saturday. The Corps of Cadets formed their companies on the playing field to cheer for both teams, led in unison by semaphore from the upper deck of the host venue. From signals above, the Corps launched into traditional pre-game cheers, but half-heartedly for the opposition. Army cadets saluted their greatest foe with a muffled, nonchalant cheer of "N-A-V-Y. Go Navy! Fight!" Then on the next semaphore command, they performed a sharp, military about-face to their side of the stadium to the rousing applause and cheers of the Army faithful. The Corps took on new life. Out came their booming cadence brazen and bold for their own: "A-R-M-Y! GooOOO ARMY! BEAT NAVY!" Throngs for Army stood and cheered wildly. The Corps marched to the empty seats awaiting them, but the parade soon broke off into a run as cadets of all classes looked to meet up with fellow classmates in the stands. Plebes are responsible for the spirit on game day.

The Mids' march-on follows, and it's evident—"nobody does march on a ship"! And if you listened closely, after the Mids raise their hats to their alternative cheer of "BEAT ARMY!", their hands drop hats back on to their heads before they align their thumbs along seams of their trousers with the muffled order from within the Brigade of, "Drop! Trou!" - inside humor from the Mids who speak in code laced with acronyms and abbreviations.

All the traditions of college football and more unfolded before us that day. Miniature tanks and ships fired bursts of blanks. Army Mules and the Navy Goats were handled along the sidelines. Cheerleaders fired up spirit on both sides. The Army band and Navy Drum Corps played their respective fight songs as Cadets and Mids sang along. They volleyed cheers at one another. The 3rd Infantry Old Guard Fife and Drum Corps from The Capitol presented the Colors as part of the pre-game festivities that year.

As for my first game action, Navy took a 12-0 lead in the first quarter, but Army overcame the deficit in the third as running back Bob Hines raced 43 yards for a touchdown, and a blocked field goal by Army's Tim Pfister resulted in an 84-yard touchdown return by Scott Beatty. A 21-yard run by Bruce Simpson and a field goal by Jim Barclay put the finishing touches on Army's 23-15 win in the 73rd edition of *college football's greatest rivalry*. The spirit and excitement witnessed on television turned out to be more intense and more colorful in person than I had envisioned.

Extra points: In 1974, I became a member of the Brigade of Midshipmen. Thanks to my underwhelming skills in math and science, I stayed for only two years. I did make the Lightweight football team, now known as Sprint Football. However, since my weight hovered seven pounds over the limit at 165, I could only practice.

I continued to attend Navy football games over the years whether at the Meadowlands, in "Crabtown" (Annapolis), versus Army in Philly, or on the road somewhere to see the Mids play. Every college football fan should experience an Army game at West Point or a Navy game in Annapolis at least once.

I've seen both Army and Navy each play in over 40 games against various teams since, some more eye-opening and thrilling (like the 28-24 Army win over Navy in 1996 that landed both teams in much-deserved bowl games) since that first meeting in 1972. It turned out that the first two eventual "steps" on my long road to achieve my eventual goal started with the greatest of all traditional rivalries in college football! No other can top it.

Turncoat and Burnout
(3) Notre Dame vs. Navy
November 2, 1974

Philadelphia – I grew up as a Notre Dame fan. On New Years Eve 1973, I had run out of my family's house into freezing weather in just a t-shirt, shorts, and socks to celebrate the Irish's 24-23 win over Alabama in the Sugar Bowl to win the 1973 National Championship!

The 1966 ND-Michigan State game was a key moment in my early life. I made a mental note before the "game of the century" that I was never going to forget that day. My father drove us to my grandparent's home thirty miles away so we could watch the game in *living color*. I read every Notre Dame book I could get my hands on, so I was steeped into the history and tradition of Fighting Irish football. I was obsessed with the notion of playing football for Notre Dame some day. At 5'9", 165 lbs after high school graduation, however, I wasn't even "Rudy" Ruediger. Neither big nor fast enough, I wanted to play ball somewhere, and a couple of small schools showed interest, but when an offer came through, though not for football, I opted for the U.S. Naval Academy as my path to the future. I actually looked Navy Head Coach George Welsh right in the eye one day after some Plebe Summer Pep rally and told him I wanted to play football for Navy. He just stared back.

November 2, 1974, became my personal day of infamy as I did something I never dreamed I would or could ever do. Navy "hosted" Notre Dame that year at Veterans Stadium in Philly. Finally, after all those years as a die-hard Notre Dame fan, I was going to get to see *my* Irish play! "*Cheer, cheer for old Notre Dame…*" I was about to see the defending national champs for whom I'd rooted so hard on that previous New Year's Eve live and in-person. Only this time, for the first time ironically, I couldn't claim them as *my* team. Since I was now a Midshipman, the Irish were the dreaded opposition. My *new* team, Navy, had to beat them. There would be no cheers "for old Notre Dame" from me for the first time ever. The 6-1 Irish came in as 30-point favorites. We were just 2-5. The Brigade was pumped up for this one, having fallen to the Irish during the eleven *long* years since Heisman winner Roger Staubach last played for Navy.

In Second Company, we approached the portal leading on to the Vet Stadium turf for the pre-game march-on. ND's male cheerleaders held their female counterparts over the entrance to show 4,000 Navy guys, especially about 1,200 female-deprived Plebes, what we were missing. Many jumped for a "touch" even though the targets were far beyond leaping capabilities. After march-on, we literally climbed the outfield wall at the Vet into our designated seats. Many boosted fellow classmates to get over the railing. One First classman, affectionately known as "Squatty" to his classmates, stepped up on a faucet head to climb the wall, but his weight tore the spigot off and spray burst out from the broken pipe sending a few guys running to avoid sitting in saturated Service Dress Blues during the game.

As one, four thousand raucous Midshipman -- including one former, recent, die-hard Fighting Irish fan -- were pumped up for today's game. Despite the daunting task ahead, we fed off a mutual appetite for the long-awaited win. We were caught up in it. Despite my years of dedication to Notre Dame, I was converted! There was no way I could root for my former favorite team on this particular day. Today, I was Navy all the way. I was a "turncoat" and proud of it—proud to be part of the Brigade. We stood and cheered our team throughout the first half to surprising success.

We forced an Irish fumble early to give ourselves good field position. We went *bananas* as kicker Steve Dykes nailed a 48-yard field goal in the first period for a 3-0 lead. The defense, led by All-American linebacker Chet Moeller, held the defending national champs in check throughout the first half. They allowed quarterback Tommy Clements only four completions on sixteen attempts, intercepting him twice. We actually held that slim lead through halftime. We Mids remained standing throughout the entire game.

Every big play, especially on defense, sent us into an uproar. We were fired up and going crazy! We went even more bonkers as our teammates on the field took a 6-0 lead over the big boys from South Bend when Dykes converted his second field goal from 37 yards away in the third quarter. Classmate Dave Hines and I embraced and jumped up and down with enthusiasm. Salivating for Blue and Gold victory after eleven years of Irish domination, we began to anticipate the taste of victory—big victory! Mass hysteria, school spirit, and a proud tradition morphed into something bigger than just eleven guys out on the playing field. Low-life Plebes, like me, and high-and-mighty "Firsties" (seniors) jumped and cheered together. This was our Navy team, and we believed in nothing less than victory. Our smaller, undermanned, outclassed 2-5 team was taking it to the vaunted Irish. However, the tide began to turn.

Early in the fourth quarter, Irish defensive end Jim Stock made two big plays on consecutive downs by breaking up a reverse for a loss, and then sacking Navy quarterback Mike Roban back at our three. Punter John

Stufflebeem, who had a great day punting for the Mids, booted it to the forty-nine, but Irishman Ron Goodman returned it to our twenty-seven. Five plays later, Notre Dame finally put the ball into the end zone on a low, five-yard pass from Clements to sliding tight end Pete Demmerle in back of the end zone. The Irish "Subway Alum" finally had their chance to cheer, but not as loud as Navy had that day. After they converted the extra point for the 7-6 lead, it was probably more a sigh of relief than a cheer.

Navy still scrapped on the field, and the Brigade still anticipated a comeback, but with 2:12 remaining, ND's freshman defensive back Randy Harrison picked off Mike Roban's pass and returned it forty yards for a touchdown to seal an Irish victory, 14-6. Though discouraged, we were proud of our team. At game's conclusion, we sang *"Navy Blue and Gold"* with more pride that day than any other time I could remember as a Midshipman. We were dejected, but proud of the effort of the team and of the spirit of the Brigade that day.

Soon after this game, Notre Dame's great, successful football coach, Ara Parseghian, decided to call it a career at South Bend. After many big victories and two national championships, a close call against Navy revealed the enormity of pressure to win at probably the most famous of all college football programs. I was a *turncoat*. Ara felt *burnt-out*. It was the end of an era – for both of us.

Extra point: Fast forward: In 2007, as I left Beaver Stadium with my daughter Alex after Penn State defeated that traditional Irish nemesis, Purdue, I heard the last two plays of triple overtime between Notre Dame and Navy on Westwood One Radio. An interference call went against the Mids on Notre Dame's two-point conversion. On the ensuing conversion attempt, Navy stuffed the Irish run. That day in South Bend, Navy had *finally* beaten the Irish, 46-44. After 43 straight losses, the streak finally ended. I cheered!

I still like to see the Irish win, and I root for them against many other foes, but over the years, the Nittany Lions and the Mids, despite my exodus from Navy after two years, remain my two favorite football teams. When Navy finally ended that streak against the Irish, I thought back to that November day in 1974. In October 2010 after personally witnessing seven losses to Notre Dame, I watched a dominant Navy team sink the Irish myself, 35-17. *Go Navy!*

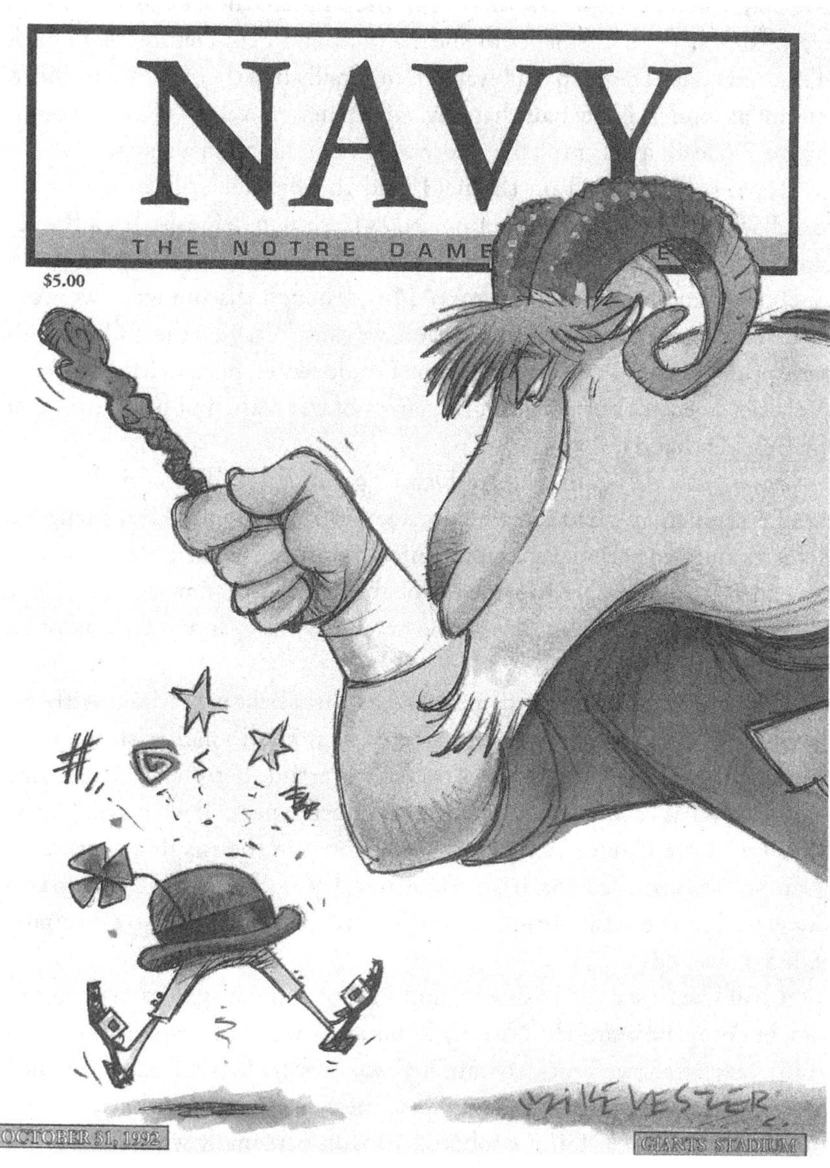

This 1992 Navy-Notre Dame program cover by Mike Lester depicts Navy clubbing the Irish, but that wishful thinking didn't occur until Navy ended their 43-game losing streak against the Irish in 2007.

Culture Shock!
(4) Georgia at (5) Auburn
November 18, 1978

Auburn, Alabama - "Oneonta?" A short, dark-haired guy curled his lip and scrunched up his nose with a wide grin while squinting at the letters on my t-shirt during a workout out at the Lakeland Hills YMCA during the summer of 1978.

"Huh? What are you talking about?" I replied. Charles Murren III pointed to the name of my current college on my bright, yellow t-shirt. How he got "Oneonta" out of J-U-N-I-A-T-A, I don't know, but it began the start of a long friendship. At least he didn't pronounce it "Juanita" as did many others at first glance of the name.

That day in the gym, Charlie was home on summer vacation from Auburn University. Like many north Jersey kids, unless you went to local Montclair State, William Paterson, or Seton Hall, you most likely went out of state in pursuit of higher education. "One thing you can give George Wallace credit for," he once told me, "is that he kept tuitions affordable in Alabama."

After years of watching Interstate 287 being built behind his home in Montville, NJ, Charlie studied for his degree in Civil Engineering at Auburn. During that summer, we talked about school, women, the future, football, working out, and other important stuff, like my future trip to Auburn for a football weekend. The perfect opportunity presented itself on the weekend before Thanksgiving, 1978. Not only would the Georgia Bulldogs, Auburn's longest, traditional SEC rival be visiting "the Plains", but Juniata was one of the rare schools organized on a trimester schedule. My semester break would begin the weekend before Thanksgiving and last through the holiday. To get to Auburn, I bought a cheap airline ticket for my first-ever flight to Columbus, Georgia. Al Di Vite, one of our cohorts from back in Boonton, NJ would fly down as well.

Charlie had the whole Auburn *cultural* experience planned for us. We bought beer at a local gas station - couldn't do that in Jersey or Pennsylvania. We got to ride on real construction equipment at night on a real highway under construction. I assumed this was a pre-requisite for Civil Engineering at Auburn. I figured that's why Charlie had keys. We ate dinner at the Barbeque House on Main Street in Auburn where the cooks rammed long, metal stakes through two whole chickens at a time in a big, flame-fired, brick oven. They were served up on paper plates with handfuls of sliced, dill pickles and six pieces of white bread. The combination not only tasted good, it coated our stomachs for the ensuing beer-fest, too! The next day, we glimpsed football traditions up close and personal taking a tour of the training facilities where we watched the AU Tigers getting taped before Friday's practice. Charlie pointed out sophomore running back James Brooks. He looked small for a guy I envisioned as an SEC running back, but eventually the speed of an SEC running back once he stepped on to the playing field explained everything.

Friday night, we ventured out to Toomer's Crossing for the traditional pep rally with the band and cheerleaders where trees filled up with streams of toilet paper. The cheerleaders were *nice-looking* for sure. I didn't see many like them at Navy or Juniata. At some house party on campus, we caught up with Charlie's Auburn pals who tried to intimidate by calling me a *Yankee*! I replied. "Let's go *Mets*!" That confused them. The Braves hadn't really caught on yet down South. Major League baseball hadn't quite reached central Alabama. This was SEC football country! We had a great time. We stopped by the *War Eagle Supper Club*, this great down-home, beat-up bar with bare plywood walls in the middle of the Plain where the Bellamy Brothers of "*Let Your Love Flow*" fame were appearing. Big-name band in a low-down place—ya gotta love it. Yes, sir. Charlie showed Al and me a great time during that first visit to "the loveliest village on the Plains."

Charlie had gotten us $2 student tickets for the game, another Auburn good deal. Before the game, Auburn fans greeted each other and parted from one another with an enthusiastic "War Eagle!" as if they were wishing one another "Merry Christmas!" We sat high in the stands of Jordan-Hare Stadium on the Auburn side at about the twenty yard-line, and boy, did three guys from Jersey stick out. In the south, a college football game is a happening, a high-class social event as well as a football game. When Southerners attended football games in those pre-Internet days, guys wore blazers, buttoned-down shirts, and loafers. Girls wore short, stylish dresses with low-cut tops which made for a more picturesque atmosphere than up north, where fans dress for comfort from the cold, especially in November. We wore flannel shirts, jeans, work boots, and ball caps among Auburn students dressed for a semi-formal affair. Al and I didn't know that this was a dress-up occasion – not that we would have dressed up if we did. Charlie knew the culture though. That's why he brought us. We wore beer-drinking clothes.

The Auburn band performed "*War Eagle!*" on the field. Charlie pointed out a friend of his in the band "playing" the tuba. He told us that the guy had no clue how to play the tuba at all, but marching guaranteed his friend to see all the Tiger games for free. The band needed a body to fill out certain formations on the field, so they gave him a tuba to march around with. And at Auburn, they don't even have to dot an "i"! Auburn cheerleaders chanted, *"Track 'em Tigers, just like beagles, give 'em hell you War Damn Eagles!"* And that was followed by, *"Weagle, Weagle, War Damn Eagle! Kick 'em in the butt big Blue! Hey!"* Southerners seem to like to throw a "damn" in there somewhere, like "*damn* Yankees!" Speaking of which, Charlie tried out for Auburn's amiable-looking mascot, Aubie the Tiger. In his angst to get crowd reaction, he hollered like a typical guy from Jersey, "Come on, *you guys*!" He knew he blew right away. His audience was more apt to get stirred up with "Come on, *y'all*!"

This turned out to be an emotional game for Auburn. The Tigers and Bulldogs share the longest rivalry in the Southeastern Conference. Auburn came into this game at 6-3 while the eighth-ranked 8-1 Bulldogs visited smelling sugar. A Bulldog win here and a Bama loss to Auburn the following week would mean an SEC championship and a Sugar Bowl bid for UGA! So emotionally-packed was this game for Auburn, Coach Doug Barfield pulled the old jersey *switch-a-roo* before taking the field to add a little more impetus for the Tigers. "Big Blue" sprinted back out on to the field after final preparations in the locker-room in new, bright, *orange* jerseys before Jordan-Hare Stadium's record crowd of 64,761. Attending my first Auburn game ever, it wasn't exactly Notre Dame coming out in green jerseys against USC, but it did make an absolute, enthusiastic impression among the Auburn faithful. They were fired up now, and so were Coach Barfield's Tigers, War Eagles, Plainsmen, or whatever one wanted to call the Auburn football team that day!

Georgia 's Rex Robinson converted two first-half field goals, but Auburn topped that with a 60-yard touchdown run by Joe Cribbs, who set a school rushing record that day with 250 yards. UGA held a 12-7 lead. On the very last play of the first half, AU fullback William Andrews broke off on what looked like a 47-yard TD run. He was in the clear to take it in for a score before being caught from behind by speedy, Georgia defensive back Bob Kelly at the one-yard line. Time expired to end the half. That tackle turned out to be a game-saver for the Dawgs.

Cribbs' second TD of the day on a two-yard run gave Auburn the lead at the end of the third period, 22-15. The defenses held from that point on until Willie McClendon scored for Georgia from the one with 5:18 remaining and cut the score, 22-21. A Georgia victory here would mean at least a share of the SEC championship and the Sugar Bowl. Georgia Coach Vince Dooley took a lot of heat for his next decision to kick for a tie rather than by going for two to win. Rex Robinson converted for the tie. Maybe Dooley's earlier failed attempt to go for two made him think otherwise, but the draw meant he would have to wait another week for Bear Bryant's 8-1 Tide to hopefully fall to Auburn in Birmingham. Neither Georgia nor Auburn scored again, and the contest ended in a 22-22 stalemate, the only tie I'd ever see in 1-A play. Thanks to overtime rules initiated in 1995 to determine an eventual winner, we'll never have to see a tie again. After sixty minutes of rock 'em, sock 'em, hard-hitting action with a championship on the line to boot, to finish with no winner and no loser is not only anti-climactic, it's downright depressing. A tie made sixty minutes of football such a waste. Afterwards, neither team gets to celebrate a victory, nor does either team get to agonize in defeat. Post-game parties either celebrate or agonize, but in the case of a tie, what do you party for? We made the party rounds on campus that night. Nothing memorable happened - probably because the game ended in a tie.

Extra point: Two visiting Jersey boys did not encounter the ultimate southern cultural shock until the very next morning: Charlie took Al and me to James Brown's Diner for the all-you-can-eat-southern breakfast in nearby Opelika. Grits at breakfast for guys from Jersey are not the memorable cultural cuisine reminisced about here, but they were assuredly a hot topic of discussion when we perused the menus. The ultimate culture shock took place out in the parking lot as Al and I digested outside in that warm November sun leaning against Charlie's old, green Ford Pinto. He was still talking to someone he knew inside the diner as we waited, when *lo and behold!* From across the parking lot sauntered this beautiful, gorgeous, drop-dead, knock-out, strawberry blonde! *Wow*! And she was walking unabashedly right towards us! She came right to us near that beat up Pinto with Garden State plates, smiled, and said, "Hey! How *y'all* doin'?" Al and I tried to recover quickly as our knees buckled like taking a hard, left jab from Joe Frazier. We recovered, and then looked at each other with smirks on our faces that said, "This doesn't happen back in Jersey!" And forget the "*y'all*" part! Mystified, still in shock, we were able to make small talk for a few minutes when suddenly this guy, supposedly her *boyfriend*, shows up and says, "Hey! How y'all doin'? " Now this definitely NEVER happens nor would ever happen back in dear old NJ. There would be screaming, cursing, ranting, or crying, and things would eventually turn physical. Something would have escalated as we probably had no right to be talking to, no less approached by, a total *"Knock-out"* like this one anywhere near her significant other! It was surreal! Where were we?

On the ride back to Auburn with Al and me still dazed, Charlie provided his insight with two words. "Holy Rollers," he deadpanned. Now, I go to Mass on Sundays, but if I ever had the notion to stay way down South in the Land of Cotton back then, I think it would have been very worthwhile to attend a few prayer meetings in the Church of the Holy Rollers, too! However, life tended to be a bit too slow for me down south at that time, and I yearned to go back home to get stuck in traffic. I just wasn't ready to make a move down there – too many cultural changes for me.

First Season Ticket Package
(6) Syracuse vs. (7) West Virginia
September 15, 1979

East Rutherford, NJ – In its fourth year of existence in 1979, Giants Stadium at the Meadowlands announced a college football schedule made up primarily of Division 1 schools. The demolition of Syracuse's ancient Archbold Stadium, built in 1907, was complete. The construction of a brand new, indoor football/basketball arena, the Carrier Dome, on the Syracuse campus in upstate New York was under way. The Orangemen were without a permanent home during the 1979 season, and the Meadowlands obliged to aid the nomads.

The Meadowlands schedule included Syracuse "home" games versus West Virginia and Penn State. With Rutgers now making its move as a full-fledged D-1 Independent, the Scarlet Knights would host a game against nearby Army. To complete its inaugural, college season football package, Garden State Bowl II was slated for December 15. The opportunities to see legitimate, major college football games in NJ for the first time in such a first class venue enticed this college football fan to buy the total package year after year.

On this day, the West Virginia Mountaineers called on the Meadowlands to visit the Orangemen in a traditional battle between eastern rivals. Without conference affiliations, teams played for as many wins as possible to earn bowl bids as Independents. The 76,000-seat venue easily engulfed the mere 10,366 that showed up that day. Charlie Murren, home from Auburn, and I listened to some old guy razzing a young, tall, geeky, SU, pain-in-the-ass fan named Myron. The old guy would croon, "My-**ron**! Hey! Myyy-**rron**!" We didn't know what instigated the old guy, but he kept at it throughout the game which turned out to be a snooze of a contest during the first half, so the razzing became the primary entertainment. With so few fans in attendance, the old guy's crooning could be heard above everything else.

Sophomore kicker Gary Anderson, who hailed from South Africa, booted two FGs for SU in the first half. Syracuse QB Bill Hurley left in the second period with an ankle injury, but Dave Warner subbed and threw a 38-yard TD pass to Art Monk, listed in the SU Grid program as a running back. He followed with a fantastic, leaping catch on the two-point conversion to give the Orange a 21-0 lead at the half. Mountaineer QB Oliver Luck finally put the visitors on the board in the fourth with a 19-yard TD pass to Ced Thomas. WVU's next drive went for 57 yards with Eldridge Dixon bulling over from the one. Now trailing, 21-14, the Mountaineers recovered a Syracuse fumble at SU's 30, but officials called the play down by contact. The Orange took advantage of the break with mighty Joe Morris, Syracuse's small, powerful, sophomore running back who ran for 166 yards that day, getting it down to the one. WVU held there, but Anderson converted his third FG of the day. Final score: 24-14, Orangemen on top.

Two-point conversion: Over the years, Meadowlands season ticket packages brought some unreachable college teams to the east so I could see them play. The convenience allowed me to attend games involving teams that would have taken me a lot longer to reach my eventual Goal. Also on that turf looking back at this game, some pretty significant names of future NFL lore performed on that day. Joe Morris played eight years including two Pro Bowl seasons in the same stadium for the New York Giants. He led the rushing attack for the Giants' first ever Super Bowl team in 1986. SU's Art Monk would spend most of his 18 Hall of Fame, NFL years as a wide receiver for the Washington Redskins amassing 12,700 yards and 68 TDs. Gary Anderson kicked footballs for the Pittsburgh Steelers for 24 seasons. Oliver Luck not only played for the Houston Oilers, today he's the Athletic Director at West Virginia. His son, Andrew, now stars at QB for a very good Stanford program.

Oh yeah, on the way out, we saw tall, geeky Myron about to get his ass whipped out in the parking lot by some stout WVU redneck who had a few beers too many. That Myron just seemed to irk everybody he crossed paths with that day.

The end of the beginning
(8) Rutgers at Princeton
September 29, 1979

Princeton, NJ - In 1979, I ventured out to finally see my home state's university, Rutgers, play for the first time. They had recently become college football's newest Division 1 program. The game would be the next-to-last of the oldest of all college football rivalries as the Scarlet Knights and the Princeton Tigers met at Princeton's Palmer Stadium for the very last time. The 1980 game in New Brunswick would be the last meeting scheduled between the two schools in this most ancient of all college football rivalries started 110 years before at Neilson Field on College Avenue in New Brunswick, NJ, "*The Birthplace of College Football.*" On November 6, 1869, Rutgers defeated Princeton, 6-4. As Charlie and I approached the 45,725-seat concrete venue that opened in 1914, he said, "So *this* has always been so close by." A little over an hour drive from where we lived, Charlie mentioned he'd attended college games at large, historic venues as far away as South Bend and Auburn, but he never realized until then that a stadium of comparable size had even existed so close to us.

Though Princeton led the overall series with a record of 53-15-1, Rutgers held a 10-8-1 edge since 1960. Under current Head Coach Frank Burns, RU was on a three-game winning streak with his personal record of 4-1-1 against Princeton. The separation between a school becoming a big program recruiting more scholarship players and one bent on maintaining scholarly traditions had already been determined. However, aside from being the first to set foot on a playing field and to win that historic game, there was not much more that the Rutgers' football program could proudly claim as a long and storied tradition.

On this overcast September day, the Tigers held on midway through the third period when the Scarlet Knights finally broke the game open with a pass from Ed McMichael to TE Brian Crockett as the Knights went on to win, 38-14. After the final tick on the clock, the natural surface in Palmer hosted the most bizarre, post-game "celebration" I have ever witnessed! No exuberance or jubilation. No back-patting of players. No surrounding the coach to carry him off the field for one final triumph at Palmer vaulting their team forward into the much-desired big-time. Instead, RU fans separated into small groups to pound the hell out of one another - not Princeton fans, but fellow Rutgers fans! The post-game celebration entailed getting someone else on the turf and pummeling the *crap* out of him. Was this indicative of future celebrations for victories at the Division 1 level? Was this a new tradition the Knights would bring with them to "big-time" college football? I never saw anything like it before or since.

Extra point: Princeton maintains its staid, Ivy League status with pride. Rutgers stepped up into D1 with the battle cry, "If we can only keep the best players in New Jersey to play for Rutgers, we'll have a great football program!" That mantra has lasted for many years.

College Football History 102
(9) Penn State vs. Syracuse
October 20, 1979

East Rutherford - The second game of the 1979 Meadowlands college football package featured perennial, eastern power Penn State visiting Syracuse during the Orangemen's nomadic season. My first Penn State game at the Meadowlands included nothing particularly memorable, but little did I have any inkling that day that this would be only the start of a long, steadfast journey following the Nittany Lions for many years to come.

PSU entered this contest at 3-2 with Head Coach Joe Paterno in his 14th season running the program, considered to be a pretty significant tenure at the time for any head college football coach at one particular school. The Orangemen came in at 4-2 in a rivalry once known as the "battle for Eastern Supremacy." Penn State, however, dominated the seven previous meetings and continued to do the same right from the beginning of this one.

Syracuse played in its second *yawner* of the season in front of a crowd at Giants Stadium, but this time they put 53,789 to sleep - five times as many as they had against West Virginia. The Nittany Lions, who fielded an awesome offensive line anchored by Mike Munchak and Irv Pankey, drove 83 yards on the opening series. Booker Moore powered over from the one. In the second period, Moore did the same from two on a drive following Gary Anderson's missed 44-yarder. QB Dayle Tate finished off the subsequent Nittany Lion drive with a 17-yard TD pass to Tom Donovan after a Lance Mehl pass interception. He followed with his second TD pass from ten yards out to TE Brad Scovill before the half ended with PSU in front, 28-0. Besides Ken Mandeville's 7-yard TD run for SU to start the third, the only Orange highlight of the game could be attributed to Art Monk's sixth catch of the day that made him the career reception leader at

Syracuse. Tate and Scovill connected for another TD in the quarter. With a 35-7 Penn State lead, the fans who fell asleep before the fourth woke up after the game was over and saw the same score as the final.

After the 1979 football season, another new acquaintance made during a workout at the Lakeland Hills YMCA helped start my long association with the Nittany Lions. As with Charlie, John Massimilla and I started our conversation in our small, cramped weight room. We hit it right off away after John mentioned where he hailed from.

"Altoona?" said I. "Do you know...?" My stories about "Altoonians" from Juniata were pretty extensive as roommates, drinking buddies, and other assorted classmates resided in the same Podunk lying 30 miles west of Juniata located in Huntingdon, Pennsylvania. John bled Blue and White as a die-hard Nittany Lion fan and alumnus. He also possessed a proud association with the University of Iowa where he was earning his master's degree in Hospital Administration.

In 1980, I attended my first game at State College, thanks to John. It was against an unlikely opponent, the Colgate Red Raiders, whom I'd seen in my first college game ever back in 1966 against Princeton. For my first game at Penn State, John, his date (name forgotten), Charlie, and I packed our stuff into the trunk of John's big, green Chevy Impala with a white, vinyl roof for our trek out to the "big Altoona." We would stay with John's family there. From experience over the years traveling out to Juniata, the boring four-and-a-half hour drive west on Route 80 through Pennsylvania was all too familiar. We came well prepared for the excursion with my big, green, beat-up Coleman cooler with a white lid. It matched John's Impala. Forty-eight Rolling Rock Nips inside were wedged between Charlie and me in the back seat. We set the record for pit stops made that night in the state of Pennsylvania which seemed like one, long cornfield. At one stop, John realized what he was missing out on in the back with Charlie and me. He insisted he and his date switch seats with us so that they could partake of what was left in the cooler (probably six nips). However, it wasn't more than a few miles before John realized how much "fun" Charlie and I already had.

"Uh... Charlie, pull over. I think I'll drive," John calmly, but firmly requested. Charlie didn't argue. He knew where he wanted to be. We happily resumed our original seating positions. None of the nips survived the rest of the trip.

I paid dearly for that liquid excursion to Altoona the next day sitting under a broiling, hot sun in windless Beaver Stadium. That day, one single, small cloud crossed the clear, blue sky during the entire game. When it briefly blotted out the sun, roasting fans cheered throughout Beaver Stadium. The most memorable highlight of the game against the 1AA Raiders came on sophomore, running back Curt Warner's breakaway run. Warner's shifty running capability broke him free past the Red Raider defense after a few nice moves for supposed, certain pay-dirt! Outracing Colgate defenders past the midfield stripe, Warner's legs suddenly went awry on the dry, plush green playing field for no apparent reason. He tumbled forward falling face first and rolled over several times until he finished lying flat on his back with legs and arms spread-eagle. He stared straight up at the clear blue, high sky over Happy Valley in front of 84,000 stunned Lion fans. He must have set the record by a running back for the most time taken to get up off the ground in the history of college football. Too embarrassed to get up and face the partisan home crowd, all was eventually forgiven as indicated by the final score of 54-10 over the Red Raiders. Warner captured All-American honors in '81 and '82 before his eight-year career in the NFL where he played for his new boss, a graduate of Juniata College, Chuck Knox.

Extra points: Through twenty-seven years of great victories, two national championships, some crushing defeats, bowl seasons, some losing seasons, promising recruits, graduating classes, Beaver Stadium expansions, revolving all-Americans - especially linebackers, electronic scoreboard upgrades, escalating ticket prices, escalating parking prices, sprawling parking lots, high-speed express lanes direct to Beaver Stadium, major traffic delays leaving late night games, Independent status, Big Ten membership, assistant coach turnovers, new blocking schemes, NCAA rule changes, and the ever-evolving BCS system, Penn State held one thing constant—Head Coach Joe Paterno. When Joe showed up with his team at Giants Stadium in 1979, he coached in his 14th season. Who could have imagined thirty-one years later, he'd still be coaching college kids for the same university he started with as an assistant back in 1951 under Head Coach Rip Engle?

Fast forward to October 27, 2001: Paterno's boys stumbled to start 0-4 in 2001. I attended two of the first four debacles. The final trek to State College in that 2001 season reeked of trepidation. That next game figured to be an opportunity to see either another humbling loss to the improving Ohio State Buckeyes in their first year under Head Coach Jim Tressel, or it could be a historic moment to see JoePa set the record to surpass Bear Bryant into coaching history. I figured that I couldn't miss this once-in-a-lifetime chance to see Paterno earn the all-time record since I had no plans to see another PSU game that season. Late in the OSU game, things looked dismal for the Lions once again.

Penn State QB Zack Mills started to work some magic in the third period for the Lions. Mills ran for a thrilling 69-yard score and threw a 26-yard TD pass before topping both with a lead changing scoring pass from 14 yards out. One problem: There were still more than 14 minutes left! With 2:55 remaining, the Buckeyes attempted a 27-yard field goal, but Nittany Lion Bryan Scott blocked it to preserve his coach's record-setting victory. The party was on! A water dousing, a handshake from Tressel, a video tribute on the big screens, hugs from his wife Sue and their grandchildren, a ride around the turf in a farm wagon, and the unveiling of the ugliest statue of Paterno that even made him laugh were presented in the glow of victory No. 324! For me, of course, it was another great experience to have witnessed a significant stretch of one of the greatest coaching feats in all of college football history. Thanks, Joe (and John)! That said, who knows how long Joe will keep plugging away defying the years? God only knows. Joe achieved win number 400 against Northwestern on November 6, 2010. I got to see that, too. God has *blessed* him.

John Van Horn flashes a "V" following Joe Paterno's 400th victory on November 6, 2010 against Northwestern in a 35-21 comeback. PSU fans Mike Breslin, Lindsay Van Horn, and Rebecca Van Horn don unique Penn State headgear to celebrate the occasion

College Football History 101
(10) Alabama vs. Auburn
December 1, 1979

Birmingham, Alabama —Records are made to be broken! Way before attending the JoePa love-fest in 2001, when he set the all-time record of total career wins among college football's greatest coaches, I had the opportunity to see the man whose record he had to break. In 1979, Paul "Bear" Bryant's Alabama Crimson Tide rode a 19-game winning streak, and Charlie Murren once again invited me down this time to see his beloved Tigers try to "Roll back the Tide!"

We hung out in Auburn for a day or so before we headed to Legion Field in Birmingham to see the fourteenth-ranked Tigers prowl into the Iron Bowl with a respectable record of 8-2, 4-1 in SEC play, to face its arch-nemesis and defending national champion, Alabama, ranked No. 1 in the nation with a record of 10-0. Alabama also brought in a 22-game SEC winning streak. Though considered a neutral site, Auburn fans vehemently disagreed as Birmingham traditionally hosted three or four Crimson Tide games every season, making it the primary home of the state university whose main campus exists in Tuscaloosa.

Unlike seeing legend-to-be Joe Paterno previously coach during his 14th season at Penn State, coming to this game we knew we were here to see a living, bona fide, coaching legend—the 65 year-old "Bear." On this day, the Bear's players walked the turf at Legion Field two hours prior to game time dressed in suits, ties, and cowboy boots for the most part, just seeming to get a feel for the playing turf. I watched from about my twenty-yard line seat in the Auburn student section as the defending champs walked from the far end zone to the one on my left, and then slowly strolled back, leaving their legendary mentor watching their return as he leaned against the goal post padding with his hands behind his back.

"Look at him! He's so drunk he can't stand up straight!" hollered an already fired-up voice from somewhere in the already packed Auburn student section. No love lost here—this was Auburn-Alabama! You not only rooted for your school here, that's the way you voted, too. There were no Republicans or Democrats—you were Auburn or Alabama!

Only a few weeks before the Auburn game on his weekly television show, Bear Bryant openly remarked, "I'd rather beat Auburn than go to ten bowls." That's quite a mouthful coming from a man who had already led his teams to 25 bowl games, including the twenty-game bowl streak he was currently guiding at Alabama, the all-time record at that time. Auburn's previous win against Bryant, 17-16 in 1972 was reportedly attributed by some to his pre-game comment that he'd "rather beat that 'cow college' than go to ten bowls." Known as the "punt, 'Bama, punt" game, Auburn scores came on two blocked punts by Bill Newton and two returns by David Langer to win the game for the Tigers.

This year, had Bear shot himself in the foot again? Auburn fans vented their feelings before this game with creativity. *"If you can't go to college, go to Alabama!"* Then they sent out their favorite chant in unison, *"Around the bowl and down the hole, roll, Tide, roll!"* The intensity felt among the 75,513 at Legion Field that day told me why. The Georgia game I attended the previous year did not project that same aura of intensity. There wasn't electricity in the stands like there was at Jordan-Hare. Instead, pure *hatred* pervaded. From across Legion Field came: *"Hey Auburn! Hey Auburn! We're gonna beat, the hell out of you!"* It sounded like they meant it, too.

Auburn took an 18-17 lead late, the only time all season that Bama trailed in the fourth quarter. The Tide offense started its next possession from its own 18. QB Steadman Shealy kept the drive alive on several critical downs before it culminated on his 8-yard keeper for a touchdown with 8:17 left. His successful two-point run put Alabama in the lead, 25-18. Auburn RB James Brooks threatened to even the score on the ensuing kickoff as he raced 64 yards before a game saving tackle by Tide Captain Don McNeal at the Alabama 31. Auburn threatened close to the goal line, but their tight end dropped an almost assured TD pass inside the Alabama five to poetically hand the ball back over to the Tide. Auburn's D held to get the ball back, but with a little over four minutes left to play, a Charlie Trotman pass on fourth down fell incomplete at the Tide's 37. Shealy and company ran out the clock to a victorious final score of 25-18.

Extra point: I'd see the Bear coach a few more times, but I'm happy to say that I'd seen him coach a game at his most rivalry-intense best.

Basketball school?

(11) North Carolina State at Penn State
November 8, 1980

State College / Raleigh, NC - The first time I saw the North Carolina State Wolfpack play, they visited Penn State's Beaver Stadium under Coach Monte Kiffin. It wasn't that memorable. Penn State won, 21-13.

Eighteen years later, I traveled to Raleigh to see NC State play again. My first Wolfpack home game at Carter-Finley Stadium was one of the most memorable of my entire tailgate tour! Fast forward to October 1, 1998:

When I think of NC State athletics, I think "hoops"—ACC basketball, the ACC Tournament, the Big Dance, Monte Towe to David Thompson on the *Alley Oop!*, Norm Sloan's team winning it all in '74, Jim Valvano racing up court after winning The Final Four in 1983. I ventured to see a game in Raleigh for the first time thinking football was something to keep State fans busy until the start of basketball season. Was I wrong!

Believe me. The Wolfpack crowd really gets into a football game at Carter-Finley Stadium. They take it seriously, and they have a lot of fun doing it, too. During each of my three games attended there, intense spirit reigned. Take that from someone who's attended games all over this fan-crazed, football country. Carter-Finley held far fewer than other venues at 51,200 in 1998, but condensed confines seemed to compress the spirit creating explosions of excitement. In between the crescendos, the place exuded non-stop spirit.

On a business trip to North Carolina, a business acquaintance, Al Warwick, invited me to come to his annual NC State tailgate party as one of about 100 guests. Al "howled" Wolfpack through and through. Syracuse showed up for a nationally televised game on a Thursday night. Aside from the anticipation of this early-season game between two ranked teams, Al had organized a first-rate, pre-game tailgate party. Good old Southern BBQ was served up along with adult beverages in large, ice-packed coolers by a sit-down buffet under a large, white tent. The hot, tasty BBQ, ice-cold drinks, and fun company provided a fantastic pre-game atmosphere, but the festive tailgate party really started hopping when NC State's marching band, "The Power Sound of the South," marched into the tent with snare drums tapping and brass horns blaring! The Power performed their traditional fight songs getting us primed for the game. The Wolfpack cheerleaders and their dance team performed routines to music including their traditional fight song, *"Red and White from State!"* "Mr. and Mrs. *Wuf*," official Wolfpack mascots, honored Al's guests with their appearances. Al had planned the exhilarating tailgate party experience perfectly, but the NC State spirit didn't end under the tent.

The high energy level filled the stadium during the entire game. The band played in the end zone throughout the game while the dance team constantly performed their rhythmic, synchronized routines. The Pack's student body stood and cheered for the entire game. Carter-Finley reveled with great football spirit, erasing my preconceived notion that NC State was nothing but a "basketball school" when it came to athletics.

The enthusiasm increased as the Pack held Syracuse's star quarterback Donovan McNabb in check. The Orangemen's Heisman candidate took a back seat that evening to Wolfpack QB Jamie Barnette who guided the home team to 525 yards of total offense - 282 through the air and 67 on the ground by himself. State's defense turned up the intensity against McNabb, too. After opening with a 66-yard touchdown drive, the Orange offense netted only 17 yards by the end of the first half. NC State enjoyed an energetic, 38-17 win.

Extra point: The atmosphere at Carter-Finley left me with quite an impression, and I returned again in 2004 to find that energy level still intact (see # 83, Texas Tech). When I was interviewed by John McGrath of the Tacoma News Tribune for the article he did about my website in the Lindy's preseason publications for 2005, he asked me to name my "bests." He shot out specific categories. "Stadium?" "Campus town?" "Tailgate party?" "Morning drive?" I had to think about each. "Best crowd?" Without hesitation I fired that one right back at him: "NC State!" The Wolfpack's Carter-Finley Stadium really *rocks*!

Blurred at Byrd—Prelude to a Championship.

(12) Clemson at (13) Maryland
November 15, 1980

College Park, Maryland - This chapter begins with apologies to Clemson fans. The only occasion my schedule ever crossed paths with their beloved Tigers occurred on this particular date. This game for me—I must confess—was more of a *party* as John and I met up with some of his old Altoona buddies attending grad school at Maryland. We were more inclined to be *celebrating* before, during, and after the game. I read the paper the next day to find out how the Terps and Tigers got to the final result, but I was *definitely* there. Many details just happened to elude my short-term memory that particular day.

Accounts I read the next day cleared the mist through which I watched this game. In this blur of a contest, Maryland's senior QB Mike Tice completed only nine passes for 144 yards, but he made them all count. Two went for TDs to split end Chris Havener and two others set up two short TD runs by All-ACC Tailback Charlie Wysocki. Maryland scored a TD in each period. It was an impressive Terrapin victory. They handled the Tigers easily winning, 34-7. Head Coach Jerry Claibourne led his team to an 8-3 finish and to its seventh bowl game in his eighth year at College Park.

Before the game played on a cold, overcast day, we enjoyed simple concoctions cut with soda that came in fine-looking plastic cups from concessions outside of Byrd which induced me to gather a prized collection of plastic souvenir, stadium cups when I got within. I first bought several of the white, 16-ounce "Snappin' Terp Territory" cups that displayed a Terrapin standing upright with claws on hips standing in front of a big, bold, red "M." More were negotiated away from other nearby fans in Byrd as I explained that I needed to collect as many as I could as wedding gifts for my future, yet unknown, bride-to-be. The ploy worked pretty well. I left Byrd with twenty-seven cups—a personal career high! They stacked neatly so that by the end of the game I could still drink from the top one while grasping number twenty-seven at the bottom.

My future wife, who wouldn't have the pleasure of meeting me eventually for five more years, just never did appreciate my effort and the benevolence of others to build this cherished collection for her. She eventually disposed of this unique gift idea along with other various works of art gathered during bachelorhood - treasures for a single guy, but unappreciated valuables viewed as "junk" in holy matrimony. A few collectible *"Snappin' Terp"* cups still reside on my garage workbench where they invaluably hold nuts, bolts, pencils, and other assorted, unidentifiable pieces of hardware - sometimes they even contained worms for fishing. However, most of my college football soda cup collection had to be disposed of to make room in kitchen cabinets for stuff like bowls, plates, coffee mugs, wine glasses, and eventually "sippy" cups. However, there is *no* way I will ever part with my cherished ticket stub and game program collections!

Extra point: This game turned out to be a significant low-point for Clemson. One week after attending Maryland's 34-7 win over the Tigers, I headed south on I-95 to go on vacation in Alabama to attend my second consecutive Iron Bowl down in Birmingham. On Sunday while driving through South Carolina, several cars passed with newly printed bumper stickers proclaiming, "Clemson 27 South Carolina 6". Unbeknownst then of course was that the recorded score on the bumper stickers represented the first of thirteen straight victories for Danny Ford's Clemson Tigers. The thirteenth, a 22-15 win over Nebraska in the 1982 Orange Bowl, earned

Clemson the 1981 National Championship. Only one year after I attended their fifth and final loss of the 1980 season by twenty-seven points, the Clemson Tigers reeled off 13 straight victories to win the NCAA title! I had witnessed the final fall of the Tigers before one of the greatest turnarounds in college football history. I only regret that I had not paid more attention to the game now instead of wasting my time putting together a supposedly cherished wedding gift that went unappreciated nine years later! Heart, effort, and a lot of vodka went into it.

A survivor of the cherished Wedding Cup Collection gathered for my unknown bride-to-be at the Maryland-Clemson game of 1980.

Bowling in The Meadowlands

(14) Houston vs. Navy
Garden State Bowl III
December 14, 1980

East Rutherford - On a cold, blustery Sunday afternoon in December, the Houston Cougars ventured to the northeast for the first time since 1962 to compete in the third edition of the Garden State Bowl at the Meadowlands. The 6-5 Cougars of the Southwestern Conference were picked by many as a Top 20 contender, but erratic play and a record-setting number of turnovers caused primarily by injuries suffered by three veer option QBs spoiled the Cougars' anticipated success. Their opponent this day would be the 8-3 Midshipmen of Navy. For the Mids, GSB III was their second bowl trip in three years under George Welsh. The Cougar's deceptive veer option offense, crafted by West Point grad and Head Coach Bill Yeoman, depended on the leadership of QB Terry Elston who optioned to a balanced running attack of TB Terald Clark and two fullbacks, Eddie Wright and David Barrett. Navy's defense ranked sixth best in the nation.

Houston took advantage of good field position in the first half. Navy's Eddie Meyers fumbled on the first play from scrimmage. Eight plays and 31 yards later, Clark scored from the one. Cougar Simon Fletcher blocked Navy's next punt. Forty-three yards later, Elston scored from the one. Cougar Tackle Leonard Mitchell thwarted any Navy offensive firepower. Two Navy fumbles, a blocked punt, and an interception resulted in a dominating 28-0 Houston lead before the first half ended. The Cougars came ready to play. The Mids atypically didn't. The Mid defense couldn't stop the Cougars' veer. Houston held Navy to total 200 yards. Clark scored again on a two-yard run in the third period. Houston gained 405 yards on 78 carries. The 5-7, 196-lb. Clark took MVP honors with 163 yards on 26 carries for 3 TDS. The game ended figuratively, 35-0, in the third period as the sky turned dark gray, as the swamp winds swirled, and as a heavy snow began to fall. Clark sat on the bench. We sat in a snow storm until the game was over.

Extra point: The cold, windy, snowy weather that December Sunday was not amenable to an outdoor tailgate party, so Charlie, Bob McKenna, Les Di Vite, and I traveled in search of beer, food, and warmth nearby. The local *Ground Round* literally burnt to the ground that week, and we drove into uncharted, downtown Secaucus. On unusually empty, snow-covered Paterson Plank Road, we pulled a "U-ie" to park on a side street next to a place called "Charlie's Corner" in the middle of downtown. It was quiet outside. We didn't know what to expect inside.

Walls and ceiling were covered by decorations commemorating every holiday of the year, not just the upcoming Christmas holiday. Previous holiday decorations remained as the next holiday went up. "Krajewski's" t-shirts with pigs screened on them hung for sale. A middle-aged couple, though she seemed younger, sang country music and Christmas carols on the small stage behind the four-sided bar. The big, busty, blond woman wore a short, red skirt and Santa cap while playing guitar and vocalizing. Her *ex-husband* played the keyboards - perfect for country music. They *were* a country song! Genesee Crème Ale was on tap along with my late, old man's favorite beer, *Schaefer*. The kitchen cooked up tasty burgers, great sausage sandwiches, and shrimp boats with fries. As it was Sunday, an NFL game was on the lone TV in the upper corner near the ladies' room. The pool table was open for play. It was a great, local neighborhood bar, and we felt right at home. It was much to our liking. The regular crowd shuffled in during the course of the late afternoon. We stayed late into the evening when a go-go dancer performed between sets of a rock band that came on stage. This was a first anywhere - a bar that displayed a poster of Pope John Paul II on the wall while a go-go dancer performed. He was smiling!

Brothers Charlie and John Krajewski inherited their family-owned, local bar. Their uncle Henry was not only the former mayor of Secaucus, but a renowned pig farmer who ran for President of the United States in the 50s. We got to know both guys pretty well as *Krajewski's* became a meeting place before and after many games at The Meadowlands. It was classic *Jersey*! Springsteen considered using the bar to film his video *"Glory Days"* a few years later, but the ceiling was too low. He chose another bar in Central Jersey and had it decorated just like *Krajewski's* to film the video. Photos of him taken with John and Charlie wound up on the wall with John Paul II later on. We loved going in for beers, extra shots on the house, and diverse entertainment on both sides of the bar. Bringing local friends or out-of-staters to *Charlie's Corner* whenever we were in the area always added to the cultural experience of visiting the Meadowlands.

My first bowl game was not very entertaining on the field as Houston totally dominated Navy. However, our serendipitous, post-game discovery that day hosted my friends and me after games attended at the Meadowlands for many years to come.

Feathers and flame

William & Mary at (15) Temple
September 5, 1981

Philadelphia - John Massimilla relocated to Abington, Pennsylvania, north of Philly to start his hospital administration career near the City of Brotherly Love. This provided a new launching pad to venture out in search of new game opportunities. Timing is everything. John's cousin, Mike Kneidinger, from Voorhees, NJ, headed up from Williamsburg, Virginia, with his fellow Indians from The College of William and Mary to open the '81 season at ancient Franklin Field in Philadelphia against the Temple Owls. I'd met Mike, the W&M starting defensive tackle, just the summer before. His father, Otto, played for Penn State under Rip Engle before he went into the football coaching profession that included stops at Delaware, Penn, and Rutgers. As the current head coach at West Chester State, John and I stayed with the family one summer weekend to attend the Philadelphia Eagles preseason camp held on the WCSU campus. We had the pleasure of partying with Mike one night and drank flaming shots together. Eventually, Mike got around to demonstrating how he could even ingest flaming potato chips! I preferred shots.

Temple's junior halfback Jim Brown, who rushed for 55 yards on 10 carries during the Owls' previous 4-7 season, exploded for 125 yards on 16 carries in this opener for both teams. He tallied four TDs as Temple scored one touchdown in the first quarter, two in the second, and three in the third. Four scores followed W&M turnovers. Brown scored on runs of 15, 1, and 30 yards. He also caught a two-yard TD pass from QB Tink Murphy. The Indians mustered only 188 yards in total offense. Mike and his merry Indians didn't put up much of a struggle against Temple that evening as it was a total romp and stomp by the Owls over the Tribe, a moniker that later politically-corrected their transition from Indians. In the end, the Owls rambled for 472 yards in their 42-0 victory.

Extra point: John caught up with Mike down in Orlando in 2006. Our night out that summer in South Jersey must have been an omen. Mike is now Chief Operating Officer for a large, well-known, international, restaurant chain. His calling evidently gravitated more toward food than football. The 42-0 William & Mary loss to Temple must have started him in that direction. That and probably his penchant for inhaling flaming potato chips!

Guinea Pigs at "The Bold Experiment"!

(16) Louisiana State at Notre Dame
September 12, 1981

South Bend, Indiana - Tony Lagratta transferred to Juniata College my senior year to become one of eight rooming together in 201 Flory in the dorm complex know as East Houses. We all got along together fabulously as we all shared common interests—drinking beer, playing sports, watching sports, partying, and harassing one another. That's all it took. Oh, we went to classes and studied once in a while, too.

Tony was a die-hard Notre Dame fan. Before my graduation in '79, we made an agreement to plan for a big tailgate party when the Irish were scheduled to play Navy at The Meadowlands in the fall of 1980. With about 60 other Notre Dame fans that came to tailgate in Lot 17B of the Meadowlands on November 1, 1980, Tony brought along his contingent of Notre Dame die-hards. They came to Jersey to join the festivities and stayed at my family's house in Boonton, NJ, the same town where two years earlier future Notre Dame Coach Charlie Weis started his football coaching career.

Missing from among Tony's entourage that day was one Dane Taylor. Tony's old classmate from Cumberland, Maryland actually followed his dream to not only matriculate at Notre Dame, but to also serve the program he loved by becoming lead student equipment manager for the Irish during his senior year. In 1977, Tony had the opportunity to attend the Notre Dame-USC game as Dane's guest when Dan Devine sparked the Irish faithful by suddenly replacing traditional blue home jerseys with new, green, game jerseys before the Irish took the field. The Fighting Irish stomped the hated Trojans, 49-19, on their way to the national championship. Tony particularly cherished a photo of himself grinning in a picture posed among the visiting USC "Song Girls" before the game.

It was not until 1981 that I paid my first visit to the hallowed grounds of the Four Horsemen, Knute Rockne, and Touchdown Jesus at the invitation of Tony and Dane. Several of us met at Tony's house in Lansdale, Pennsylvania to board our mobile home-away-from-home, and picked up some more guys on the way to South Bend. By mid-morning Friday, we parked in an RV lot on the Notre Dame campus, ready to experience the historical culture of a Notre Dame, football weekend. For our contingent, this Notre Dame game presented the opportunity to witness a much anticipated historical event in the annals of Fighting Irish football. We were in South Bend to help usher in "the Bold Experiment," the first game ever under new head coach Gerry Faust. Faust, the highly acclaimed high school football coach from Cincinnati's nationally-known, powerhouse oft times referred to as the "Moeller Steamroller," came on board to keep the loyal sons marching onward to victory. In his 18 years at the helm of Moeller, his Crusader teams won 174 games and lost only 17. How could such a coaching juggernaut be stopped? He would do no wrong, so it seemed. Despite no collegiate coaching experience, the Notre Dame administration and faithful followers expected Faust to produce the same magical results at the highest level of NCAA football. He was undoubtedly their man, so it seemed.

We visited Notre Dame Stadium, the school library featuring "Touchdown Jesus," the Golden Dome, the campus bookstore, The Convocation Center, the Chapel, and even some of the dorms where players lived. We walked all over the place. We all looked forward to the traditional Notre Dame pep rally that evening. During one of our forays across the green, well-groomed campus, our group literally crossed paths with none other than the man who would definitely lead Irish football to new heights. Smiling, happy, affable Gerry Faust led his freshman players to some event across campus, but he stopped, shook all our hands and chatted for several minutes. One of the die-hards declared later that it was "like meeting the Pope!"

That chance meeting left me with a memory more enduring than Faust's eventual, five-year career at Notre Dame. While some of the guys hobnobbed with the new mentor of the Fighting Irish football program, I eyeballed his group of freshman Irishmen. My thought: which, if any of these guys would go on to eventual stardom? It happens in every program. Some guys rise to the top and others will eventually "wash-out" quickly, never to be associated with football lore again. I noted the one freshman closest to me. This "roly-poly" kid, who looked like he never picked up a razor blade before, had this big, quiet, goofy, just happy-to-be-here smile across his face. He didn't strike me as athletic, but he was a big kid, definitely a lineman. I thought let me find out who this guy is and see if he ever makes anything of himself, or if he just becomes a footnote in the annals of Notre Dame, football history. When I bought the <u>Notre Dame vs. LSU Official Game Program</u> the next day, I perused pictures of the Notre Dame roster to identify him for future reference. Found his picture—"82 Mark Bavaro TE/DL—Freshman." I made a mental note of it. Could I pick out football talent or what? Not only did Mark Bavaro achieve All-American honors his junior and senior seasons at Notre Dame, he became an All-Pro TE twice with the New York Giants during a 9-year NFL career.

That evening, we stood in the middle of the renowned Notre Dame pep rally with a clear view to the speakers on the stage. For Gerry Faust and me, it was our first. As he spoke, the crowd continuously cheered. I couldn't hear a word he said, and I doubt anyone else did, or even cared. The Irish fans were pumped up! Whatever Gerry said didn't matter. He was going to do everything right for Notre Dame. No team could stop the Fighting Irish now, not with Faust! He coached the Gold and Blue and proved his prowess based on a lifetime, high school record of 174-17. Irish eyes envisioned national championship after national championship. Irish eyes have seen Leprechauns with pots of gold at the ends of rainbows, too!

The game against Louisiana State reinforced Irish hopes. An LSU fumble on its first series resulted in a 7-yard Notre Dame TD pass from Blair Kiel to Larry Moriarity. Phil Carter and Tony Hunter followed with one-yard TD runs in the first and second quarters for a 20-0 ND lead at halftime. Tim Koegel threw a six-yarder in the third to Dave Condemi. Both players played for Faust at Moeller. Faust shuffled in 65 players during the course of the game. LSU eventually put up the final six points with 23 seconds remaining. A two-point conversion failed. Despite the late TD by LSU to make the final 27-9, the ND crowd turned up its chants of "Gerry!Gerry!Gerry!"

The partisan crowd cheered the Irish and their 1-0 coach. They believed they had witnessed the beginning of what they anticipated. Fans were thrilled. Players were thrilled. Gerry Faust was thrilled, but not seemingly concerned about 100+ yards in penalties, or numerous turnovers on offense, especially two INTs among Blair Kiel's six passes. The new coach overlooked these nuances and focused only on the success of his final score over a now 0-2 opponent. Gerry Stovall's Tigers would end the season 3-7-1. With No. 1 Michigan's 21-14 upset loss at the hands of Wisconsin that day, all was right for the Irish. They vaulted to No. 1 in all the polls the following Monday. The cheering didn't last long though.

Extra point: After witnessing the initial success of the "Bold Experiment", our excited but weary band of tailgaters headed home in our rented, mobile home from that memorable, "historic" weekend. Along Route 80 before we *even* left Indiana, a loud, deafening roar started from beneath the vehicle followed by a loud explosion! We pulled over to find that a rubber retread let loose from one of the tires. Luckily, we had double axles and four tires on each. Another exploded and let loose in Ohio. It happened again in Pennsylvania. We left remnants of rubber retreads in each state on our way back. Luckily, we made it through our ordeal in one piece. The same could not be said for a formerly, successful, high school coach applying his skill at one of the greatest, traditional powers in college football. Faust and the Fighting Irish lost the very next week to Michigan, and it got worse after that. The Irish finished the season at 5-6. "Oust Faust!" eventually became the cry in South Bend over the next few years, but the administration lived up to its five-year commitment to the beleaguered head coach who was eventually fired in 1985. In retrospect, we were the first witnesses to the "Bold Experimental Failure." A 30-26-1 record, two minor bowl games, and no national championships were not the intentions Notre Dame bargained for when Gerry Faust signed up. After his team's win over LSU, the wheels on our "bus" never came off. The same couldn't be said for Gerry Faust's career at Notre Dame.

With apologies to LSU fans, there's not much to dwell on here from the Tigers' perspective, but I did make it down to Baton Rouge in 2008 for their 34-24 win over Mississippi State. I found the tailgating there *is* what it's all cracked up to be. Special thanks to Mike and Carol Barish for inviting me to tailgate with their friends and family at the mobile home called the *G&G Express,* also affectionately known as "Stinky".

Low-scoring affairs

(17) Virginia at Rutgers
September 18, 1981

East Rutherford - I took a date to The Meadowlands to see 2-0 Rutgers host 0-1 Virginia. In the final period, Virginia had the ball fourth and short at Rutgers' sixteen. Head Coach Dick Bestwick decided since his Cavalier defense put the stops to RU all evening, he would put the easy three up on the scoreboard and hope for his defense to maintain its stinginess. Wayne Morrison trotted out on to the field to give his team the lead with a fairly routine 33-yard kick. *Wide right*! Like the previous season, Rutgers' Alex Falcinelli got his chance to give the Scarlet Knights a late lead after a Morrison miss. With 3:02 left in the game, his kick sailed through the uprights from thirty-seven yards away. During the final three minutes, Bestwick's defense held, but so did Rutgers'. Both offenses remained as ineffective as they had during the first fifty-seven minutes of the game. In the end, the final score laid claim to the lowest scoring affair ever witnessed in over thirty years of watching intercollegiate play. Final score: Rutgers 3, Virginia 0.

Extra point: Results of the date - like the Cavaliers, I did not score.

Comeback at the Coaching Combine

Syracuse at (18) Pittsburgh
October 24, 1981

Pittsburgh – My Juniata College friends Toni-Anne Svetkovich and Cheryl Ondrejek graduated a year after me and roomed together while they attended the University of Pittsburgh for post-grad studies. They invited me out to the 'Burgh as I told them I'd be interested in seeing the Panthers play a game at Pitt Stadium. Under head coach Jackie Sherrill, Pitt ranked second in the nation when I rolled into town to see them play a familiar team, Syracuse, who was struggling with a record of 1-4-1.

SU drove to score on their opening possession on Gary Anderson's 36-yard FG. Surprisingly, the underdogs did not let up on their second possession against a staunch Panther defense that allowed only 18 yards per game. Joe Morris ran it in from seven yards out to take a surprising 10-0 lead at the end of the first following a 65-yard scoring drive. After "Snuffy" Anderson's 32-yard field goal for Pitt in the second, it was all Dan Marino and the Panther *D* for the balance of the game. A 13-yard TD pass to John Brown and a 13-yarder to Julius Dawkins following Dan Short's INT before the half gave Pitt a lead it never relinquished. Neither team scored in the third, but in the fourth, Marino sealed the game with a 5-yard spot pass to Dwight Collins before stepping out of the end zone. Marino threw for 282 yards and three TD passes that day, but Syracuse kept the high-scoring Panthers in check with four interceptions. Syracuse's 22 passing yards on only two completions along with two INTs kept Pitt's record unblemished at 6-0. In the end, Morris impressed with 128 yards on the ground against the formidable Pitt defense. The Pitt Panthers remained in the national championship race winning 23-10.

Extra point: In retrospect, an analysis of coaching staffs on both sidelines during that game indicates that Syracuse Coach Dick MacPherson and Pitt Coach Jackie Sherrill both surrounded themselves with a wealth of great, young coaching talent. From Syracuse, in action over subsequent years along prestigious sidelines: Gary Blackney coached Bowling Green before he became Ralph Friedgen's defensive coordinator at Maryland; Clarence Brooks became a defensive assistant for the Baltimore Ravens; Ivan Fears coached running backs for the New England Patriots in four Super Bowls; George O'Leary now coaches Central Florida; and finally, Jim Tressel coached both Youngstown State and Ohio State to respective 1AA and 1A National Championships. On the Pitt side, defensive coordinator Serafino

"Foge " Fazio stepped in as head coach of his alma mater after Sherrill left. Bob Davies also went on to a tenuous stint as Notre Dame Head Coach before ending up as a television game analyst on ESPN; George Pugh, Pitt's tight end coach, was seen as wide receivers coach 27 years later with the Houston Cougars in the second Texas Bowl; Andy Urbanic, RB coach, spent 19 years as head of football operations for at Florida State; and Mike Sherman, a grad assistant, went on to become Head Coach of the Green Bay Packers for six years before returning to the collegiate ranks at Texas A&M. Over thirty years, it's been interesting to trace the careers of coaches to see who makes it to the top of their profession. Even more interesting is to see who has the ability to stay.

Sentimental Souvenirs
(19) Wake Forest at Richmond
November 14, 1981

Richmond, Virginia – I hadn't seen Charlie Murren since the previous season. He relocated to Atlanta after graduating from Auburn and came back to Jersey to visit in the fall. Along with his friend T.J. Nelligan from Charlie's hometown of Montville, we took the opportunity to travel down to Virginia to see T.J.'s alma mater, Richmond, host the Demon Deacons of Wake Forest at Richmond City Stadium. We tailgated before the game with a large group of T.J.'s friends at UR's homecoming. "Go Spiders" painter hats were handed out and we walked off with plenty of extras "found" later to give out to acquaintances back home as souvenirs. Friends appreciated the unique football gift idea.

The Spiders, considered a mid-level D1 program, held on to a 15-7 lead late into the third period until the Deacons offense came alive with a vengeance. Within eleven minutes, Wake rallied with 27 unanswered points. Gary Schofield tossed a seven-yard TD pass to FB Dan Dougherty. Next, he fired an eleven-yard completion to split end Tim Ryan before the end of the third. To start the fourth, Wayne McMillan scampered twelve yards for the Deacons' third TD, and WR Kenny Duckett hauled in a 28-yard scoring pass from back-up QB David Webber for the final score and a 34-15 lead. Richmond scored one more time on Steve Krainock's 31-yard TD pass to Clayton White for the 34-22 final.

For me, souvenirs we collected provided lasting memories of this game. The "Go Spiders" painter hats were novel gifts appreciated by many when we went home. John Massimilla's housemate, Jack, wore his to a concert at the Spectrum in Philly where he was greeted by enthusiastic, Spider fans in a restroom wiggling their fingers and waving their hands up and down while shouting "Go Spiders!" in traditional UR fashion. Jack stated he was not in a convenient position to return their "salutes". Also, Charlie and I decided we needed to have one of the homecoming banners hanging from the stadium fence after the game as a memento. We set our sights on one, but some sweet-looking, young girl pleaded with me not to take it as I unhooked it from the stadium fence. Looking into her teary eyes, I spied Charlie with a devilish grin waving to me from about 50 yards behind the begging babe. The belly of his jacket was fully extended. He had stuffed a confiscated consolation prize underneath. We got our souvenir! On the white linen had been hand-painted a large, blue spider web with large, red lettering, "Mary Washington College says Go Spiders!" Dozens of girls had signed the banner, but none left phone numbers from the all-girl school located about 50 miles north in Fredericksburg. Too bad! We could have stopped by on the way home.

That banner hung as tapestry in my bachelor apartment back in Elizabeth, NJ until 1989 when my new wife and married life moved in. It's a shame how all the neat things you collect along the way during bachelorhood suddenly get categorized as "garbage" when marriage sets in. Along with my Snappin' Terp Territory cup collection and other assorted stadium, collectible cups, I lost my wooden reel lamp stands, garter belts caught at weddings, a lobster trap TV stand, souvenir beer mugs, and especially my prized, autographed "Go Spiders" banner. These nostalgic collectibles depicted cherished memories of bachelorhood and college football excursions in my one bedroom apartment. As a good buddy of mine from work, Greg Hardman, mused when he first stopped in for a beer after one of our softball games, "Well if anybody came in here for the first time and didn't know you, they'd know two things you like right away - football and drinking!" Souvenir collections tell no lies.

Extra point: As for Charlie's friend, T.J. Nelligan, I found out years later that he heads up a successful sports media company of his own, Nelligan Associates. I wonder if our weekend adventure to the Wake Forest-Richmond game helped him develop an appreciation for sports marketing? The Spider paint hats turned out to be very popular. *Go Spiders* (arms up and down, fingers wiggling)!

Orange streak and "Wild Horses"

(20) Tennessee vs. (21) Wisconsin
Garden State Bowl IV
December 14, 1981

East Rutherford - Garden State Bowl IV was billed as Big Ten Strength versus SEC Speed. For me, it was a chance to watch two big-time programs play for the first time. Only 38,780 other fans joined me and John Massimilla in the cavernous stadium. Being an Iowa Hawkeye as well as a PSU alum, John was rooting for the Badgers on a "pro Big 10" ticket. We perched in great seats for the game since buying the season ticket package that year put us ten rows up from the 40-yard line behind the Wisconsin bench. Kenny Gallagher, Bob "Polecat" Marcello, and I retained those six great seats for every college game we saw at Giants Stadium through 2002.

The Badgers took a 7-3 lead on a 68-yard drive in the first period, but on the ensuing kickoff, we watched orange-clad, US Olympian track team member Willie Gault streak 87-yards down the sideline right in front of us for a Tennessee TD that's still the best return I've ever seen. In the second period, UT QB Steve Alatorre threw a 43-yard TD pass to a diving Anthony Hancock followed by a two-point conversion pass to TE Mike "Go" Cofer. Mike "Stop" Cofer played linebacker for the Vols. Two Fuad Reveiz FGs gave Tennessee a 21-7 halftime lead. In the final period, backup Badger QB Randy Wright fired a six-yard TD pass to Jeff Nault and an 11-yard TD pass to Thad McFadden to tie the game. With 8:23 left, Alatorre finished a drive with a six-yard touchdown run. When the Vols got the ball back with over five minutes in the game, they ate up the clock, and Jimmy Colquitt punted down to the UW one with less than a minute to play. Time ran out for the Badgers, and Tennessee triumphed, 28-21 in the fourth Garden State Bowl.

As memorable as Willie Gault's kickoff return that day was the halftime performance by the University of Wisconsin Marching Band, referred to by their band director Mike Leckrone in the bowl program as "a team of wild horses." They nearly blew John and me out of our tenth row seats. Their brass section was loud and strong! It might have been because of where we sat, but to this day, I remember that team of wild horses more than any other D-1A marching unit I've seen perform at a college football game.

Extra point: This would turn out to be the last Garden State Bowl played. Within the next year, the N.J. Sports and Exposition Authority announced it finalized negotiations with the NCAA to initiate the first edition of a pre-season "bowl" that officially became known as The Kickoff Classic. Now, I'd have opportunities each fall to possibly add one or two more teams from far away for my football-viewing pleasure. It also provided me with more opportunities to visit Krajewski's before or after each game.

You Call *This* a *Classic*?
(22) Nebraska vs. Penn State
Kickoff Classic I
August 29, 1983

East Rutherford - My 1982 season was void of new teams as games played in East Rutherford, Annapolis, New Brunswick, and State College featured games between teams already seen. That season ended, however, in a significant game between 9-1 Pittsburgh at 9-1 Penn State. Facing Dan Marino at quarterback, the Lions defeated the Panthers 19-10. Even with an early 42-21 loss at Alabama, this victory led to Penn State's first-ever national championship (despite undefeated seasons in 1969 and 1970). The deal was sweetly coated at the Sugar Bowl where Joe Paterno's Nittany Lions beat previously undefeated Georgia and Heisman winner Herschel Walker, 27-23.

Since Penn State had just come off a national championship and maintained a huge fan base within easy driving distance, the new Kickoff Classic game committee invited the defending champs to the play in the inaugural, pre-season game. Nebraska was also an excellent choice for the New Jersey venue because several key players from their solid program would get a chance to play in front of their home state fans. The New Jersey Sports and Exposition Authority along with the NCAA expected to capitalize on this potential, financial bonanza.

The Classic now offered me the opportunity to see teams from other regions for the first time. The proximity and the atmosphere allowed for great tailgating, but to be honest, it lacked in new, fun opportunities to experience adventures traveling to different college campuses. Under meager budget constraints, however, it worked to my advantage in my early college football endeavor. I would make up for limited travels later on. As a result, for most of my Meadowlands experiences I focus on the games and players more than the collegiate atmosphere surrounding the action.

After every college football season, a phenomenon known as "graduation" tends to deplete experienced rosters. Many players graduate, and others just ran out of eligibility of some sort. This particular year, Penn State was seriously impacted. Last spring, the NCAA's leading rusher, Curt Warner, graduated. Last year's starting QB, Todd Blackledge, also moved on with a degree. The Lions' second, third, and fourth leading receivers all left with diplomas. In all, seven offensive starters from 1982 graduated and were replaced in 1983 by inexperienced underclassmen. Meanwhile, the Huskers brought back a strong returning core, and their last loss prior to their current 10-game winning streak came at the hands of the '82 Lions who beat them with only four seconds remaining in a 27-24 win. The experienced Huskers brought added incentive coming into this game at Giants Stadium. Penn State showed up with a revamped roster to kickoff a new season.

Nebraska RB Mike Rozier of Camden, NJ started his monster 1983 season with a mere 71 yards against Penn State before he'd rush for over 100 yards in each of the following eleven games to win the Heisman. QB Turner Gill passed for 158 yards and a TD completing 11 of 14 passes while gaining 53 yards and a TD on the ground. Second-team QB Nate Mason saw action in the second period and also led the Huskers to scoring drives on a 20-yard pass and a 21-yard run.

The financial bonanza at the ticket office before 71,123 fans unfolded into a boring, one-sided blow-out. The Huskers enjoyed a 44-6 laugher over the "defending champs" on their way to an 11-0 regular season. You call this a *classic?*

Two-point conversion: Rozier became only the second player in NCAA history ever to rush for over 2,000 yards in a season with 2,149. His 29 touchdowns set a Nebraska seasonal record. In 2006, he was inducted into the College Football Hall of Fame along with the opposing coach from this first Kickoff Classic, Joe Paterno. Rozier became the second of fifteen Heisman winners I'd get to see play through 2007, and despite his mere 71 yards, his was one of the better Heisman performances I would ever witness from a statistical standpoint. I'd see some other great names perform, but not at their best.

In the 1983 national championship at the Orange Bowl, NU Head coach Tom Osbourne called for a gutsy, two-point conversion for the win in the waning moments, but the attempt failed. The undefeated Huskers fell to Miami, 31-30.

"How's the corn ...?"
(23) Iowa at Penn State
September 17, 1983

State College - John Massimilla, my buddy Greg Hardman, an Army vet who now worked with me at Alpha Wire, and I sat in the thick of the visitors' section at Beaver Stadium again, but more Hawkeye fans showed up this time than Colgate Red Raider followers had during our first visit to State College in 1980. Unlike that earlier visit, today we dressed in "Iowa camouflage" since John had just presented me with a black and gold Hawkeye t-shirt from his second alma mater. We figured we'd just blend in among all the Iowa folks. The disguise worked. While waiting in the port-a-john out line in the parking lot, a friendly PSU fan, undoubtedly a farmer, acknowledged my attire: "How's the corn growing out in Iowa this year?"

"Well, I don't know about Iowa, but it looked pretty healthy in Jersey when I drove out yesterday." I replied too honestly.

"Hmmph!" He grumbled and looked away. "I thought you were from Iowa."

Sorry! But not as sorry as the two of us would feel after the game. The Hawkeyes racked up 587 yards under fifth-year head coach Hayden Fry. Quarterback Chuck Long threw for an Iowa record of 345 yards and two TDs completing 16 passes on 30 attempts. Long ran for a TD as well. Owen Gill rushed for 131 yards and a TD. PSU QB Doug Strang finished with 254 passing yards and three TDs of his own. Iowa overcame a 21-14 halftime deficit scoring three of four TDs following Penn State fumbles in the second half. Their impressive offense outscored the Lions, 42-34, for the win.

Long would lead his team on their way to a second-place finish in the Big Ten and 14th in the nation. Penn State's loss marked the first time since 1964 they'd lost their first three games, making it a first for a Paterno-coached team, but the Lions recovered by winning seven of their next eight before playing Pitt to a 24-24 tie in the season finale. They defeated the Washington Huskies in the Aloha Bowl.

Extra point: After the game that night, we all partied around State College. Greg and I crashed on couches at John's brother Joe's apartment on Beaver Ave. Joe, being hospitable, slept on a pile of blankets on the floor between us. When we woke up the next morning, Joe sat up on his pile of blankets – dazed!

"You - S.O.B.'s! I couldn't sleep last night! One of you would snore, and when one would stop, the other would start – only *louder*! You did it all night long, you *sonsofbitches*!" Neither Greg nor I heard anything. We both slept soundly. The secret to a good night's sleep during a road trip like this was to party hard after the game and to fall asleep before anyone else. Greg and I were tailgate party veterans. Joe was still in college. We drove back to Jersey the next day well-rested. Joe had to stay awake to study for an exam on Monday. I noticed that the corn *did* look pretty healthy on our way back home.

How 'bout those Hurricanes?

(24) Miami (FL) vs. Auburn
Kickoff Classic II
August 27, 1984

East Rutherford - Over the years, I became pretty adept at planning tailgate parties for 20 to 100 or more people. Most big ones were held at The Meadowlands, and the Kickoff Classic offered a great, late summer reason to party! With family and close friends, the last weekend of the unofficial end of summer was usually spent at the Jersey shore. Happy, relaxed, well-tanned vacationers had to be enticed to break away from the comforts of a bungalow near the beach to a tailgate party on the pavement at the Meadowlands. Charlie Murren came up to root for his Tigers from his new home down in Georgia, now settled in with his wife Lynda and Charles Murren IV. To stimulate interests of the beach-goers, the *Tour from the Shore* promised home-made *Hurricanes,* concoctions discovered at *Mardi Gras* in New Orleans in 1979, seemingly appropriate for the Tigers' competition that night, the Miami *Hurricanes.*

The second Kickoff Classic would start at 9 p.m. We started our tailgate party around 4 p.m. Friends in the area started arriving soon after work, joining us vacationers. We had booked an entire row of about thirty seats for most of the revelers. Others had pre-purchased seats in other sections around the stadium. Bob "Polecat" Marcello, Kenny Gallagher, and myself sat in our season-package seats ten rows up from the forty. The pre-game Hurricanes made with three rums, fruit punch, and other juices were a big hit in the parking lot, especially among women. The rum drinks flowed quite smoothly along with many beers. The Miami Hurricane football team had been flowing quite smoothly on the gridiron since the previous season as well.

For the second time in two years, The Kickoff Classic had invited a reigning national champion, but the 'Canes constituted a more formidable returning champion than last year's Penn State edition. Miami had concluded the 1983 season by knocking off 12-0 Nebraska in the Orange Bowl, 31-30, and leap-frogged several teams including Auburn, jumping from No. 5 to No. 1 – much to the dissatisfaction of the Auburn faithful. Sophomore QB Bernie Kosar, the Orange Bowl MVP, along with his entire offensive line known as the "Blitzbusters", returned intact for the Classic. The big change from the 1983 version of the Hurricanes, however, took place right at the top. Former Head Coach Howard Schnellenberger, who had turned the floundering program around, left for supposedly greener pastures in a new, pro league called the USFL. After scouring the nation, Miami replaced him with former Oklahoma State Head Coach Jimmy Johnson. We were attending his Hurricane debut. On the flip side, Auburn entered this game ranked as pre-season No. 1 in several polls. Its formidable rushing tandem of TB Bo Jackson and FB Tommie Agee provided one of the best one-two punches in college football. The Kickoff Classic's _Official Game Program_ proclaimed this game as" No. 1 (Auburn) versus No. 1-1/2". The AP poll reflected otherwise, pushing Miami down to the tenth spot.

Despite Kickoff Classic ticket sales dropping by some 20,000 due most likely to the absence of a "local" team, this year's Classic stood up to its billing much better than last year's. Kosar tossed TD passes of 17 yards in the first quarter and of eight in the second to WR Stanley Shakespeare. Auburn's only TD came on a 31-yard pass in the second. AU's Robert McGinty kicked FGs from 42 and 36 yards away in the second and third period. The other two AU points came on a safety when Miami snapped a punt over the punter's head for a safety. The vengeful Tigers enjoyed a 15-14 lead going into the fourth. Miami's defense held Bo Jackson to 96 yards on 20 carries before knocking him out of the game in the final period. The Cane's Alonzo Highsmith ran for 140 yards. Miami's Greg Cox scored on a 45-yard FG to start the final period, but McGinty matched the distance with his to retake a lead for AU. With 6:08 in the final period Cox converted a 25-yarder. DE Julio Cortez recovered an Auburn fumble on a pitch with less than three minutes left. From there, Kosar, who finished the game with 329 passing yards on 22 of 38 attempts, led Miami down to the Auburn two as time expired to preserve the 20-18 Classic victory.

As for our pre-game Hurricane celebration that started five hours before kickoff, everyone had a good time during our tailgate - probably too good a time. We polished off all the rum mixed with Hurricane "juices".

At halftime, when one of our partiers up from the shore, Laura Dixon, ventured over to visit most of our fellow revelers sitting in the full row of tickets purchased for the game, she came upon an unexpected sight. The entire row had fallen asleep! They truly enjoyed the tailgate experience, but most of them had no inkling as to what happened during the game. *Hey! How 'bout those Hurricanes?*

Two-point conversion: For his performance, Kosar earned the William J. Flynn Award as the game's MVP. Despite Miami's 8-5 finish for the season, he eventually finished second in the Heisman balloting, coming in second to none other than Boston College's Doug Flutie, whose famous "Hail Mary" pass to Doug Phelan that season defeated Miami, 47-45. Miami finished the season ranked No. 18.

Under Johnson, the program would become as infamous for its arrogant swagger as it was hated for its 52-9 record and 1987 national championship under his guidance. In the annals of my personal college football history, I've seen the Hurricanes play on the road seven times against the likes of Ohio State, Penn State, and Pitt, but to this day, they are the only undefeated team I've seen in a minimum of six contests.

From Wishbone to "Dodge-ball"
(25) Texas vs. Penn State
September 29, 1984

East Rutherford - One week after its loss to Miami, preseason No. 1 Auburn hosted No. 2 Texas, falling to the supposed rebuilding Southwestern Conference's Longhorns, 35-27. Two weeks after that big win over the Tigers, Texas ventured to the New Jersey Meadowlands to "host" 3-0 Penn State. "Host?" you ask.

According to the Official Game Program, in 1978 Joe Paterno called Bob Harter, CEO of the Meadowlands, to inquire about available open dates in 1984. It just so happened that the Lions and the Horns were looking for a date to play one another, and UT's AD and former Head Coach Darrel Royal sought a game in the northeast, but he insisted on a site other than State College, Pennsylvania. The Meadowlands obliged, and one of their many open Saturdays got booked. Three weeks before the game at a meeting of the Metropolitan Football Writers Association, a coin flip determined the "host" team. Texas won rights to wear their home, burnt orange jerseys and to take the bench on the sideline opposite the press box.[1] Neither of these home team "advantages" affected the outcome of this game, however.

The running tandem of Terry Orr and Jerome Johnson excelled against the Lions that day as the Longhorn backs ran for 108 and 72 yards respectively. The days of the Texas Wishbone offense were officially over as Head Coach Fred Akers had transitioned the Southwest Conference power to a pro style attack. UT confirmed the successful transition in the second period when QB Todd Dodge linked up with William Harris for an 84-yard TD pass, third longest in Texas history. The Longhorns introduced their own version of "*Dodgeball*" that day with a quarterback who could pass. PSU was held to 273 total yards of offense, but most of them came late in the second half after Texas had the game under control. It took a late field goal to keep Paterno's non-shutout streak intact in the 28-3 loss.

Extra Point: The wide-open passing attack Todd Dodge brought to North Texas State from Southlake (TX) HS as the Head Coach for the Mean Green in 2007 translated into no success there. Like Gerry Faust at Notre Dame, Dodge's previous success marked by high school championships and scholar-athletes playing in college and beyond, especially quarterbacks, did not equate to comparable success at the collegiate level. His wide-open offensive philosophy at NTSU resulted in a record of 8-40 over four seasons before he was asked to seek other opportunities.

Classic Lesson: Bring us your Quarterback!

(26) Brigham Young vs. (27) Boston College
Kickoff Classic III
August 29, 1985

East Rutherford - The Meadowlands administration should have learned at least one lesson from Kickoff Classics I and II. To have a successful, competitive game on the field, be sure the teams invited return with some star power intact, especially at quarterback. Nebraska and Miami did and won. Auburn competed with a returning starter. Penn State imploded with inexperience at that position and others.

Lavelle Edward's Brigham Young Cougars came to the Meadowlands fresh off their first National Championship with a record of 13-0. They were loaded to the hilt with key returning letterman including four receivers

1 "Six years and a flip! ", *Texas vs. Penn State Official Game Program* (29 September 1985), p. 25.

with 168 receptions among them. Tossing passes to the likes of WRs Glen Kozlowski and Mark Bellini came from 1984's No. 1 QB, BYU's Robbie Bosco. Boston College traveled down Interstate 95 following a great 10-2 season finishing No. 5 with a 45-28 Cotton Bowl victory over Houston. Missing from Classic III, however, was the field general who led the Eagles to new, soaring heights - last year's Heisman Trophy Winner, Doug Flutie. To the Canadian Football League went Flutie with his 233 completions, 3,454 yards, and 27 TDs from 1984. His favorite target at the end of his "Hail Mary "pass against Miami, Gerard Phelan, also graduated. Jack Bicknell's BC Eagles came to the Classic with Senior QB Shawn Halloran at the helm – three of six passing in 1984 for a grand total of 19 yards. Wonder why the Eagles were missing from the pre-season polls?

Long passes from Bosco to Kozlowski set up BYU's first three scores. The duo completed a bomb to get to the six to score first on a six-yard TD pass from Bosco to Bellini. The second came on a short run after another long completion to Kozlowski. BC knotted the score 14-14 in the third on Tryon Stratton's five-yard run. A 51-yard pass to Kozlowski put BYU at the 12 and a second TD pass to Bellini followed on the next play for a 21-14 lead. Bosco connected with Kozlowski for a 22-yard TD to extend the lead and finished off BC with a final score of 28-14. Bosco finished with a career high of 508 passing yards completing 35 of 53 including three TD passes. Kozlowski hauled in 10 catches for 241 yards. Bellini tallied 9 receptions for 111. Halloran started off slow in his first start at BC and completed 18 of 37 for 165 yards. His three INTs were topped by Bosco's four. Despite the turnovers, the experienced passing attack made the difference in this game. For the season too - BYU went on to a record of 11-3. BC finished the season with a record of 4-8. The Classic turned out to be a microcosm of both teams' seasons. The main difference – Bosco returned to BYU. Flutie flew the BC coop. Early season success in college football generally means having an experienced QB. Selection committee, please note!

Extra points: Regretfully, I didn't get to see Doug Flutie play during his collegiate career. His brother, Darren, played on the 1984 BC Eagle team at WR. I attended the 1982 Princeton-Brown game where Doug's brother, Bill, played wide receiver for the Bruins when Princeton defeated them, 28-23, in a very competitive game. In 2008, I watched Bill's son, Billy, play for Boston College his freshman year against Maryland in the final home game. Doug's nephew made up for what I never got to see twenty-six years earlier. As holder on the field goal unit, Billy faked a pitch over his head and rolled right to throw a 34-yard TD strike in the Eagles' 28-21 win. I can actually say I saw *Flutie* throw a touchdown pass in college even though it was 26 years after the *original* Flutie won the Heisman!

"Hayseeds" no more!
(28) North Carolina at Navy
September 7, 1985

Annapolis, Maryland - One week after the Classic, my traveling bone took me back to familiar haunts in Annapolis. The North Carolina Tar Heels visited *Crabtown* as the next team I'd see for the first time, but a couple of significant firsts for Navy highlighted this contest. The 7 p.m. kickoff made it the first night football game played under newly-installed lights at 27 year-old Navy-Marine Corps Memorial Stadium. This game also marked the first time a Navy player participated under *red-shirt* status. All-American RB and co-captain Napoleon McCallum achieved honors during his junior season of 1983 averaging 216.8 rushing yards per game, but his senior season of 1984 ended when he broke his ankle in the second game forcing him to sit out the remainder of the season. USNA had never granted red-shirt status to any player before, but his status as a star in the Navy football program made him an exception, and talented he was. In addition to being the featured back, Navy's record-setting running back also returned punts and kickoffs.

The Mids and Tar Heels opened the '85 season and knotted the score 7-7 at the half. UNC fumbled the second half kickoff return and Navy's Andre Stokes recovered at UNC's 17, but Navy gave the ball right back. UNC QB Kevin Anthony took advantage immediately connecting with WR Earl Winfield for an 82-yard TD pass. UNC scored again to extend the lead, 21-7. Navy scored two quick TDs in the final minutes of play. After failing the first extra point, Coach Gary Tranquil called for a two-point conversion pass to try to knot the score after the second, but the play was nullified by an ineligible receiver downfield call. The Heels held on to win the first night game in Annapolis, 21-19.

Speaking of holding on, the game program's cover featured artwork depicting a typical "North Carolinian". The unsuspecting Tar Heel is tripped up in front of Navy's famed icon, Tecumseh, who is depicted having mischievously *tarred* the ground to trap him. Both of his work boot *heels* stuck hard to the *goo* causing him to unexpectedly fall forward. The unshaven character depicted on the cover wearing a Carolina blue shirt falls forward with his beat-up hat and corn cobb pipe with a look of shock on his face. This caused a stir by some nearby UNC fans who had asked to check out my game program's cover.

"Hey, that's not fair! That's a *Hayseed!*" One Tar Heel fan laughed loudest as he pointed out the picture to his wife and friends seated beside them. Feigning being offended, their amusement reflected the state of North Carolina's current transition under way from an agricultural to a high-tech based economy. Significant changes had started to take place there and continued over the years. Keep the hat, a pipe, and a Carolina blue shirt, but instead of a "Hayseed", in subsequent years you could depict a Tar Heel as possibly a research scientist, a banker, or an engineer. It signaled change, progress, and prosperity in North Carolina – a good sign for the rest of the country as well.

Extra points: Navy's Napolean McCallum set an NCAA career, all-purpose, yardage record with 7,172 yards before he graduated. The L.A. Raiders drafted him in 1986, and he rushed for 536 yards his rookie year sharing backfield duties with Marcus Allen while serving in the US Navy. He played pro ball full time in 1990 after he finished his Navy commitment. His NFL career came to a horrific ending with a serious leg injury suffered on the season premiere of *Monday Night Football* in 1994.

This program cover for the 1985 Navy-North Carolina game by artist Bill Garner depicting a "typical" Tar Heel drew some laughs from UNC fans visiting Annapolis.

"No-Show Bo", again!
(29) Florida at Auburn
November 2, 1985

Auburn, Alabama – Life was certainly a-changin', especially for some of my friends. Charlie Murren and I continued to stay in touch, and we talked about me heading down South again some weekend for an Auburn game. But Charlie no longer had any youthful contacts back at his alma mater where we could find a place to crash. Instead, after he picked me up in Atlanta, he took me to Snellville, where he and Lynda not only had Charlie IV, but baby daughters Megan and Laura. Lynda's sister and her two little kids stayed with them while Charlie and I crossed the Alabama state line to rehash some fond weekends back at Auburn. As far as the game was concerned, it provided my first gander at the visiting Florida Gators. On paper, this promised to be a typically brutal SEC affair.

Florida (6-0-1), on NCAA probation, visited "the Plains" ranked second in the nation. Of all teams, their lone "setback" came in a 28-28 tie at home to lowly Rutgers who eventually finished the season at 2-8-1. Auburn (6-1) hosted the Gators with a 14-game unbeaten streak at home. The Tigers' lone loss came at the hands of Tennessee, a team Florida had beaten in a close game, 17-10. Heisman candidate Bo Jackson already amassed 1,402 yards and 13 TDs on 198 carries for AU. This game had SEC championship implications written all over it.

With all the pre-game hype focused on offense, defense dominated right from the start. Florida led 7-3 entering the final period. Heisman hopeful "No-Show" Bo Jackson rushed for only 48 yards on 15 carries in the first half. He left the game for good after a no-gain in the third quarter. Just like the Kickoff Classic in 1983, Jackson could neither score nor answer the bell physically near the end of a tight game. Auburn grabbed a 10-7 lead early in the final period, but QB Kerwin Bell led the Gators on a 61-yard scoring TD drive to take the lead with his second scoring pass of the game to WR Ray McDonald from 8 yards out. The Gators won the big one, 14-10.

Extra point: We listened to Auburn fans lambaste Jackson on the radio call-in show after the game for his ineffective performance. Bo Jackson was a great athlete in college and in the pros, but regretfully, my timing was off both times to see him play at his best during his Auburn football career.

"No-Show Bo" rushed for 1,786 yards that season, second highest ever in an SEC season. He won the Heisman. Auburn retired his "34" football jersey in 1992 in tribute to his 4,303-yard career. I got short-changed both times I saw him play. Bo rushed for only 144 yards on 36 carries and no TDs in two games – maybe it was me.

He went on to become a professional star in both football and baseball as he split seasons between the L.A. Raiders and the Kansas City Royals, among other baseball teams. A hip replacement eventually ended his athletic career. In 1989, he was named MVP in Major League Baseball's All-Star Game, being the second of only two players to hit a home run and to steal a base in the Mid-summer Classic. The other player is Willie Mays.

Down to the wire...and beyond!

Alabama vs. (30) Ohio State
Kickoff Classic IV
August 27, 1986

East Rutherford – Long before overtime was even a figment of the NCAA's imagination in 1995, the fourth Kickoff Classic provided action after regulation time had already expired. Two great college football programs clashed at The Meadowlands for their first-ever regular season meeting despite long, storied football traditions. The Alabama Crimson Tide and the Ohio State Buckeyes combined for more than 1,200 wins, with only one of these played between them. The Tide had defeated OSU in the 1978 Sugar Bowl, 35-6. Both schools now played for coaches marking time behind the bona fide legends who coached that game eight years earlier. After the 1978 season, Earle Bruce took the reins from the legendary Woody Hayes, who had amassed 239 OSU wins. Bruce kept the program running strong with his own 65-19 record. Ray Perkins, a former Alabama player for legendary coach Paul "Bear" Bryant with his 323 wins, stepped in after his late, great coach's retirement in 1982. Both teams came to tangle following strong seasons and bowl wins. Returning with experienced, star-studded rosters, the Buckeyes and The Tide opened the 1986 season with legitimate shots at the national title.

Trailing 16-10 with only 55 seconds remaining and starting from his own 21, QB Jim Karsatos led his Buckeyes into Tide territory. As time expired, Alabama's Derrick Thomas was flagged for defensive pass interference giving Ohio State one more chance with no time left on the clock. On the next play, Thomas was called for pass interference a second time on the drive. Ohio State remained alive for a possible tying touchdown and the winning extra point to boot (pardon the pun). At Alabama's 18,

Karsatos caught a glimpse of Cris Carter open in the end zone. As he fired the ball, fast-closing DB Chris Goode, who replaced Thomas, and Britton Cooper, knocked the ball down. 'Bama's win in the season opener gave them the edge in the early season polls.

This Classic actually came down to - and even went beyond - the wire. Three plays were run with no time left on the clock. The selection committee came up with the right formula in Alabama's 16-10 thriller for their second win in their second meeting with Ohio State. The final result could be attributed to returning experience in the kicking game. Two misses by the OSU freshman Pat O'Morrow and a botched hold of a snap on a third by Carter negated nine possible Buckeye points. In this defensive struggle, it seemed appropriate that a stalwart defender be picked as the game's MVP. LB Chris Spielman of Ohio State became the first defender to capture the honor. He not only became the first defensive player of two ever in the Classic to win the award with his sixteen tackles and one interception, but he also became the only member of the losing team to ever win the award.

Extra point: At the end of the season, despite identical 10-3 records and a head-to-head loss, Ohio State finished at No. 6 and No. 7 in the AP and UPI polls respectively. The Crimson Tide finished No. 9 in both.

Low-budget Bearcats

(31) Cincinnati at Penn State
September 19, 1987

State College - For over one full year, not one new, unseen team had been added to my schedule, but I couldn't complain about my 1986 travels after the Alabama-Ohio State game. I watched Penn State and Joe Paterno win three of their 12 victories on the way to their second National Championship in four years. Paterno was 32nd now among active 1-A coaches in wins with a 200-45-2 record. I pieced together my usual Penn State plans before the '87 season with John Massimilla. As usual, I selected "good" games balanced with the "bad" and the "ugly". This year, the good games were against Alabama and Notre Dame. The bad, well not so bad, was against West Virginia, but the ugly was definitely against Cincinnati.

Along with my buddy Fred Bacchetta, whom I'd known since I was six, and his wife Emilie, my girlfriend Laurie and I traveled as a foursome to State College to see the defending national champs play ordinarily mediocre Cincinnati. It was an unremarkable 41-0 rain-soaked PSU victory against a team with an offense expected to threaten under the controls of "Heisman Candidate" Danny McCoin – not even close! The most memorable detail about this trip was seeing a Bearcat DB talking on a pay phone in the hallway at our hotel in Lamar, Pennsylvania the morning before the game. I always booked economy –class hotels and less. During my many pre-game overnight stays, I had never even seen a visiting team at a hotel I stayed in. You need no better proof to confirm that the University of Cincinnati was definitely a low budget football program!

Extra point: The most significant aspect of the Cincinnati Bearcats in the annals of my personal history is how they lost and lost big! Besides the 41-0 loss in State College, Syracuse smoked them during my first Carrier Dome trip in October 1997, 63-21. However, the Bearcats' third loss provided the charm when they visited the Black Knights of the Hudson on October 9, 2004 in a Conference-USA game.

Army, on a 19-game losing streak, led 41-29 going into the final period. The Bearcats drove to the Army nine, but on a fourth and eight, Gino Guidugli's pass was batted away. After a two-yard loss, Army went to the swing pass to the right side and Tielor Robinson got great blocking downfield to ramble 93 yards for Army's final TD of the day. The Black Knights of the Hudson won, 48-29. The Corps erupted! Cannons exploded! The goal post nearest the Corps went down quickly in a sea of gray. Disassembled, an upright was paraded around the stadium by giddy Cadets. It met the same fate as the other as both ended up at the bottom of Lusk Reservoir. Half the Corps had never, ever seen their team win a football game. For them, it was a long-awaited first. For Cincinnati, it was another loss - not to an overpowering favorite, but to an underwhelming underdog. No matter who I watched the Bearcats compete against, the result was always the same—a lop-sided loss.

Getting their kicks

(32) Kentucky at Rutgers
September 26, 1987

East Rutherford - In 1987, the Meadowlands offered a four-game ticket package presenting two new teams I could add to my Goal on back-to-back weekends. On this particular Saturday, the Kentucky Wildcats entered the swamplands to claw at the Scarlet Knights of Rutgers. One week later, the Duke Blue Devils were scheduled to joust with the Knights.

As written earlier, while the Meadowlands presented convenience for me travel-wise, offered great tailgating, and hosted some great teams to catch "big-time" college football, the atmosphere there could hardly compete with the spirit and traditions of a campus game on a Saturday afternoon. While Army-Navy or a visit from Notre Dame can make a neutral setting a little more special, the canned atmosphere of an off-campus pro stadium tends to sanitize the collegiate environment. Fans miss the spirit and tradition of games on campus. It's just not the same.

Since both games at The Meadowlands kicked off on Saturday evenings, the start times presented opportunities to attend other local games during the afternoons to revel in a campus atmosphere. On this particular date, my girlfriend Laurie accompanied me to Bethlehem, Pennsylvania to see the Holy Cross Crusaders led by Heisman candidate Gordie Lockbaum wallop usually tough Lehigh, 63-6, in the Engineer's ancient Taylor Stadium. At the conclusion of this Colonial League blow-out, we headed to East Rutherford to see the big 1A game at the big stadium. Only 21,230 other fans showed up.

The Kentucky Wildcats (2-0) featured the backfield tandem of 5'7" Mark Higgs and Ivy Joe Hunter, fresh from wins over Utah State and Indiana. RU (1-1) countered with Harry Henderson averaging 7.3 yards per carry for 226 yards, but the Knights accrued only 13 points thus far against Cincinnati and Syracuse. Last year, kickers sent this Kentucky –Rutgers match to a 16-16 final. RU's Doug Giesler and UK's Joey Worley both booted three FGs at Commonwealth Stadium. Giesler knocked through a 37-yarder for the RU lead with 2:18 left, but Worley finished the scoring with one tick remaining from 32 yards to knot the final score. Would these two teams battle to the wire once again this year?

Worley would eventually put his "foot" on this season's final score, but Giesler, though still on RU's roster, would stand on the sideline. Carmen Sclafani took over the Scarlet Knights' kicking duties. His field goals of 28 and 46 yards along with Scott Erney's 29-yard pass to WR Eric Young accounted for the Knights' 12-7 lead in the third period. Wildcat TE Charlie Darrington's 10-yard scoring reception from QB Kevin Dooley put Kentucky back in the lead. Dooley's subsequent, successful two-point conversion to flanker Dee Smith put the Wildcats up, 15-12. Like greased lightning, RU return man Brian Cobb zoomed 94 yards to the Kentucky four. RB Dwight Giles carried it in from there, and the Knights retook the lead, 19-15. Both defenses held until 6:42 remained until Worley attempted to start another kicking duel with a 37-yarder good for three points. Ahead

19-18, Sclafani was called on to extend the lead to four for RU with 1:08 remaining, but a roughing the kicker call assessed against the Wildcats gave the Scarlet a new set of downs. RU ran the clock out to hold on to the one-point victory.

Extra point: Rutgers finished the season at 6-5 in Dick Anderson's fourth year as Head Coach. Kentucky Head Coach Jerry Claiborne, who had coached Maryland when I saw them play Clemson in 1980, faced the task of cleaning up a program targeted for recruiting violations. In 1989, he retired from Kentucky with a record of 41-46-3 including the 5-6 mark left by his squad of 1987. With a career mark of 179-122-8 at three schools, Claiborne was inducted into the College Football Hall of Fame in 2000. Anderson returned to Penn State in 1989 as an assistant where he still coaches the offensive line entering the 2011 season.

Welcome "New Ball Coach"

(33) Duke at Rutgers
October 3, 1987

East Rutherford - Another college football "two-fer", this one consisted of two D1 games. I squeezed in the Wake Forest-Army game at West Point before heading down the Palisades Parkway in dreary rain immediately afterwards to catch the Duke Blue Devils play Rutgers at Giants Stadium. Despite being a decent match-up between fledging programs, the fans stayed away from Giants Stadium in droves. New Head Coach and former Heisman Trophy winner Steve Spurrier coached Duke in his first season.

That evening, I avoided my prime, rain-soaked seats ten rows up from the 40 on the press box side for drier climes under the mezzanine. Everyone else in attendance had the same idea. Looking down from my dry, covered perch, not one red seat visible above or below the mezzanine in the 76,000-seat stadium supported a single human being.

With so few attendees, Rutgers and Duke players seemed to be playing in front of their families, a few close friends, and one die-hard college football fan. Maybe five or six thousand showed up in the rain that night, but the no-shows didn't miss much – offensively any way. Following a pass interference call by Duke in the fourth quarter, Rutgers TB Harry Henderson scored on a two-yard TD run with 5:41 left for the only score of the game. RU recorded its 500th win in school history, 7-0.

Extra point: Besides the historic win for RU that rainy night at The

Meadowlands, the game provided two other historical footnotes to my experiences: Spurrier's 5-6 Duke team of 1987 would be his only losing squad ever at any school; and the 7-0 loss represented the only time the "Old Ball Coach" would ever get shut out until his South Carolina squad lost to Georgia, 18-0, in 2006! How many can claim to have ever seen Steve Spurrier coach during a losing season or get shut out? Along with about only 5,000 others, I can say that I saw both!

"♫ Yogi Bear is smarter than the average bear...♫ "
Nebraska vs. (34) Texas A&M
Kickoff Classic VI
August 27, 1988

East Rutherford - The Aggies of Texas A&M, winners of three consecutive Southwestern Conference titles, literally marched into The Meadowlands to kickoff the 1988 season against the first team to ever return to play a second Kickoff Classic, the Nebraska Cornhuskers. The selection committee did an excellent job choosing competitive teams for its sixth season opener within the NCAA constraints to invite each major conference within the first seven years of the Classic.

Like Ohio State's traditional dotting of the "i" in *Script* Ohio by "the best dam band in the land" (their description, not mine), the Kickoff Classic introduced the NY-NJ metropolitan area's college football followers to the *Fightin' Texas A&M Aggie Band*. The precision, military unit in campaign hats, brown tunics, khaki trousers, and whose seniors wore polished, knee-high, tan riding boots, performed impressively to the *"Aggie War Hymn"* marching in tight precision formations. What struck me funny, however, is how their proud War Hymn reminded me of the "Yogi Bear Cartoon" theme song, but with a more methodical beat. Next time you get a chance to hear it, try singing along, *"Yogi bear is smarter than the average bear, Yogi Bear is always in the Ranger's hair, Have a picnic basket you will find him there,♫..."* I'm sure it's just a coincidence, but those words enter my mind whenever I hear the Aggies play their war hymn. I haven't taken the time to learn the real words because I always liked the lyrics to *Yogi Bear.*

The game turned out to be a little bit Yogi Bearish, but I'd say it reminded me more of his sidekick, *Boo-Boo*. Nebraska failed to score after recovering two A&M fumbles in the first half to trail, 7-6. NU QB Steve Taylor threw a one-yard TD pass to Nate Turner early in the third. Early in the fourth, he connected with TE Todd Millikan who carried two defenders into the end zone on a 20-yard pass play. A 20-7 Husker lead woke up the Aggie offense after the special teams unit recovered a Husker fumble on a punt return at the 44. A&M RB Randy Simmons narrowed the margin, 20-14, on a 2-yard run with 10:15 left. NU's Greg Barrios booted his third FG of the contest, a 48-yarder for a Classic field goal record to finalize the scoring at 23-14 with just over seven minutes left. Both defenses prevented any further serious scoring threats.

Extra point: Nebraska QB Steve Taylor garnered the Flynn Award as MVP in one of the Classic's more lackluster offensive MVP performances. The voters for MVP evidently could not see their way to select another defensive player despite the pre-game hype over the reputations of the linebackers featured in this Kickoff Classic. Despite LB John Roper's impressive reputation and stats at A&M, he never gained any notoriety during a six-year NFL career. Despite two All-American seasons at linebacker for Nebraska, Broderick Thomas, picked sixth overall in 1989 by the Tampa Bay Buccaneers, never earned any All-Pro honors. Stardom at the collegiate level never guarantees the same beyond. The pros play at an extraordinarily higher level, but I'll take college football's traditions, intensity, spirit, and pageantry over the Sunday version - even if an occasional fight song does remind me of a cartoon show song. Also, after attending Saturday gridiron battles, I find Sundays convenient for recovering so I can return to work on Mondays rested to block and tackle the issues preventing me from getting my job done.

"Wunderbride" and "Wunderkind"

(35) Southern Cal vs. Syracuse
August 31, 1990

East Rutherford – Before I reflect on my memory of watching USC play for the first time, let me mention that 1989 turned out to be another season void of new teams for me. Primarily two big events occurred in my life that year. I was in my second year of grad school attending Seton Hall University at night to work on my MBA. Many weekends focused on papers, studies, and projects depriving me of football. Even bigger, I was adjusting to life as a married man. Laurie became my wife in August 1989, and two weeks after we returned from our honeymoon in Hawaii, we attended the next Kickoff Classic between Notre Dame and Virginia as husband and wife. Ten days after that, we attended the BYU-Navy game in Annapolis with Fred and Emilie Bacchetta. Laurie knew what she was getting into, and I was getting her acclimated that I was still going to enjoy college football weekends with or without her. As time marched on you'll read it got more challenging for me to keep up with my endeavor. I had three more years of grad school that reined me in at first, so I couldn't travel as much anyway and stayed local if I could attend a game at all. A year after that, we had our first baby, Alexandra, and two years after her, Eric arrived. So times were more challenging for me on the football front, but I continued to enjoy fall weekends as much as I could and not always with the blessing of Laurie, who constantly reminded me that she should be exalted for the sacrifices she was making. She claimed no other woman would put up with it, but I wasn't pulling any punches either – I did this before I knew her and while we dated, so why did she think I was going to stop now? From that point on, she made it known that she was the self-proclaimed "St. Laurie", a moniker that you'll find out that even I would agree she deserved at times. So when the reference is made from here on out, you'll understand that *St. Laurie* is my wife – unofficial "patron saint of college football widows".

The USC Trojans ventured east for their first trip in 39 years to become the first Pac-10 team to participate in the annual Kickoff Classic. Their appearance would fulfill the obligation of the Classic to invite all seven major conferences as participants. Known as *Tailback U.* for its tradition of outstanding Heisman running backs, this year's offensive spotlight fell upon QB Todd Marinovich. The Trojans appeared with their starting sophomore QB known in certain circles as "*Robo QB*", or as "America's first test-tube athlete." In his mother's womb, Todd Marinovich was raised by his father, Marv, a former USC and AFL lineman, to be the "purest" natural athlete possible. He committed his wife to give up cigarette smoking and insisted she consume a high protein diet. As a youngster, Todd's dad planned strict work-out regimens and ensured no fast food products ever entered his son's body. Marv's admitted goal was for his son to make him the first high school athlete ever to be pictured on the *Wheaties* cereal box – seriously![2]

The opposition for the Trojans that evening would be the former, short-term denizens of the Meadowlands, the Syracuse Orangemen. With USC leading 14-10 in the third period, the teams traded field goals before

---

2 Anonymous, *Todd Marinovich*,http:// www.biographicon.com/history/lpdc4/Todd_Marinovich (Jan. 2008).

Marinovich threw a 46-yard scoring strike to flanker Gary Wellman for the 24-13 lead. In the final period, LB Scott Ross and company held the Orangemen to a field goal, and the Trojans scored the last ten points to seal the victory in Kickoff Classic VIII, 34-16. Neither team lived up to pre-season expectations although the Orangemen won the Aloha Bowl defeating Arizona, 28-0. The Trojans fell 17-16 in the Sun Bowl to Michigan State. However, the most intriguing epilogue to this game is the plight of the game's MVP, "Robo QB" Marinovich, who eventually earned the appellation, Todd "Marijuanovich".[3]

The strain of Marinovich's relationship with Head Coach Larry Smith gradually intensified, and after encounters with the law for drug abuse and rape charges, the prodigy raised from the womb to become a football player first and foremost, opted early for the NFL draft in 1991. The Raiders, the same organization for whom his father had played in 1965, drafted him in the first round. He signed for $2.27 million. His debut in the final game of his first season would be the highlight of his NFL career. He threw three TD passes before his release in 1992. He flirted with the Canadian and Arena Football Leagues for a few years, but he did more than flirt off the field as he was served with three paternity suits and arrested for more drug abuse convictions. In 2004, ESPN rated him seventh among "*The 25 Biggest Sports Flops*". Exactly seventeen years after his Kickoff Classic MVP Award, the 38-year old Marinovich was arrested for felony possession and resisting arrest on the Newport Beach, California pier after being stopped for skateboarding in a "No Skateboarding Zone"![4]Despite or perhaps because of his parents' selective and controlled cultivation, the 38-year old Marinovich still hadn't grown up. There's a lesson here somewhere.

Extra Point: In 2008, a younger brother, Mikhail Marinovich, a highly recruited tight end was offered scholarships by USC and Texas Tech among others. Eighteen years after his brother's MVP Kickoff Classic performance, Mikhail ended up, ironically, on the roster of Syracuse, USC's opponent that night. He's seen little action as a DE entering his senior season in 2011.

---

3 Ibid

4 Ibid

1986 postgame tailgate celebration at Johnny's in Boonton. From left to right: Doris from Taunton, Mass, brother-in-law Gunther Neumann (see team #71), the Author, St. Laurie, sisters Mary Kay and Nancy

Tico TKOs Tekay

(36) Michigan State at Rutgers
September 29, 1990

East Rutherford - What always makes college football most fun for me is the enthusiasm of fans. Whenever I went to a game in a neutral setting like The Meadowlands, I always found it a plus to invite friends or acquaintances affiliated with one of the opposing schools. To the Michigan State versus Rutgers game, I invited along a good business acquaintance, a friend to this day who had played basketball for the Spartans for two seasons in the '70s. Jack Hessler follows sports and enjoys reminiscing about his experiences growing up and playing basketball as a kid in the Detroit area. He remembers a young gym rat with great basketball skills who hung around the courts at Jack's high school. The kid was known then as "E.J.," short for Earvin Johnson, who later took on a more "Magical" nickname.

Jack and his buddy Gino came down from New Hampshire to join St. Laurie and me for a tailgate at the Meadowlands. That day we'd watch Jack's former school take on Rutgers (2-1) as the Scarlet Knights still tried to make a significant mark in big-time college football ("If only we can keep the best players in New Jersey..." continued the rant). A win over the

22nd-ranked Spartans would definitely give notice that the Scarlet Knights program was turning around – hope eternal for RU fans.

For Rutgers, this was the second of three games to be played at The Meadowlands, and sophomore RB Tekay Dorsey led RU in rushing with 228 yards and a 4.5 average per carry. Hopes were high for the home team, but this night belonged to Tekay's counterpart - Michigan State running back Tico Duckett. The sophomore tore up the Scarlet Knight defense that night with a career-high 229 rushing yards and a TD. His big run in the third period set up the go-ahead score by FB Rob Roy. Michigan State scored on each of its four second-half possessions. The Spartans whipped the Knights back to reality with a 34-10 victory and captured their 500th overall win. They finished the season strong with six straight wins including the Sun Bowl victory over USC and its Wunderkind. RU never recovered from the thrashing they suffered that day at the hands of Tico and the Spartans. They finished the season at 3-8.

Extra point: MSU did not appear on my slate again until 2002 in a Big Ten game at Penn State. As for Rutgers, I would see them play many more times over the years trumpeting their battle cry, "If only we can keep the best players in New Jersey ..."

Yellow Jacket fumble-fest

Penn State vs. (37) Georgia Tech
August 27, 1991

East Rutherford - The Kickoff Classic invited its fifth defending national champion to its ninth edition as Georgia Tech came in with Head Coach Bobby Ross, recipient of the 1990 Bobby Dodd Coach of the Year Award, following a storybook, 11-0-1 season in1990 (Why are all southern football coaches named Robert or Bob always called "Bobby"? - i.e., Bowden, Ross, Johnson, and Dodd. Usually if you don't call a true Southerner by his given name, you get a dirty look or you hear about it). The Yellow Jackets crushed Nebraska in the Florida Citrus Bowl, 45-21, to earn the No. 1 ranking in the final UPI Coaches poll. The polls split the national championship that season, however, as the AP writers poll selected 11-1-1 Colorado. The Buffs played a schedule arguably better than Georgia Tech's, and they also beat Nebraska in Lincoln, 27-12, during the regular season.

Penn State led 13-3 into the second half. In the third quarter, PSU QB Tony Sacca continued to fire away, throwing for three touchdowns following three straight Georgia Tech turnovers. The first touchdown followed one of QB Shawn Jones's three fumbles. Sacca flipped a five-yard scoring pass to O.J. McDuffie. Following Matt Baggett's interception, Sacca lofted a tight spiral down the right sideline to a leaping, twisting, turning, diving McDuffie for an exciting, 39-yard touchdown catch. On the subsequent drive, OLB Rich McKinzie forced Jones's next fumble and one play later, Sacca's screen pass to RB Richie Anderson resulted in a 52-yard catch and run to give the Nittany Lions a commanding 34-3 lead.

Much as Nebraska had done in Kickoff Classic I, the team with good, experienced playmakers returning from a solid season built a comfortable lead in the third period. In the fourth quarter, Tech made the score respectable by scoring three touchdowns to make the final 34-22 in favor of Penn State.

Extra point: Immediately after that season, Ross left Tech to become head coach of the San Diego Chargers. In 1995, he coached the Chargers to Super Bowl XXIX. After years of frustration with professional attitudes, he returned to the college ranks. In 2004, I saw him coach Army late in his career as the highest paid employee of the federal government.

King of the Commander-in-Chief's Trophy

(38) Air Force at Navy
October 12, 1991

Annapolis - In 1975, as a Third Classman in the Brigade of Midshipmen, I had helped cheer Navy on to victory over Air Force at RFK Stadium in D.C. where our team shut down the Falcons for a 17-0 win. Navy won the second of the fourth Commander-in-Chief's Trophy (The 1974 season resulted in a three-way tie). Since 1972, the Trophy is awarded to the winner of the round-robin rivalry among the three military academies for football supremacy.

By 1991, Navy had taken home the Trophy five times, but the last time was back in 1981. Air Force dominated academy football now, taking the hardware back to Colorado Springs six times since, including three of the previous four seasons. Air Force had become a much-improved team since 1984 when offensive coordinator Fisher DeBerry took over the head coaching job. He had turned Falcon football fortunes around by implementing his vaunted wishbone attack that best suited the quick, smart, smaller athletes the academies recruited. Since 1984, DeBerry had guided the Falcons to a 55-30-1 record and five bowl games.

To this game came St. Laurie, her brother Tom, his wife Linda, and their son, five-year old Brian Bramhall to see the "rivalry" between the 5-1 Falcons against 0-4 Navy at Navy-Marine Corps Memorial Stadium. On top of the rivalry, today marked the 1,000th game in Navy football history. Fans of all factions came to see this one. Tailgating next to us were some die-hard Michigan fans who got caught up in singing *"Hail to the Victors!"* for some reason until I reminded them of their 51-31 loss two weeks earlier to Florida State. I performed the "Tomahawk chop" and *Seminole War Chant* at them. They ceased their singing. The pre-game festivities included a flyover by a squadron of F-14 Tomcats commanded by former Navy punter, Lt. Commander John Stufflebeem, USNA class of 1975. He punted against Notre Dame in the 14-6 loss chronicled earlier. In 1973, he was the punter in Navy's 800th game that was played against these same Air Force Falcons when the Mids came away with a 42-6 romp. Eighteen years later at this game, he flew over Annapolis where the final score would be similar. During Operation Desert Storm, Admiral Stufflebeem regularly reported the status of the military events on national television as a military advisor to the White House.

Navy Coach George Chaump threw a curve at Air Force and started Plebe Jim Kubiak at quarterback for the first time. In front of the second largest crowd in Navy-Marine Corps Stadium, Navy trailed their second biggest rival, 7-6, at half time. Kubiak fumbled on the second play of the second half, and the Falcons capitalized with Jason Jones' seven-yard TD run. Navy turned the ball over four more times in the half giving the USAFA good field position each time. Falcon QB Rob Perez completed only two of six passes on the day, but one was a 40-yard TD to Bobby Thomas to take a 25-6 lead by the end of the third. The visitors didn't need to pass. Their vaunted wishbone finished the day with 407 yards rushing. Air Force sank Navy, 46-6, the most points ever scored in this traditional rivalry.

It was the tenth straight time the Falcons bested the Mids. In 1991, Air Force won its fourth consecutive CIC Trophy. Under the tutelage of Fisher DeBerry, their domination over their sister academies didn't stop then. During the next eleven football campaigns, USAFA swept Army and Navy nine times to keep the Trophy in Colorado Springs.

Two-point conversion: In 1998, DeBerry coached the Falcons to a 12-1 record and a number 13 ranking. That season, Air Force dominated Army at West Point, 35-7, with the same adults and now 12-year old Brian in attendance once again. Tom, St. Laurie's brother, thought he had some influence over parking matters by putting up a banner across his windshield proclaiming his status as a former Army Sergeant figuring the NCOs directing traffic would find him a prime spot. That got us a space in *general* parking just like everyone else!

It's hard to know if the two dominant Air Force victories attended by young Brian over Navy and Army had any influence on his life, but eight years later, he served his country in his first tour of duty with the 177th Fighter Wing of the US Air Force in Iraq as a Fire Fighter extinguishing flames and avoiding mortar fire. Two years after, he served as a Staff Sergeant on a second tour in Kuwait.

Fisher DeBerry coached the Falcons until the end of the 2006 season. During his 23 seasons leading the Falcons, his team won the CIC Trophy outright 14 times and shared it once. He finished with a combined record of 34-8 against Army and Navy to become the winningest coach in service academy history with a record of 169-109-1.

This side of the Rainbow

(39) Florida State vs. (40) Kansas
Kickoff Classic XI
August 26, 1993

East Rutherford/New Orleans -When the Kansas Jayhawks came to The Meadowlands in 1993, Dorothy's words from the *Wizard of Oz* never rang truer: "Something tells me we're not in Kansas any more, Toto." No kidding, Jayhawks! You're in the swamps of Jersey playing preseason No. 1 Florida State coming off an 11-1 season with Heisman Trophy candidate Charlie Ward at QB, *my Pretties*! And while *Scarecrow* didn't have to worry about balls of fire today, it was 118 degrees on the playing surface.

This year's Kickoff Classic added two more schools to my ever-growing life list. While I enjoyed adding the Jayhawks, Kansas didn't. They got rolled flatter than their home-state prairie. FSU rolled to an easy 42-0 win. If you can believe this, the highlight of the game for KU was a goal-line stand. Bobby Bowden's squad rolled on to "*somewhere over the rainbow*" defeating undefeated Nebraska in the Orange Bowl for the National Championship at the end of the season. That Kickoff Classic romp was definitely not my most memorable FSU game. Fast-forward to January 2, 1996:

St. Laurie and I traveled to New Orleans to see No.1-ranked FSU play

No. 3-ranked Florida in the Sugar Bowl for the National Championship of 1995. Although my saintly wife didn't know she was helping rack up points, we got the tickets through a credit card rewards program. One day, she noticed that we had accumulated enough points for a toaster oven. What? I wasn't running up credit card expenses and paying interest to burn bread! "No way! We're going to a bowl game!" She was stunned, but before she could counter, I was ready. With a growing balance of frequent flier miles, I told her we had saved enough points for at least one ticket to New Orleans. Having booked her parents to watch our kids and three days at an inexpensive hotel in the Big Easy, this proved easier than expected. (Nebraska originally expected to be in New Orleans, but flamed out at the last minute by losing the Big 12 title game to Texas). St. Laurie was tempted. She had always wanted to go to *Brennan's* in The French Quarter for breakfast, her favorite meal of the day! She definitely wanted "in" despite having to go to a football game.

It's hard to find a bad place to eat in New Orleans. When we arrived, we hit a restaurant specializing in crepes and drank authentic Hurricanes at *Pat O'Brien's*. We spent New Year's Eve celebrating at Jimmy Buffet's *Margaritaville*. Despite having no kids along, we visited the New Orleans Zoo. *Brennan's* breakfast was expensive, but it was a once-in-a-lifetime experience for its turtle soup and *Bananas Foster*. Thanks to my ... well... our spending and a championship bowl game, we enjoyed a great mini-vacation in New Orleans.

On Saturday night, we watched the Gators, led by Heisman winner Danny Wuerffel, torch the Seminoles with three TDs and 306 yards completing 18 of 34. Only 33 days earlier, the Seminoles dished out some hard shots to the resilient quarterback in Tallahassee for their 24-21 win. FSU emerged as the only undefeated team left standing at the end of regular season to jump to No. 1 with their victory. In the rematch, former Heisman winner Spurrier, coaching his Heisman-winning QB (a college football first), set him up in the shot gun to offset the FSU rush. The strategy paid off. Florida won its first national championship, 52-20. In New Orleans, Florida State, like Kansas in The Meadowlands, found itself somewhere on *this* side of "the Rainbow".

Ten + one = Big Ten?
(41) Minnesota at Penn State
September 4, 1993

State College - The Minnesota Golden Gophers visited Beaver Stadium not only for the first time in their first game ever versus Penn State, but they visited as the Nittany Lions' first opponent from their new conference, the Big Ten. PSU decided to give up 106 years of Independent status to join up with the ten major, traditional, Midwestern football programs that had been playing each other for conference championships since 1953. Personally, I had mixed emotions about the move into conference play. First, if the Lions were to join a conference, my preference leaned to continue to see them play Syracuse, WVU, Pitt, and Boston College who could only get stronger playing each other while building on solid and thriving traditions. Likewise, I always enjoyed seeing games against the aforementioned, but I also enjoyed the flexibility Penn State had of scheduling diverse opponents each year like Notre Dame, Alabama, Texas, Nebraska, Miami, and a few others. Seeing the Lions host basically the same schedule of Midwestern teams every other year really didn't thrill me. Michigan and Ohio State games would surely be exciting rivalries, but Indiana, Northwestern, and Illinois every other year could become monotonous. The scheduling flexibility Penn State surrendered to join conference play took away possibilities to see big-time games with *national* implications. Now the focus narrowed on vying for a conference championship before setting sights on a national championship.

I realized that one advantage the entry of Penn State into the Big Ten provided was a major possibility of going to the Rose Bowl. I called my good friend Jim Lewis, who was relocating from New York City to California. I told Jim that when the Lions beat Ohio State and Michigan in the same season, get ready because we're going to the Rose Bowl! Those words would prove to be prophetic.

WR Bobby Engram had a big day for Penn State against Minnesota returning to the lineup after a one-year suspension by Coach Paterno. He nabbed four TD catches from John Sacca to set a new school record. His first went for 29-yards on a screen pass on PSU's first play from scrimmage following Derek Bochna's INT. The next came on the very next series with a fantastic, diving catch for a 32-yard score. He added two more TDs among his eight receptions for 165 yards. That was plenty for Penn State to start 1-0 in Big Ten play with a 38-20 win.

Extra point: The 95,387 fans this day received commemorative medallions. One side read, "Penn State vs. Minnesota, Nittany Lions' First Big Ten Conference Game." The flip side read: "I was there, Beaver Stadium, September 4, 1993." Of course, Penn State joining a conference that already had a great name and 10 teams presented a numerical challenge. The Lions, of course, became the 11th Big *Ten* team. John Massimilla pointed out the Big Ten logo on the scoreboard to show me that the powers-that-be compensated by overlaying the digit "1" along each side of the "T" in Big Ten to indicate 11 schools. Does this make sense? Besides tradition, why not Big Eleven? Of course, they can't add one more and become the Big Twelve – the name's already taken. Why can't these institutions of academia be more creative? Leave numbers out for flexibility. How about "Monsters of the Midwest"? Would some Bears in Chicago be upset? All right, "Big Monsters of the Midwest." Use some imagination.

Rush hour in Un-Happy Valley

(42) Michigan at Penn State
October 16, 1993

State College - The Nittany Lions remained undefeated and ranked No. 7 in their inaugural Big Ten season leading up to their first showdown with Michigan, winner of the most Big Ten championships (37) since the start of conference before the turn of the 20th century. It was time to find out if the Nittany Lions could challenge the Wolverines for some of their traditional territory. This would also be the first PSU game for three people who made the trip up with St. Laurie and me.

With only two tickets for the first really significant Big Ten showdown at Beaver Stadium, we planned to bring our six-month old daughter, Alex, to meet our Penn State tailgating partners, John and Kelle. Since Laurie planned to spend her day hanging out in the parking lot with Alex, we brought along our two neighbors, John and Jan Hosler, for the overnight trip. Affectionately known as Grandma Jan and Pop-pop John to the kids over the years, I still refer to John as "the Superintendent." With adjacent properties, I was never lacking for tools, and even more, for advice for any job around the house or yard. The plan for this game was for John to join me at the game while Jan would hang out with Laurie and Alex to tailgate. This plan benefited us more than anticipated. With a noon time start and a record-setting crowd of 96,719 converging into State College all at about the same time, all roads leading into Beaver Stadium parking lots were backed up by 10 a.m. Traffic crawled. Full parking lots caused most tailgaters to diverge from their normal parking arrangements. State College was not prepared to absorb this sudden vehicular surge for expanded capacity with an early kickoff.

Kickoff approached as we crept along Route 322 to our usual parking lot, but I realized we weren't going to make it on time. Our arrangements paid off though. St. Laurie took over the driver's seat, and John and I took the tickets and hopped out of the mini-van to start our hike to Beaver Stadium. In the age before cell phones, we planned to meet Laurie, Jan, and the baby by the traffic light next to the intramural gym after the game. John and I parked our fannies in our aluminum bleacher seats just minutes before kickoff. We didn't miss a play in PSU's 1,000th football game, but we arrived so late that all programs for this game were already sold out. It's one of few missing from my cherished collection.

The Lions led early, but U of M's Derrick Alexander returned a punt 48 yards to cut State's lead, 10-7. In the third, Michigan's Mercury Hayes made a diving catch in the end zone on a 16-yard pass from Todd Collins to take a 14-10 lead. After that, the Lions challenged Michigan's staunch defense, pounding up front with plunges close to the goal line. The Wolverines stuffed Kerry Collins quarterback sneaks twice, and twice more, they stopped Ki-Jana Carter at the one in a potential comeback series for a goal line stand. PSU struggled to contain Michigan's powerful rushing attack. Tyrone Wheatley gained 192 yards, one of the highest totals ever given up by Penn State. The Lions closed the score at 14-13 with a Craig Fayak FG, but Todd Collins threw a TD pass to Che Foster to end the scoring with 5:12 left. Penn State suffered its first Big Ten loss, 21-13.

It would not be the last time the 18th-ranked Wolverines would leave Happy Valley denizens unhappy when I watched the two play, or tried to. In 1999, I drove up to State College the night before another noon start, but I missed the 31-27 Wolverine victory led by QB Tom Brady because my four-year old son, Eric, woke up sick to his stomach several times during the course of the night in our hotel room. I sold the tickets in the hotel lobby the next morning for face value and took him home. The 2001 game was the worst for PSU as the Wolverine defense showed no fear of the Lions' offense, shutting them out 20-0 to create the first 0-4 start for a Paterno-coached team in 36 years. In 2006, Michigan defeated Penn State at one of its celebrated Beaver Stadium "white-outs," a 17-10 win where the

Lions got down to their third-string QB. By far, no team has brought more unhappiness to Happy Valley than the Michigan Wolverines.

Extra point: The inaugural Big Ten season turned out somewhat successful for the Lions, who finished 10-2 overall, 6-2 in the conference. Wisconsin, who the Lions didn't play, won the conference to move on to the Rose Bowl. The one blemish on the Badgers 10-1-1 season record came at the hands of the Minnesota Golden Gophers, 28-21, as Jim Wacker's club finished the season at 4-7. Maybe there would be more competition than just the Buckeyes and the Wolverines in the Big Ten for the Nittany Lions after all.

Dirty Looks
(43) Indiana at Penn State
November 6, 1993

State College - When Penn State joined the Big Ten, no doubt PSU fans expected to witness key battles against Michigan and Ohio State over the years. The Indiana Hoosiers, on the other hand, were expected be an automatic "W". Basketball, of course, would be an entirely different matter.

As an indication of their football reputation, the Hoosiers came to State College as Penn State's Homecoming opponent that first season, and as for my "trade-off" to balance my tickets for the "good" game against Michigan, I took tickets for the "bad" game against Indiana. But shockingly, IU not only showed up in Happy Valley for a game that had bearing on the Big Ten conference championship, they came in ranked at No.17 in the nation, two spots ahead of Penn State! It was their best start (7-1, 4-1 Big Ten) since their Big Ten Conference championship of 1967. They showed up to play a PSU team that hadn't scored a TD in six quarters, compliments of the Wolverine and Buckeye defenses.

On this cold Saturday in early November, St. Laurie and I bundled up our seven-month old baby girl in a pink snowsuit and woolen cap. No one else could go with me that weekend and no one was available to baby-sit, not for free any way. We packed up all the stuff that came along with Alex in the mini-van. The three of us would share our two seats next to John and Kelle up in section EJ of Beaver Stadium. With parking such a fiasco at the Michigan game, we had little time to catch up with them before or after that game. With our two tickets and our pink bundle of joy in a snowsuit with spread-eagle arms and legs, we got on line with the rest of the crowd to enter our gate and ascend the ramps and stairs all the way up to row 87. Without the option of a sitter and desiring to catch up with friends at the game, we thought nothing of lugging our tiny tot into the stadium. She wouldn't take up any extra space as she was going to be sitting or laying across our laps the entire game. She was barely able to sit up by herself - especially in her snowsuit-straight jacket! However, leers we got from ticket takers and some hesitancy on their part indicated either that we weren't supposed to be doing this, or they were unsure that we could do this. Looks made me wary. I said nothing, and they said nothing. What was the big deal? I didn't notice if anyone else was carrying a baby in, but what did that mean? Maybe nobody else was crazy enough to bring their seven-month old out on a cold, wintry afternoon to watch a football game, or maybe they had all found baby-sitters! Alex lay across our laps during of the game, flat on her back mostly sleeping. When she was awake, she was happy and taking in all the action around our seats. People reacted typically to seeing a little baby, especially when she smiled at them. Most people were still focused on the game action anyway, so she didn't bother anybody.

Penn State jumped out to a 17-3 first quarter lead, but Indiana tied it at 17-17. State led again, 31-17, late in the third. However, the Hoosiers tied it again with a Big Ten-record, 99-yard touchdown pass from John Paci to Thomas Lewis. Suffice to say I saw a record that will never be broken even though it happened against the beloved Lions. Paci threw for 379 yards and Lewis finished with 285 of those on 12 catches for two TDs. Penn State regained the lead when Kerry Collins connected with Bobby Engram on a 45-yard score with 6:25 left. The Hoosiers didn't quit though, threatening until Tony Pittman intercepted inside the 10-yard line to preserve a hard-fought win for the Lions. They came away with an unexpectedly competitive, but satisfying Homecoming win, 38-31, over the surprising seventeenth-ranked Hoosiers.

As for my baby girl's first Beaver Stadium visit, we carried her out that day under the steel beams, posts, and bleachers. She noticed the echoes surrounding her and let out a sharp "Eh!" of her own. She heard her little voice ricochet back from the stadium walls and was enthralled to hear the sound bounce back. Sixteen years later, she was still intrigued by her own voice. She's always singing!

Extra points: With this win and three more Big Ten victories afterwards, PSU finished its first season in the conference at 9-2, 6-2, and went on to defeat Tennessee in the Citrus Bowl, 31-13. They finished eighth in the nation ahead of No. 11 Ohio State (10-1-1) and No. 21 Michigan (8-4), the two new rivals they had lost to in conference play.

Alex and I shared memorable times going to Penn State games together since. She insisted on trying to see at least one Penn State football game with me every year when she could. I have several fond memories taking Alex to State College, and since her Mom and I brought her into Beaver Stadium bundled up in that little pink snowsuit for the first time, the dirty looks have subsided. She always had her own ticket! We're sure it wasn't just us, but after carrying our little pink bundle up all those ramps and stairs to have her lay across our laps, mostly napping, stadium policy was now clearly announced over public address system that everyone entering the stadium, regardless of age, had to have a ticket. Anyone at PSU ever check the cost of a baby-sitter these days? It could cost you a lot more than a ticket. It's surprising that they haven't set up a child-care center for game days yet. Surely the cost will be comparable, if not higher, than the price of admission once some university official comes up with that money-making scheme.

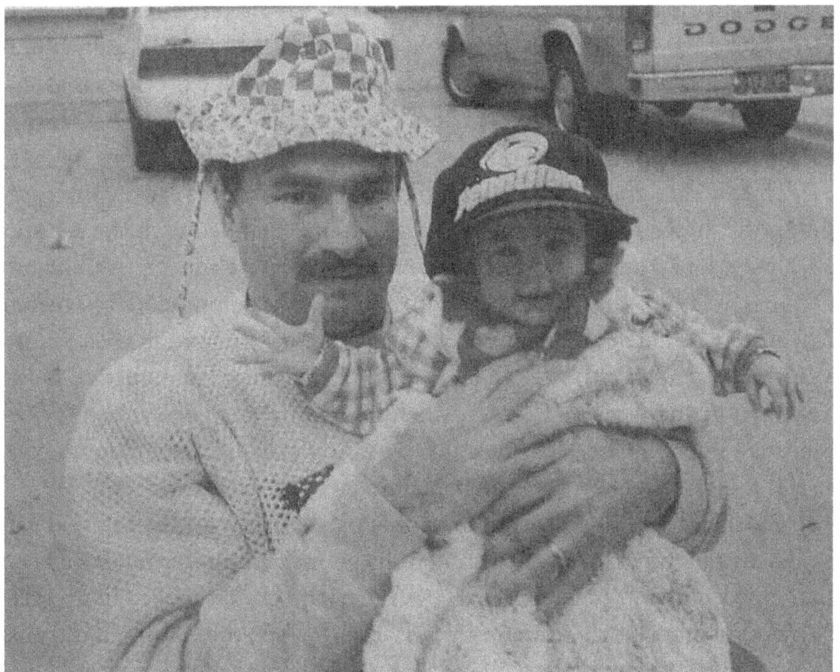

This little girl needs a ticket! Alex remained in the parking lot with her Mom and Grandma Jan during the Michigan game before I caught up with her after the game. Three weeks later, she napped on our laps for most of the game against Indiana.

Upset! Upset! Upset!
(44) Louisville at Army
October 15, 1994

West Point, New York - On this sunny, cool, brilliant fall Saturday on the Hudson River, Army, on a four-game losing streak, trailed the Cardinals, 29-23, after allowing Louisville to score two rushing TDs and two two-point conversions within 34 seconds. Cardinal QB Marty Lowe was hot with 19 completions for 245 yards, but for the Cadets, Kurt Heiss was also on target with a 37-yard FG and two more from 30 yards. Army's Ronnie McAda fired a 10-yard TD pass to FB Joe Ross to tie the score with 3:17 remaining. Heiss booted the extra point for a 30-29 Black Knight lead. The Cardinals drove to retaliate, but Louisville's Anthony Shelman fumbled a pitch for a nine-yard loss at Army's 28. A second U of L possession ended with David Aker's 46-yard FG attempt wide right with 1:35 left. The Black Knights ran out the clock for an exciting, Army upset.

I got to enjoy it this particular Saturday with good friends Tracy and Dave Headden. St. Laurie was back at home taking care of 18 month-old Alex who had already attended her first three games the previous season. With our second kid expected in about six months, St. Laurie just wasn't up for a short trip to West Point with a toddler.

This wasn't the most memorable game I saw between Army and Louisville, however. That came five years later and ended with the second of "Upset! Upset! Upset!" On a dark, chilly, overcast Thursday evening on October 7, 1999, the Army-Louisville game, to accommodate television scheduling, would be the first weekday night game ever played at West Point. With my friends Paul Zordan and Jim Baker visiting from upstate New York, we sat on the visitors' side to watch this Conference-USA clash. With Heisman hopeful Chris Redman at QB for Louisville and Army coming in at 1-3, the game looked like a mismatch in favor of the Cardinals.

Shockingly, Army's offense looked unstoppable in the first half as Michael Wallace ran around, over, and through the poor-tackling Cardinal defense. In their second year of Conference-USA play, the Cadets looked like world beaters that night as they built a 45-17 lead. However, the Cardinals did not go away in the second half to make what would for one of the wildest, most exciting games ever played at Michie Stadium. Paul and Jim noted the key to Louisville's offense in the second half was TE Ibn Green. Wherever he lined up, the Cards followed. With that strategy, Louisville rallied in the second half with 28 unanswered points on two one-yard runs by RB Frank

Moreau and two TD passes from Redman, one to Green and one to WR Lavell Boyd to tie the game late in regulation, 45-45. On a night of firsts at Michie Stadium, both teams played in their first overtime periods ever. On their first possession, Louisville took a seven-point lead on a ten-yard run by Moreau, but Army QB Joe Gerena capped the extra Army possession with a nine-yard TD pass to Brandon Rooney. To start the second OT period, Gerena, who played a heady game for Army, didn't let up as he posted a seven-yard TD run to take a 59-52 lead for the Cadets. Louisville's next possession got to the Army eight to set up a fourth and seven. Redman stepped up into a pocket and fired to a seemingly wide-open Boyd at the back of the end zone. As Army's Derrick Goodwin closed quickly, Boyd went high, had the ball in his hands, but he and the ball hit the turf at the same instant. The Corps roared! Howitzer volleys fired from across Lusk Reservoir. Army won a thriller on its first weekday night game and in its first overtime game ever. In the annals of my personal game history, the one-hundred and eleven points totaled the most ever scored in one game. It was a fantastic, exciting football game – long scoring plays, big lead, big comeback, and not one, but two overtime periods. Fans moved from one end zone to the other to be closer to the action when the teams went from the south end zone to the north in the extra periods. College football couldn't get much more exciting than this!

Extra point: As for the third of the memorable triumvirate of Louisville upsets, there was another Thursday night game in 2006 played along a different river, the banks of the Old Raritan. The Knights that evening wore scarlet, not black. This contest was played in front of a much larger television audience because the stakes weren't only for a possible Big East conference championship, but for even bigger BCS bowl possibilities. In the end, a 25-7 Cardinal lead turned into a 28-25 Rutgers' victory for the second biggest win in the history of the program that started everything back in 1869. Make that the third "Upset!" for the Cardinals on the short-ends of "Upset! Upset! Upset!"

Doormat
(45) Northwestern at Penn State
November 19, 1994

State College - As expected when Penn State joined the Big Ten, one team that could be counted on to give the Lions a "W" in the win column year after year was Northwestern, the one private institution playing football for years against bigger state institutions with bigger stadiums, larger student bodies, larger state budgets, and lower academic standards. During my college years, *Sports Illustrated* featured an article about the beleaguered Wildcat football and basketball programs. It included a photo where a bit of humor was added to a sign somewhere along Interstate 70. Below "Interstate 70", someone painted "Northwestern 0"! Things hadn't changed much for NU since.

Despite the losing seasons every year since 1971 including an NCAA record-setting 34-game losing streak from 1979 to 1982, the Wildcats stuck it out in the Big Ten (I watched Columbia erase their record in 1986 when they lost to Princeton for their 35th straight loss on the way to 44!). NU became the school traditionally "traded-off" in our annual ticket plan for balance to get Michigan or Ohio State tickets. The 1994 season was no exception. However, the Wildcat game against Penn State presented historical significance to the Lions. Ranked No. 2 in the nation with a 9-0 record, 6-0 in the Big Ten, a win here would make the Lions outright conference champs of the Big Ten for the first time and send them on their way to The Rose Bowl despite the possibility of losses to the Wildcats or Michigan State in their final two games.

The Wildcats would not disappoint the Lions in their first visit to Happy Valley. Four first half turnovers by NU resulted in 28 points for PSU. S Kim Herring picked up a Wildcat fumble and raced 80 yards for a touchdown. Bobby Engram scored a 50-yard TD after catching a short pass from Kerry Collins. Ki-jana Carter scored two more TDs in the second period sandwiched around Brian Milne's 11-yard run to take a 38-3 halftime lead, but the Wildcats had outgained the Lions by 65 yards! State's tackling was horrible. Interceptions and fumbles halted NU drives. The Cats scored on Tim Hughes's 22-yard TD pass to Chris Gamble in the third and on Bobby Jackson's two-yard run with 1:28 remaining in the game. Carter scored from the one again for PSU in between. The Lions extended the nation's longest winning streak to fifteen games with a 45-17 victory. Despite the score, however, PSU did not jump to No. 1 because its defense, suffering the losses of four starters already to injury and losing a fifth in this game, allowed 475 yards of total offense to Northwestern, who finished the season in typical Wildcat fashion at 3-7-1. With their Big Ten record of 2-6, the Wildcats finished just ahead of 1-7 Minnesota, missing their typical, last-place finish as Big Ten doormat.

Rose-colored Frog
Penn State vs. (46) Oregon
The Rose Bowl
January 2, 1995

Pasadena, California –In 1993, my friend Jim Lewis, who I'd known since second-grade, moved from New York City to beautiful downtown Burbank, California. Jim wrote for The Jim Henson Company, creators of the Muppets. Of course, I had mixed emotions about my friend's relocation. I was sorry he was moving so far away, but I also realized that we now had real Rose Bowl possibilities. My prophetic words to Jim Lewis to go to California to attend the Rose Bowl with him became reality in 1994 after Penn State defeated Michigan and Ohio State to win the Big Ten to get invited to play in the Rose Bowl on the second day of 1995. The Rose Bowl is never played on Sunday.

When my wish came true, I called him. He said, "If you're still serious, let me know. I *may* have a connection." Would I be any more serious? The next long distance conversation went like this:

"I'll make a call, but how many tickets do we need?" Jim asked.

"Well, there are you and I, and I know John Massimilla will definitely go. Laurie says she's not interested in the game, of course, but says that she's always wanted to go to the Rose Bowl Parade."

"I'll ask if we can get tickets for that, too. How many?"

"Well, you and Judy, me and Laurie, Alex, John, maybe Kelle..." Jim decided to ask for eight.

"I can't promise you anything. I'll probably call you back next week." We had our second conversation the very next day.

"I called this guy and I told him that some Penn State friends of mine were interested to come out for the game, and I'd like to see if we can possibly get any tickets?"

"Sure! How many would you like?" responded Jimmy's contact.

"Three."

"How's the fifty-yard line halfway up?"

"Great! How much do you want for them?"

"Don't worry about that. You and your friends will come as my guests. Would you like seats for the parade as well?"

Wow! This was bigger than the time a few of us as 14-year olds went to Madison Square Garden and were told by an usher to give him a buck and go to gate 105 and ask for "Ike". Jimmy couldn't have come up with a better contact. W.H. "Bud" Griest happened to be the Vice Chairman of the Tournament of Roses Committee that year. The following year, Bud would be Chairman. The Chairman gets to select the Grand Marshal for his parade. The only consideration that we needed to make for the tickets was not to divulge who Bud's Grand Marshal would be in 1996 Tournament of Roses. The secret was safe with me and I never let the cat, or I can now say frog, out of the bag. *Kermit the Frog* was Bud's choice as Grand Marshal. My old Boonton pal Jimmy was artistically responsible for "Kermie" at that time. So thanks to the green frog, I saw the green and gold Ducks play for the first time - and in the Rose Bowl!

The fabulous Rose Parade came first. We enjoyed reserved parking spaces and reserved bleacher seats below the television cameras. The PSU and Oregon bands came along to cheers from their respective fans. Horse units, US Marines, Morris Brown University, and other marching bands were great, but I have to admit that I found myself very amazed seeing the floats in person for the first time. I know it struck a chord with my little daughter, as for a very long time Alex would remember the event as "bears and flowers."

After the parade and a short drive to the stadium, we enjoyed a great, buffet lunch under a huge bubble in the parking lot as guests of Big Ten and PAC 10 officials and Grand Marshal Chi-Chi Rodriguez, the golfing legend. Saint Laurie, Jim's wife Judy, and Alex left after lunch, not that they had any interest in watching a football game to begin with, but Laurie and Judy were both awaiting arrivals of baby boys in the spring. Jimmy, John, and I headed to the Rose Bowl to meet Bud at our seats. There we presented him with a Penn State sweatshirt as a token of our appreciation. He graciously accepted, but for obvious reasons did not put it on to maintain his neutrality. We couldn't put him on the spot, but we hoped that he'd wear it eventually.

The 81st edition of the oldest bowl game in history started off with an explosion. Penn State RB Ki-Jana Carter broke a tackle at the line of scrimmage and raced 83 yards for a touchdown. Things couldn't get started any better than that for the disrespected Lions who led the nation offensively with 47.8 points and 526.2 yards per game. When Carter scored again in the second half, John, Jimmy, and I celebrated among the Rose Bowl attendees sitting in our "neutral" section. Locals, mostly USC fans, turned to look at us to wonder why anybody in their section was cheering. We roared for the Lions!

Ki-Jana Carter tied a Rose Bowl record with three rushing TDs for the Lions among his 156 yards on 21 carries. Oregon QB Danny O'Neill riddled Penn State's defense completing 41 of 61 passes for 456 yards and two TD passes. He shattered 13 Rose Bowl records. Tied at 14 early in the third, Ambrose Fletcher returned a kickoff 72 yards for Penn State. Carter ran it in from 17 yards. Later in the third, S Chuck Penzenik intercepted an O'Neil pass, his second of the day, and returned it to the Ducks' 13. Carter took it in from the three for a 28-14 lead. With a Brett Conway FG and Jon Witman's TD run of nine yards, Penn State went on to defeat the "Quack Attack", 38-20, to finish the season 12-0, the fifth undefeated season ever in Coach Paterno's illustrious career.

From a personal perspective, this Rose Bowl experience was the opportunity of a lifetime—first-class all the way! We couldn't thank Bud enough for his great hospitality, and before we parted at the end of the post-game celebration, he told us, "The next time Penn State plays in the Rose Bowl, you guys are invited back any time."

I left Bud with this thought, "Bud, no matter who's playing, I'll be glad to come back any time!"

A year later, Kermit the Frog presided over Northwestern's first trip to Pasadena since 1949 to face the nearby Trojans of USC. Regretfully, the Lions did not return until 2008, and even more so, we couldn't track down Bud. If I ever do get back to the "Granddaddy of 'em all", I'm sure it will never top the experience enjoyed on January 2, 1995. I got to see Team No. 46, the Ducks from the University of Oregon, thanks to my acquaintance with Kermit the Frog.

Two-point conversion: PSU's win set off controversy though as undefeated PSU finally let loose on the media charging that they were as deserving of the national championship as was Nebraska. Their arguments exposed the weakness of a national championship determined along television network alignments and bowl coalition ties with which the Rose Bowl was not affiliated. Despite the arguments, Nebraska was crowned as national champs even though two undefeated teams remained standing at the end of the 1994 season. Even Cornhusker Head Coach Tom Osborne was quoted succinctly, "People in college football ought to be smart enough to get the No. 1 and No. 2 teams together."[5] Powers-that-be formed Bowl Championship Series which isn't exactly perfect, but it's better than deciding with secret ballots.

Little did I know at the time that I had watched that game with a

5 "Osbornespeak", *News Record*, January 3, 1995, page B3.

celebrity. My pal James Lewis won an Emmy award in 1998 for Outstanding Children's Programming for his work on *Muppets Tonight*. He was nominated again in 2003 for *Kermit's Swamp Years*.

Brad's Bullies
(47) Vanderbilt at (48) South Carolina
October 21, 1995

Columbia, SC - The year 1995 offered me a new career opportunity that caused me to pull up roots from my native New Jersey to start work with a company in the middle of nowhere—Hemingway, SC. I first moved down by myself as St. Laurie stayed in NJ waiting for baby number two, Eric, to arrive in May. By September, we finally got everyone settled into a condo complex along the coast in Georgetown, SC, half way between Myrtle Beach and Charleston, both great areas for different reasons. The incentive to relocate was for a better salary in an area with a much lower cost of living. Yeah, right! It was to get closer to SEC and ACC games. Okay, not really, but it sure did help make seeing more teams a reality and re-settling somewhat bearable for me any way. South Carolina, Clemson, and The Citadel for affordable Southern Conference games fell within driving range. I still planned to fly north once or twice a year to catch a game at the Meadowlands or at Penn State, or both.

Settling into our new neighborhood which included some "friendly local" alligators who sunned themselves in the condo complex, it was impossible to leave Laurie and the kids alone on weekends, so when the first, few opportunities presented themselves to go to games, we all went together. With a two-year old and a five-month old, trips to Clemson didn't make sense at the time. The South Carolina Gamecocks played games about two hours closer in Columbia, and when Mike Morgan and his wife Pam invited us to go to a game, we jumped at the chance. The Gamecocks would host the perennially hapless Vanderbilt Commodores, whom I missed on a previous visit to The Meadowlands because of some grad school conflict years earlier.

A big crowd showed up at Williams-Brice Stadium that day despite the ineptitude, or maybe *because* of the ineptitude, of the competition. South Carolina Head Coach Brad Scott entered this weekend 3-3-1 by beating the likes of Louisiana Tech, 68-21, Kent, 77-14, and Mississippi State, 65-39!

With 0-5 Vanderbilt showing up in the capitol of the Palmetto State, what else could be expected from Scott?

It certainly turned out to be a nice day weather-wise. We tailgated and checked out the "Carolina Cockabooses" before the game. Catering is offered with all the comforts of home—furnishings, heat, AC, running water, and cable TV. It was an interesting side trip on the way to the stadium.

As the onslaught took place with Eric and Alex trading places on our laps, I struck up a conversation with the USC season ticket holder sitting to my left. My voice gave it away that I wasn't from South Carolina. After I explained how we were in the process of settling in from New Jersey, our conversation turned to South Carolina basketball. He spoke of how much he and the Gamecocks both missed their New York City connection over the years since Frank McGuire's days. The coach from NYC recruited players from the metropolitan area when he coached the Gamecock basketball program up until 1980. Basically, we discussed some good college hoops during a bad college football game. USC's Steve Taneyhill threw for two TDs and 187 yards in the first period alone! His first tied a school record of 21 TDs for the season and blew away the record before the day was out. He threw for five all together to tie his own South Carolina game record set previously in the LA Tech blow-out. He finished 31 of 54 for 354 yards. We watched SC tear up the hapless Commodores, 52-14. Funny thing though, despite all this supposed offense, the Gamecocks 4-3-1 record never improved in the win column for the balance of the season. They took advantage of weak competition like Vanderbilt, but couldn't get by any team of equal or better talent. Like bullies who beat up on the much weaker kids, the Gamecocks got their tail feathers kicked in by the likes of Florida, Tennessee, and Clemson by a combined score of 157-45 to end their season 4-6-1. Head Coach Brad Scott stayed for five seasons and left with a 23-32 record, but evidently, the win column was very suspect.

What can I say about Vanderbilt? The Commodores performed typically as the SEC bottom-feeders that they are. However, to the delight of *Vandy* fans, I can also say that I've seen them play at the extreme opposite of their quintessential selves. The five-month old on my lap in 1995 was almost as big as me in 2008 and by my side in Nashville at the Music City Bowl. We watched the Commodores defeat Boston College, 16-14. For VU, the bowl bid was only their fourth ever and the victory was their first in the post-season since 1955. Eric and I probably saw the greatest game in the history of Vanderbilt football!

Extra point: My move to South Carolina ended about a month later.

The job opportunity was not as anticipated, the housing market in NJ was very slow, and our home there had not yet been sold. The living expenses from the company only lasted three months, and St. Laurie had left her job with the arrival of Eric, so things got very tight financially, to say the least. Luckily, my resume still circulated, and another company back in Jersey offered me a better position. It was a welcome relief after a tumultuous time—new job, no job for the wife, new baby, buying a house, selling a house, new surroundings, and looking for a new job again! Having a young family with new needs and a paucity of college football opportunities close by in South Carolina, I was pretty fortunate that things turned out the way they did.

Though all Jersey had as far as college football was the oldest but most anemic of all Division 1A programs in the country, Rutgers, within a driving range of four hours or less, there were nine different 1A campuses and even more good 1AA football schools, not to mention some competitive Division II and Division III programs. Also one of the best sports complexes hosting both major college football games and two pro football teams exists not far right in the swamps of Jersey.

I learned South Carolina is great for nice, relaxing vacations near the beach about eight months out of the year, but New Jersey is the Birthplace of College Football, and its greatest fan!

Seeing Red!
(49) Purdue at Penn State
October 12, 1996

State College - The Purdue Boilermakers showed up in State College to play the Nittany Lions in 1996 for the first time since 1952. St. Laurie and I met up with our friends Darryl and Kim Reigel to tailgate in Happy Valley without any of our kids. Darryl, a friend since our days at Juniata, and Kim, a Pitt grad, had three daughters and lived about 15 miles from us in Jersey. Finally on a rare occasion, we made plans to drop the kids off with extended families that weekend and made a date to tailgate in State College for fun and refreshments - kid-free! The Lions won their sixth of seven games that day, 31-14, bouncing back from their only loss the week before to Ohio State.

Four years later on September 30, 2000, the Penn State-Purdue game became etched in my memory for an unusual encounter that day. Purdue

QB Drew Brees had one final chance to bump off the Lions his senior season playing at State College after losing his two previous starts against them. Would he overcome the Lions with an overwhelming performance in his last stop at Penn State? Would his third start be the charm for Coach Tiller and the rest of the Boilermakers? I looked forward to the game. Brees had had great statistical games versus the Lions the two previous seasons, but the Boilermakers met their demise both times, 31-13 and 31-25. St. Laurie and I also looked forward to tailgating with some other good friends.

Business associate Barbara Glazar, a Purdue alum with a degree in chemical engineering, and her husband, Denny, were joining us in the Happy Valley parking lot to tailgate before the 3:30 pm kickoff. Barbara liked to reminisce about her fantastic trip to the Rose Bowl as a student, the last time the Boilermakers made it to Pasadena when they faced USC on January 1, 1967. Her husband, Denny, introduced us to a new brew, *Dogfish Head Ale* from a Rehoboth Beach, DE brewery—good stuff, very good stuff! Bob Jones, another business associate, lifetime PSU season-ticket holder, and Slippery Rock grad, planned to meet us to tailgate along with his Mom, a die-hard Penn State fan for many years. Like St. Laurie on many weekends, Bob's wife Lisa stayed home carting three kids around to various events. St. Laurie and I looked especially forward to our tailgating that day because it would be the first time that we would get to unfold our new, red canopy for our first football tailgate party that season. However, a strange thing happened in the parking lot that remains a mystery to us to this day. Only one conclusion seems to make any sense.

By mid-morning we were unfolding the frame of our tent in a lot north of the stadium just west of the Agricultural school buildings. Traffic was lighter than usual coming into the Beaver Stadium parking lots that day. On the positive side, a 3:30 kickoff meant everyone didn't converge into State College at the same time. On the negative side, traffic was light because Penn State was off to its worst start ever, 1-4. A week earlier, Ohio State hammered the Lions, 45-6, in Ohio Stadium. On top of that, PSU freshman CB Adam Taliaferro suffered a severe spinal injury with 1:39 left in that game. He was removed from the stadium on a stretcher and transported to Ohio State Medical Center where he underwent surgery for a cervical spinal injury. By the following Saturday, it was still too early to tell if the 18-year old athlete would ever be able to walk again.

Maybe the outcome of the previous week's defeat and misfortune had something to do with what happened to us next. Some guy walked up to us and congenially started a conversation while we rigged the red canopy up over our out-stretched frame. Next, the guy says, "I have to warn you that these canopies cause traffic problems and are not allowed here. I have to ask that you put it away. If you don't take it down right away, I'll have to get security people and confiscate it." What? Now I'd been attending Penn State games in Happy Valley for twenty years, and one of the reasons it's "Happy" is because a lot of people come up and gather on football weekends in RVs, vans, trucks, and cars to set up tents, grills, kegs, and more to enjoy themselves before and after Nittany Lion football games. However, this was my first time in this particular lot. There weren't a lot of tailgaters around yet, but I looked around trying to disprove that this guy was not telling the truth. I couldn't to my surprise! There wasn't an awning of any kind now in sight. Was it too early still? Did this parking lot have different rules than others? Did the school suddenly change the rules just because *I* finally brought a canopy to tailgate under? I had a hard time believing the school initiated such a new policy, but this guy said they were now banned because they created traffic problems? No kidding! All of a sudden I have this nice, new, "red" canopy that we bought primarily for tailgating, and suddenly, it's forbidden? I looked around for more security people, but noticed none. I was really getting pissed off, but since I couldn't disprove this mystery man, yet, and not wanting to get into a physical confrontation over a tent, I acquiesced. We pulled out a cooler full of beers and snacks. Thank the Lord food and alcohol weren't banned. We drank somewhat dumbfounded as the guy headed toward the road where traffic was finally starting to build. He just kept walking never to be seen again. Calming down a little, I left St. Laurie to wait for our guests as I walked eagerly to the crest of a hill for a vantage point to witness a tent-less Happy Valley Saturday. Who was this guy kidding, and where did he come from? Overlooking the lots to the east, blue and white canopies filled the landscape galore! What the...? Blue and white? Was that this guy's issue? Did this idiot see a scarlet canopy as an association with last weekend's dreadful loss to the Ohio State Buckeyes? Was that the reason for his threat? By the time I got back to our car, a couple new rows of tailgaters had begun to form behind us. Tables, chairs, coolers, grills, AND canopies started to fill traffic lanes. We took our frame back out and rigged the red canopy on top among all the blue, white, gray, and probably black and gold ones as well. The guy never came back. It had to be the strangest damned experience I'd ever had in any parking lot. It still ticks me off thinking about it today!

QB Rashard Casey took it in from the two and PSU closed out the third period ahead of Purdue, 22-13. Drew Brees brought his team back on the next drive culminating in a 39-yard TD pass to Vinny Sutherland with 11:30 left to close the gap, 22-20. His completion tied the Big Ten record for touchdown passes with 74. Purdue's Travis Dorsch missed a 46-yard FG attempt. The game wasn't over until the final play of the game. Brees tossed one last "Hail Mary" into the end zone, and James Boyd batted the ball to the ground for State. Brees finished his collegiate career against Penn State at 0-3 despite career Big Ten passing records including most completions, yards, and touchdowns. The emotional week after Taliaferro's severe injury probably played a hand also in helping the struggling Lions defeat a team ranked higher than them for the first time since 1996.

With Barbara, Denny, and the Joneses, we partied late under our red canopy after Penn State's second win and Purdue's second loss of the season. Cars crept out of the parking lot slowly since most stayed to watch the final outcome decided on the final play. I still wonder if the color of our canopy caused that mysterious jerk to make threats to confiscate it. That guy was there one minute and gone the next. I still see red over the whole incident. It was weird.

Extra point: I attended the opening game at Beaver Stadium the following season to watch a poorly played 33-7 loss by the Lions to eventual National Champ Miami. The Canes dominated the Lions to the point where ABC-TV switched coverage at halftime to the Oregon-Wisconsin game. The bad news for Penn State football was that they continued on to their second consecutive, losing season with a record of 5-6. The great news for Penn State football that opening night – over 100,000 people stood and cheered for Adam Taliaferro when he *walked* out of the Beaver Stadium tunnel prior to the kickoff.

"Two lanes" to Success— Express and Detour

(50) Tulane at Army
October 19, 1996

West Point - A nor'easter battered the entire east coast including the banks of the Hudson this Saturday afternoon, but Tulane showed up as a team I had not seen play yet. With St. Laurie and Fred Bacchetta, my close friend since grade school, we ignored the weather and headed up to West Point despite the extreme elements. Fred's wife, Emilie, had to back out as a couple of their four kids had gotten sick that weekend. Fred came nonetheless as we had planned this little football excursion to get together for the first time in quite a while. Entering West Point's main gate near Thayer Hotel in a single line, we laughed as traffic cops shouted at each and every vehicle, "Two lanes! Two lanes! Two lanes!" It sounded like they'd be the only ones cheering for the visitors that day among the 23,532 braving the rotten, cold, stormy weather at Army's Homecoming. Tulane visited the Point for the first time in 22 years. A rare Army team awaited the Green Wave after all that time. For only the second time since the two foes last met, the Cadet record stood at 5-0! One week after churning out 546 yards against Rutgers with their deceiving wishbone attack, Army led the nation in rushing with 367.6 yards per game. A 2-3 Tulane forged the Army opposition today.

Driving rains and gusting winds would keep both passing games under wraps during the entire game. That advantage played into Army's strengths - a triple option rushing attack and a strong defense against the run. Army led 20-3 going into the final period before RB Bobby Williams scored on TD runs of three and of fourteen yards among his game-high 111 yards on 17 carries. Tulane could only muster one lone touchdown late in the game with a TD pass to finish off the scoring to end it, 34-10. The Black Knights prevailed still undefeated. In a manner of speaking Army and Tulane's 1996 seasons continued down separate "Two lanes! Two lanes!" After meeting on that miserable day in West Point, Army took the express lane to a bowl game that season finishing with a very successful 10-2 record including the Independence Bowl resulting in a close loss to Alabama. For his leadership, Army Coach Bob Sutton won the Bobby Dodd Coach of the Year Award. Tulane took a detour after that loss hitting more bumps before things smoothed out. The Green Wave's 1996 season continued to tailspin resulting in a 2-9 finish. Tulane relieved Buddy Teevens of his head coaching duties at the end of the season and replaced him with Florida State offensive coordinator Tommy Bowden, son of Bobby. The Wave's football fortunes turned the very next season with a respectable 7-4 record. In 1998, they finished 12-0 as QB Shaun King led them to victories right through to a Liberty Bowl win over BYU, good for No. 7 in the nation. Bowden left for Clemson after only his second season at Tulane to play an ACC showdown every year against his old man. As of 2010, neither Army nor Tulane has even come close to their respective finishes of 1996 or 1998 until Army finished 7-6 with a win over SMU in the 2010 Bell Helicopter Armed Forces Bowl. Tulane's had only two winning seasons since.

Extra point: At some point during that rainy, bone-chilling nor'easter at West Point, St. Laurie decided the deluge was too uncomfortable and she retreated to the warmer, drier confines of our mini-van parked along the stone wall on Thayer Road running through campus. Fred and I stayed literally to the bitter end. As you hopefully understand by now, games don't count if I don't stay until time expires in the fourth quarter (college shirts aren't "official" either unless you buy them on campus). Cold, wet, and somewhat disoriented after seeing Tulane play for the first time, Fred and I jogged down Mills Road toward what we thought was a short-cut to find the mini-van with the engine on and the heater running. Instead, we ended up in some *cul-de-sac*. On big white cement steps of each residence, names and ranks of the heads of each household were stenciled in big, black letters. The first one to our right read "Head Football Coach Bob Sutton." It didn't look like anyone at the household planned a victory celebration any time soon, not that we were invited. So we jogged back out and down the hill to the next left which finally led us to our warm sanctuary on wheels. Laurie slept curled up in a blanket with the engine running and the heater on. Thank you! Our journey to recovery was more like Tulane's than Army's that day. We took a *detour* instead of the *express* lane.

From the Ashes

(51) Marshall at Army
September 6, 1997

West Point - My late father grew up in Lyndhurst, New Jersey about five miles from the mouth of the Lincoln Tunnel. Both sets of my grandparents lived in that same town during the 1970s. My father always spoke with great pride about the athletes and teams that came from his old hometown over the years. During the height of my youth baseball career in the late '60s growing up in Boonton Township, he took me to see a few games one weekend when the Lyndhurst American Legion baseball team played in the state championship tournament in nearby Dover. The Lyndhurst lineup consisted of players playing college baseball as freshmen at Notre Dame, Seton Hall, Princeton, and Lafayette, among others. The team's catcher was a broad-shouldered kid with a *gun* for an arm who went to "some small school down south," according to my father, who was a former sports editor for the local paper near Lyndhurst, The South Bergen News.

Ted Shoebridge played catcher for the Lyndhurst Legion. Between Legion baseball and a semi-pro baseball circuit known as the Metropolitan

League that played at Bergen County Park in Lyndhurst, we saw many of these same players compete over the next few years during various visits to my father's parents' house. As an All-Star catcher in youth baseball still learning the position myself, I focused on Shoebridge playing catcher when I watched those teams play. He was a solid hitter, a hustler, and a take-charge leader on the field. In one, quick motion from the crouch, he'd spring straight up, take one short stride, and bring his arm up straight over the top in a split second to nail runners trying to steal second. Surely pro scouts drooled. As a 12-year old, I didn't emulate the Reds' Johnny Bench or the Mets' Jerry Grote, two of my favorites when I was behind the plate. I was Ted Shoebridge!

In the fall of my first season playing football as a high school freshman, I remember hearing the news about the horrific plane crash in West Virginia in which most of the Marshall team perished on their return trip from East Carolina on November 14, 1970. But it became more poignant the following Monday. For some reason, our varsity team hosted a game on Monday instead of Saturday, and we freshman were in attendance in the stands. After the game, my father came by to pick me up. He asked, "Do you know *who* died in that Marshall plane crash?" I never really had heard much about Marshall until the news of the tragedy much less knew of anyone who went there. Before I could give it much thought, he blurted out, "Ted Shoebridge." I was shocked! Until that moment, I never knew that the "small school down south" Shoebridge attended was Marshall. Nor did I even know that the baseball prospect I admired with a rifle of an arm also played quarterback for that college. Head Coach Rick Tolley was revitalizing the Herd football program. He expanded the program's recruiting efforts to states rarely considered before – New Jersey, Texas, Alabama, and Florida. On that terrible day in college football history, Shoebridge had led a comeback against ECU that fell short in a 17-14 loss. He came off the bench in the second half and completed 14 of 32 attempts for 188 yards and a 16-yard TD. His Lyndhurst High School teammate, Marcelo Lajterman, doubled as kicker and punter for The Herd. At the crash site, Shoebridge's body was never recovered. I remember a photograph in *The Sporting News* after the tragedy showing his parents presenting a huge floral arrangement at the Marshall campus.

Fast forward to West Point on September 6, 1997, twenty years and a day since my father passed away and almost 27 years after the horrible plane crash that took the lives of Ted Shoebridge, Marcelo Lajterman, and seventy-three other people retuning from a college football game played in

Greenville, NC. The Thundering Herd football program rebuilt itself from the ashes and was on the verge of taking on a new challenge. As depicted in the 2007 movie release *"We are Marshall,"* the efforts to continue the football program began immediately after the loss of 34 players, 5 coaches, and 5 staff members. From 1971 to 1981, the program never achieved more than four wins in a season. In 1982, the school administration decided to take a step back to play at the 1AA level, a move that revived the football program to new heights in the long term. The program thrived even winning the national title in 1992. Under first-year Head Coach Bob Pruett, they won it again going 15-0 in 1996. In 1997, Marshall returned to Division 1A as a member of the Mid-American Conference where they played years before from 1954 to 1969. Today's game against Army was their second in their return to 1A football since 1980.

Marshall sophomore wide receiver Randy Moss showed his speed early by catching a short pass from QB Chad Pennington and streaking past Army defenders for a 90-yard touchdown. Another Pennington TD pass was countered by Army TD runs by Joe Hewitt and Ty Amey, but missed extra points kept The Herd in the lead, 14-12. In the third, Moss did it again catching a short pass and hurdling an Army defender for an exciting, 79-yard score. Later, Hewitt then got creamed by NT Larry McCloud, fumbled, and suffered a concussion as Herd LB Ricky Hall picked up the loose ball to sprint 43 yards for a score giving Marshall a 28-12 lead. Army actually outgained Marshall that day, 527-337 yards, but the visitors came up with the big, scoring plays. Marshall earned its first D-1 victory since 1980, 35-25. Moss and Pennington would have a lot to do with that early Marshall success back into big-time football. During the 1999 NFL Draft Show, ESPN continuously highlighted the two big plays Dave Headden and I witnessed that day when Moss took two short Pennington passes and turned them into two long touchdowns against Army. Moss got drafted by the Minnesota Vikings. Pennington got drafted by the New York Jets. The rest is now pro football history.

To witness the beginning of Marshall's rebirth in 1A football was a highlight amongst my own annals of college football history. Under Head Coach Bob Pruett, re-entry into Division 1A football for the next eight years resulted in a 79-23 record, five MAC Championships, five bowl wins, and a couple of Top 25 finishes proving that the Thundering Herd had made it back from the ashes that horrific day in 1970. I'm sure Rick Tolley, Ted Shoebridge, and their Herd teammates would be proud that the Marshall team of 1997 revitalized what they had set out to do back in 1970.

Extra point: On November 14, 2009, 39 years to the day of the tragedy, my friend Steve Ciesla and I drove down to Huntington, West Virginia to attend the annual Memorial on campus and the Marshall-Southern Mississippi game (won by USM, 27-20). The ceremony is held near the Memorial fountain that gets turned off every year on the anniversary of the tragedy. We met Ted's brother, Tom, who was presented with a memento, a memorial quilt. A player who was injured and missed the game spoke about memories of his teammates. The team and the date will never be forgotten in Huntington. We were glad that we had the chance to be there. It's a solemn and beautiful occasion to remember the many young lives and those that perished with them that day in 1970.

The Marshall Memorial Fountain on the 39th anniversary of the Marshall plane crash.

What she said!
(52) Southern Mississippi at Penn State
September 5, 1998

State College - With only two game tickets, St. Laurie and I drove to State College with five-year old Alex and three-year old Eric for a family weekend. Penn State hosted Southern Mississippi's Golden Eagles in the season opener for both teams. The pool was still open at the hotel we'd stay at, and we planned to visit Knoebel's in Elysburg, Pennsylvania, an amusement park with old-time rides for the kids.

My personal connections with Southern Miss were fleeting over the years but memorable none the less. My grade-school gym teacher, Bob Exum, who arranged my first college football trip to see Colgate play Princeton in fifth grade and who later coached me in basketball and baseball, attended Southern Miss. He played baseball for the Eagles. Too many times we heard the story of how he and shortstop Don Kessinger, later of Chicago Cub fame, took so many ground balls to work their double-play combination. He was one of the first to encourage my college football fandom even more by fanning the flames with our debates over where the best football was played—in my North or in *his* South!

Another Southern Miss memory came on my 1979 return trip from *Mardi Gras* with my college pal, Pat Daly. Stopping at various college campuses down and back to New Orleans to break up the long drives, we checked out the "sights." Our stop in Hattiesburg placed far out in front as a unanimous No. 1 for girl-watching. We saw more gorgeous women there in our half-hour stop than any other campus we visited. I can't remember how many times I "fell in love" that morning. If you can believe this, I still have the Southern Miss t-shirt with a Golden Eagle on a blue background strutting proudly forward tucked away in my dresser drawer. I actually still wear it once in a while thirty years later. After our *Mardi Gras* trip, Pat and I selected the University of New Orleans as the best campus, picked Virginia Tech's bookstore as the best among the dozen or so schools we stopped at, and chose Southern Miss by far the tops for the women.

The plan for our family journey in 1998, due to the announced ticket policy at Beaver Stadium, required me to bring both kids, now ages five and three, to our two seats for one half each. St. Laurie would be content to hang around the car and meet me near the gate for our halftime kid exchange. One ticket could serve both kids, and they could sit on my lap or sit in their own seat now that they would officially be in possession of their own ticket.

It was a warm, comfortable, sunny day as we tailgated before the 3:30 start time for the nationally televised game. We parked in a field opened for the first time for football that was still used by the Agricultural School—*dairy farming* to be precise. As game time neared, we packed everything back into the car, took what we needed, and walked to the stadium so we could synchronize our halftime plan to exchange kids. We left with plenty of time since it would be a long walk for short legs. I held Alex's hand and took the lead as 3-year old Eric would walk for a while before wanting Mom to pick him up. Alex would join me for the first half, and Eric would join me after halftime.

As we approached the exit from our tailgate on to East Park Avenue leading to Beaver Stadium, lines of fans waited about seven or eight deep for their turns in the port-o-johns. Appropriately near the portable toilets were large piles of cow manure freshly heaped so fans could avoid squashing cow chips while grilling or feasting before the much-anticipated opener between No. 13 Penn State and No. 21 Southern Miss. However, the ground near the port-o-potties not only consisted of cow dung evidently flattened by vehicles entering the lot from that gate, but it became soft, wet, and cow manure stinky. As we passed patient people poised and pondering to pee, I kind of anticipated the next words from my little *kindergartner* even before they came out of her mouth. Her timing was impeccable. "Boy, Dad, there sure is a lot of *COW POOP* around here!" The silent lines lit up with laughter. What the adults quietly tolerated, a five year-old had no qualms about announcing the obvious. As the saying goes: "Out of the mouths of babes". We had some good laughs about the preparation of a new parking area on the way to Beaver Stadium. Alex's words not only accurately described the conditions in our dairy land parking lot, but they were also prophetic regarding how the Golden Eagles would perform that day!

A trio of inexperienced Penn State running backs, Cordell Mitchell, Omar Easy, and freshman Eric McCoo, replacing graduated Curtis Enis, combined for 213 yards on the ground. FB Mike Ceremele scored two TDs on short runs behind a line that dominated the Eagles. The Eagle passing game lived up somewhat to the hype as Lee Roberts and Sherrod Gideon connected 13 times for 176 yards, but PSU's defense halted any progress after each reception. Both players set school bests that day. Gideon set school marks in career receptions (100) and yards (1,684). Roberts broke Brett Favre's single game record with 27 completions. None of his 289 yards cracked the end zone. The Lions roared in a dominating 34-6 win.

Extra point: It turned out to be an up and down season for the Golden

Eagles who fell far short of their pre-season expectations. And how they started that season couldn't have been depicted any better than how my five-year old described what she saw outside the stadium before she went in.

From "the cradle"...
(53) Miami (Ohio) at Army
September 12, 1998

West Point - For the second week in a row, the entire family traveled on another football excursion. This trip was much closer and four tickets allowed us to all attend the game together. The sun shone brightly at West Point which is a rare occurrence whenever I attend games there. We took to our seats in the south end zone well before all the traditional, pre-game festivities. Everything seemed ok until other fans approached us and made me realize that we were sitting in the wrong seats. That wasn't the first time I'd done that at Michie. Sometimes the section numbering system there screws me up. My kids and wife let me know about it.

Miami's head coach Randy Walker followed a long line of successful coaches at the school in Oxford, Ohio who went on to achieve high marks in both college and the NFL. Known as the "cradle of coaches", Miami of Ohio launched the careers of Sid Gillman, Paul Brown, Weeb Ewbank, Woody Hayes, Bo Schembechler, John Pont, Ara Parseghian, and Army's legendary Earl "Red" Blaik. Michie's playing surface bears Blaik's name today.

In the third period with a 10-7 lead, Army drove to Miami's 29. Out of field goal range, Army Coach Bob Sutton called a play on fourth and short, but the Hawks stopped Bobby Williams at the line of scrimmage. On Miami's ensuing possession, we watched Travis Prentice burst through the middle and sprint right toward us for a 45-yard TD jaunt. Before the period ended, Army cut the lead on Eric Olsen's 32-yard FG, 14-13. Both defenses held fast to hinder any further scoring threats, and the Red Hawks sealed their second victory of the young season on their way to a 10-1 record. Terribly, no bowl bids came Miami's way that season. How "bowl eligibility" has changed since!

Junior Travis Prentice finished his Red Hawk career after the 1999 season with 5,596 yards on 1,138 carries to capture school, conference and NCAA records. His 862 consecutive touches without any fumbles were considered by many to be his most impressive personal stat.

Extra point: On June 29, 2006, 52-year old Randy Walker, the head coach that day who left Miami to take over Northwestern in 1999, died from a sudden heart attack. Walker was well liked and would be deeply missed by the Wildcat players and staff in the program he started to improve. His assistant and former NU LB, Pat Fitzgerald, whom I watched perform as an All-American in 1996, took over the program as the youngest head coach in D1A football at age 31. When Northwestern visited Penn State that season, I saw the youngest coach against the oldest, 80-year old Joe Paterno! When Walker left Miami in 1999 to take over at NU, his defensive coordinator, Terry Hoeppner, took his place. In March 2007, Hoeppner, another successful Miami coach who moved on to take over at Indiana, passed away from brain cancer he fought for several months. He inspired his Hoosier players on to the program's first bowl game in fourteen years. He lived his life and left behind his players with the mantra, "Don't quit!"[6]

Even after death, the spirit of two great leaders of young men from the Miami Red Hawk program left behind legacies that encouraged their teams to always play hard and to never give up – lessons learned at "the Cradle of Coaches."

Greatest Game Ever!

(54) Virginia Tech at Syracuse
November 14, 1998

Syracuse, NY - Over the years, I attended thirteen Syracuse games. The Orangemen always played as road warriors whether they "hosted" games at the Meadowlands while the Carrier Dome was under construction or played there in Kickoff Classics. I traveled to see them play at venues in Annapolis, State College, Pittsburgh, and Raleigh. Finally in 1998, 23 years after seeing them play in Annapolis, did I finally get to see them play not one, but two games in the Carrier Dome. Bernie Olszyk, a friend from work, purchased a season-ticket package at Syracuse while his daughter, Heather, attended school there. Initially with "Bernardo," we witnessed a typical 63-21 blow-out of Cincinnati in the Dome, but five weeks later, Les DiVite and I attended the most exciting football game I ever witnessed in over 30 years attending college football games. It set my high standard for excitement.

---

6 Terry Hutchens, "Indiana football coach Terry Hoeppner dies," http://www.usatoday.com/sports/college/football/bigten/2007-06-19-in-hoeppner-obit_N.htm (20 June 2007)

Les and I trekked up I-81, and unlike the previous trip to Syracuse, we shunned the satellite parking lots for a chance to park closer to the stadium. As luck would have it, we turned on a street near the SUNY Upstate Medical Center not more than a stone's throw from The Dome. A nurse who must have just come off her shift approached her parked car along Adams Street. We slowed to stop, she waved, got in her car, left, and we had a free parking space literally in the "shadows" of the Carrier Dome. I always looked for ways to minimize expenses so I could continue to afford to do this. One other pre-game note of interest, this was the first time in twenty years attending an on-campus athletic facility that sold beer! We took seats chosen personally by Bernardo in Section 328, Row H, high above the end zone sitting right between the uprights in the south end of the Dome. They turned out to be perfect for the game about to unfold before us.

This important Big East match-up took place between the 6-3 Orangemen led by QB Donovan McNabb against the vaunted defense of the 7-1 Virginia Tech Hokies. As expected, Frank Beamer's special teams were forces to be reckoned with. His punt-return team already had nine blocked punts to their credit. McNabb started the game with the thumb on his throwing hand wrapped, but the bandage came off early in the contest. Trailing early 3-0 in the first period, Virginia Tech FB Jarret Ferguson broke through a hole over left tackle, and sprinted away from us untouched for a 76-yard TD run—wearing only one shoe for 60 of those yards no less! By game's end, his run would account for more than fifty percent of Tech's rushing yards. What's more, this one jaunt also totaled more than twice the passing yardage that the Hokies' QB Al Clark would throw for that night.

You wouldn't expect this to be such an exciting game with such an anemic offense, but this night's game would epitomize classic "Beamer Ball" – big, special-team plays. Right below us, on Syracuse's ensuing possession to start the second quarter, VT's Anthony Midget blocked the SU punt into the end zone where Ricky Hall recovered it for the Tech lead, 14-3. Before the first half ended, Beamer's *defense* would get the chance to strike. Syracuse moved into field-goal range. On an attempted reverse, WR Maurice Jackson had the ball knocked from his grasp into the air by FS Keion Carpenter. CB Loren Johnson picked it off in mid-air and sprinted 78 yards for the defensive TD to take a 21-3 Virginia Tech lead. Syracuse responded with a FG, a 36-yarder by Nate Trout to dent the Hokie lead, 21-6. The majority of the 49,336 in attendance this evening expressed extreme discontent for the Orange and Blue as the teams left for intermission. Coach Paul Pasquoloni's troops knew their first half offensive performance was dismal. Aside from Jarret's run, the SU defense held Tech in check, but Donavan McNabb and the offense would have to step things up. Were they up for the task?

In the third, the Orangemen defense continued to stifle the Hokies, and McNabb finally got the Orange into the end zone with a one-yard scoring pass to his TE Stephen Brominski to complete a 10-play drive. A second 10-play drive resulted in three more points as Trout converted again from 30. By the end of the third period, Syracuse only trailed by five, 21-16. With twelve minutes left to play, the Orange finally took the lead on a one-yard plunge on fourth down by FB Rob Konrad. The 22-21 lead lasted briefly. Beamer's special team defense team found another way to take it back! Loren Johnson played the culprit once again when he picked off McNabb's pass attempt on a two-point conversion and raced away from us for Tech's 99-yard two-point conversion. On another unusual, long play, Tech re-took the lead just like that, 23-22. Following the two-point turnaround, the Hokies' offense finally came through with its second score, a 49-yard FG by PK Shayne Graham at the end of a short 29-yard drive.

With 4:33 left in the game, the Orange started from their 17-yard line trailing, 26-22. They'd have to play for the TD to have a shot to win the Big East conference still within reach. A second conference loss would eliminate them from contention. On a fourth and six from his 46, McNabb came up big with a 39-yard run for a fresh set of downs at Tech's fifteen. On his hands and knees along the sideline, McNabb puked. A 14-yard pass to Maurice Jackson brought the Orange to the one-yard line right below our vantage point. McNabb heaved some more – not the ball, his guts. With less than a minute remaining, the Hokies stopped a Konrad run for no gain. After an incompletion to Brominski, Syracuse moved half a yard closer courtesy of a VT penalty. McNabb bootlegged left only to be sacked by DE Corey Moore, the Big East's Defensive Player of the Year, for a 12-yard loss. No time-outs remained. The Orange hustled back to the line of scrimmage. McNabb spiked the ball. The clock stopped with time remaining for only one more play on fourth down. This was it. McNabb rolled to his right, stopped, suddenly looked all the way back to his left, turned, jumped, and floated a pass high to Brominski. He positioned himself in front of LB Michael Hawkes. Brominski went high to make the grab. He pulled it in while falling to the ground, and clutched it to his chest for the most exciting finish imaginable! No time left. No extra point needed! The SU squad piled on top of Brominski. Syracuse students raced on to the field in celebration.

Hokie players collapsed to the turf in disbelief. It was a wild, unforgettable finish—a true classic determined on the game's final play, 28-26!

Extra point: My primary purpose to attend this game was to see Virginia Tech play for the first time. I was starting to try to specifically schedule teams I hadn't seen play. Yet, this game became a classic featuring a number of unusual, exciting scoring plays leading to a classic finish for the ages. In his *FoxSports.com* article, *"100 Greatest Finishes"*, Pete Fiutak rated this game No. 58 among the elite in this category. Each game required three primary requirements: 1.) won on a final play or drive; 2.) played for some significance; and 3.) remembered in college football history.[7] Syracuse won the Big East championship. In over three hundred college football games, none topped Syracuse versus Virginia Tech in excitement from beginning to end in the quest to "see 'em all!" I was there. I remember! How can I forget?

"Want to get away?"
(55) Arizona at Penn State
Pigskin "Classic"
August 28, 1999

State College – Arizona visited Penn State in the '99 opener as a twelfth game added under the auspices of the Pigskin Classic started ten seasons earlier. It was a copy-cat to the original Kickoff Classic. More copy-cats followed, causing the ultimate demise of the "Classics" when the NCAA eventually determined every team could play a twelfth game starting in 2003. Not only was this my first Pigskin Classic, but the following day, I headed back to The Meadowlands to see Miami (F.) play Ohio State in Kickoff Classic XVII.

With four year-old Eric, I traveled to State College for what surely promised to be a great season opener with implications already on the national championship. PSU ranked third in the AP pre-season poll and fourth in the ESPN/USA Today Coaches Poll. Their season-opening opponent, the Arizona Wildcats, claimed the exact opposite in the preseason polls – fourth in the AP and third in the Coaches Poll. This game looked to be a real *"Classic"*.

The Wildcats returned 17 starters from the previous season's 12-1 team

7 Pete Fiutak, "100 Greatest College Football Finishes," http://cfn.scout.com/2/657471.html (9 July2007)

with Dick Tomey's heralded "Desert Swarm" defense. Penn State drove 80 yards on its first possession with Chafie Fields taking a short pass 37 yards after a missed Arizona tackle for an early lead. The Lions didn't stop there. Fields took an inside reverse through the Swarm for a 70-yard TD run. In the second period, Travis Forney kicked a 31-yard FG. Kevin Thompson tossed a 60-yard TD pass to Larry Johnson, and Leo Mills followed with a one-yard run to put the Lions ahead at halftime, 31-0. This game looked to be a real "Classic" - *Not!* Arizona which averaged 31 points per game in '98 didn't score until the game's final minute, and Penn State ran roughshod on, over, and through the Desert Swarm defense for 504 yards of offense, winning 41-7. Fields, a receiver, rushed for 110 yards on three carries and caught three passes for 76. Arizona's Trung Canidate, winner of the Pac-10 rushing title the year before, tallied 31 yards on 10 carries. These Cats weren't just beaten, they were embarrassed. They left with their proverbial tails between their legs.

Not long after taking my sweaty son back to the parking lot to eat, drink, and play catch while letting the Beaver Stadium parking lots empty, a sight I'd never seen before or since appeared in the sky over Happy Valley. It couldn't have been more than a half an hour after time expired, but a Boeing 737 rose above the tree line northeast of the stadium, got altitude, took a sharp turn in the direction of Tucson, Arizona to high-tail it quickly out of central Pennsylvania. Only a few years before, the state of Pennsylvania extended the runways at State College airport at the behest of the Big Ten who wanted to travel direct on larger jets. I doubt Arizona players even had enough time to shower! I envisioned a bunch of sweaty players strapped into their seats still wearing pads. The Cat contingent tucked tails embarrassed and jetted quickly out of Happy Valley trying to leave a very bad start behind. I couldn't see what airline it was, but their quick departure reminded me of one airline's ad campaign seen on TV a few years later – "Want to get away?"

Extra point: Looking back, it didn't pay for the Wildcats to leave in such a hurry. Expectations fell far short of any championships as they stumbled along to a bowl-less 6-6 season. Since that Wildcat letdown, I never witnessed the departure of any visiting contingent of winners or losers bolt that fast from Happy Valley on such a big jet airliner!

Location! Location! Location!
(56) Central Michigan at Syracuse
September 11, 1999

Syracuse, NY - Bernie Olszyk, Steve Ciesla, and I ventured up to Syracuse to watch the Chippewas of Central Michigan wander into upstate New York to play the Orangemen for their first time ever. I hoped that CMU could give the Orange a tussle as they had done to Michigan State in years past with a couple of upset wins. It was also a farewell celebration of sorts. This would be the final season Bernie purchased season tickets at the Carrier Dome. His daughter Heather entered her senior year at Syracuse's Newhouse School of Public Communications majoring in Journalism. The highlight of our final trip to Syracuse together came before the 8 pm kickoff.

Bernie, Steve, and I picked up beer and food in town before meeting Heather at what she proclaimed as the best "tailgate" spot on the entire Syracuse campus. She still insists that her apartment was the best and most coveted among all SU students – 708 Comstock Avenue. Located on the same street as the Schine Student Center, we parked in the small, private lot behind the two-story residence. Then, three 40-plus year-old guys barged into his daughter's *supposed*, downstairs apartment with sub sandwiches, buckets of fried chicken, and cases of beer, ready to pig-out and party before the game. Wrong apartment! Guys lived here, but they weren't in. Hearing the commotion, Heather came downstairs to get us. Bernie looked around to see if the guys had anything else we might need before ascending. We started to set up our "tailgate" on Heather's screened-in deck overlooking Comstock. Evidently though, no one had been there since spring semester. Dust, pollen, and dirt coated the floor and furnishings. Three guys way over college-age ready to feast had to do a little house-cleaning first. Steve and I swept off the deck, and Bernie barged back into the boys' apartment downstairs to get a roll of paper towels to wipe down the table and chairs. The girls didn't have paper towels! We cleaned up so we could finally feast on the deck of 708 Comstock.

Eventually, we strolled over to the Carrier Dome nearby to watch the Orange home opener. The Chippewas punted on their first four possessions and the Orangemen capitalized. Troy Nunes threw a 15-yard scoring pass to Pat Woodcock for the first Syracuse score. CMU dropped a punt next to set up Nate Trout's 39-yard FG. WR Quinton Spotwood, returning from an injury that kept him out the previous season, hauled in a long pass from Nunes for a 56-yard TD. CMU finally countered on Pete Sheperd's 17-yard

TD pass to Eric Flowers to reduce the SU lead to 17-7 in the second period, but the Chips never scored again. Nunes threw his third of four TD passes to Spotwood on a 34-yard pass and DB Will Allen recovered a blocked punt in the end zone for a 31-7 lead at the half. Central Michigan turned out to be the right remedy to end the Syracuse opening game, losing streak at five. Syracuse swamped the Chippewas, 47-7.

Two-point conversion: As for Heather, she did well after graduating with her degree from the Newhouse School, alma mater of other profound pundits like Bob Costas, Dick Stockton, Mike Tirico, and the Emmy Award-winning James Lewis III. Excited about her first job interview after graduation, she called her Dad to announce taking a position with a publication she referred to as *"Cigar, Fishing, and Auto."* Interesting combination, thought Bernardo. I wondered if they could add *college football.* He checked the magazine racks at airports during one of his frequent business trips as a glass peddler. For the life of him, he couldn't find a copy of that publication. He perused the newsstands again. Wait a minute! He called his daughter from his cell phone. "Don't you mean *Cigar Aficionado*?" he inquired.

"That's it!" she replied. His next question was, "How much did I spend to send you to that school?"

A few years later, Bernie found out he contributed a little more to Heather's education than he knew of. According to Heather, our tailgate party at 708 Comstock was nothing compared to what she described as "one of the best and biggest parties in SU history" thrown there by her and her roommates before graduation. She gave credit where credit was due though. Bernie's monetary contribution helped pay for a few kegs, and in his honor, Syracuse University students toasted Bernie Olszyk at the best tailgate spot on the Syracuse campus, 708 Comstock. What an honor!

By the way, Paul, one of the guys who lived downstairs, became Bernardo's future son-in-law. And all Bernie took from his apartment was a roll of paper towels!

Pirates of the Hudson!
(57) East Carolina at Army
October 2, 1999

West Point - The surprise team of Conference-USA sailed up the Hudson with their big guns ready, battle-tested, and Hurricane-proofed. The East

Carolina Pirates invaded the banks of the Hudson sporting a 4-0 record including a 27-23 come-from-behind win the week before over the Miami Hurricanes to vault into the AP Poll at No. 19!

Led by QB David Garrard, ECU took a 19-0 fourth-quarter lead. Army cut the Pirate lead to 19-7 with less than ten minutes left. A sack of Army's Joe Gerena forced the ball loose and was picked clean off the turf by DT Norris McCleary for 40-yard East Carolina TD return. The Black Knights cut the lead to 26-14 on a one-yard run by Gerena capping a 65-yard drive. The Cadet onside kick however was poorly executed, and ECU's Marcellus Harris pirated the loose ball off the turf 10 yards downfield with an escort of blockers to sail down the sideline to put any Army comeback out of reach. Army's defense held the Pirate runners to only 52 yards, but 300 passing yards by David Garrard and two loose balls picked clean off Army's playing surface made the difference in the victory for the purple Pirates who shivered the Black Knights' timbers along the Hudson that fall Saturday. ECU out-dueled the Knights, 33-14.

Extra point: Too bad for Army, but it was another chance to say we saw another future NFL star from a non-powerhouse play in person. Randy Moss, Chad Pennington, Travis Prentice, and now David Garrard – I got to see a few prominent pros play at West Point.

Try this at your local super market!

(58) New Mexico State at Army
October 23, 1999

West Point – Three weeks later on a brilliant, fall Saturday morning with good friends and football fans Charlie Roberts and Dave Headden, we drove up to West Point. Charlie grew up attending many Yale games with his grandfather who lived within walking distance of the Yale Bowl and became an avid Eli fan. As a boy, Dave remembered attending many games at West Point driving up with his Dad from his home in Jersey. We headed up the NY State Thruway this morning to meet up with "Slippery Rock" Bob Jones to make our football foursome. New Mexico State came all the way out from Las Cruces to play the Cadets, so I benefited by adding the Aggies to my growing list of teams seen.

With two cars loaded with food, grills, and coolers of beer, we exited before the first toll on the Thruway to take Route 6 East to West Point's Stony Lonesome Gate, the back entrance to the huge, historic college campus/military base. At the Point, you never know where you'll end up parking for an Army football game once you enter the military reservation patrolled and directed by Military Police. Today's parking space turned out to be one of the most memorable of all locations I've parked in at an Army football game.

As we entered the Stony Lonesome Gate, traffic just crawled along. I feared it would take us forever to get to a parking space to start tailgating. I was sure that they were going to direct us all the way out to the farthest reaches of tailgating lots down along the river by the water treatment plant where I'd parked several times before. We'd have to unpack, eat fast, re-pack, and walk to a bus to get to the game on time. The bus might even get caught in traffic—been there, done that! To my surprise, an MP in front of me suddenly directed me to turn my car with his very military-like signal to take an immediate left turn. I made sure he directed Bob to follow me into the same lot that looked like a busy, local super market. Sure enough, we ended up in the middle of the West Point Post Exchange (PX) parking lot. The PX is the military equivalent to your friendly neighborhood supermarket. We unloaded chairs, coolers, grills, a table, and food into the adjacent parking space. Army wives loaded kids and groceries into cars bound for home. We had the radio blasting as we tailgated. Try drinking beer and grilling burgers at 10 a.m. some Saturday morning at your local grocery store among women pushing shopping carts and carrying grocery bags with kids in tow. See how quickly you're appreciated. I can imagine a few irate homemakers in over-sized SUVs challenging for a convenient parking space filled with coolers, a table, and chairs on a crowded Saturday morning. Other guys might join you for a few beers. That is until their wives or more likely the local cops show up. The beauty of this, however, was that the military cops directed us here! The experience was surreal. We cooked out and drank beer as families around us did their grocery shopping. I can hear St. Laurie complaining already if she ever witnessed this at our local super market! On the other hand, she'd probably laugh, shake her head, and realize the people partying were friends of ours. To get ready for the game, we put our stuff away and caught our school bus alongside the PX for the climb up the steep hill to Michie Stadium.

Army's record-setting Michael Wallace scored from six yards out to open the second period. The Cadets again appeared unstoppable. The offense was reminiscent of the first half of their 59-52 win seen only sixteen days earlier on Thursday night against Louisville. Omari Thompson's 72-yard run gave Army a 28-6 lead by halftime. State put up two field goals and a TD after intermission, but Army scored the final TD on Calvin Smith's 25-yard burst in the fourth. The Cadets nailed the Aggies with their fourth loss of the season, 35-18.

After the game, we went back for a few more beers back in the PX parking lot. The store was now closed and only a few other cars remained for post-game cook-outs. I think back to that day when we had the grill going and drank beers in the super market parking lot. Only at West Point could we ever savor such a tailgate experience. Where else would local law enforcement direct you to have a party with alcoholic beverages in a super market parking lot? Try this at your local supermarket—I *dare* you!

Extra Point: The PX no longer exists in that location at West Point.

Watch a blow-out, fix a flat

(59) Louisiana Tech at Penn State
September 9, 2000

State College - Before the 2000 season, a review of my personal history showed that I had seen almost half the 114 teams in 1-A football play. This season finally started my first concerted effort to kick off my goal to "see 'em all!" I identified eight teams as possibilities to see play at nearby fields in 2000. In previous years, I reviewed the Penn State home schedule with John Massimilla to determine which games I'd prefer to see in State College. My priorities were to see good games and balance them with lesser games. Now "The Goal" became my new focus. The Nittany Lions' home schedule wasn't particularly enticing before the 2000 season began, but the Louisiana Tech Bulldogs and the Fighting Illini would be added as new teams on my new *bucket* list.

Tech came first. They scored first following a Penn State fumble on Brian Stallworth's 10-yard pass to Sean Cangelosi for a quick 7-0 lead against 0-2 PSU. That was it for the Bulldogs. Rashard Casey followed Larry Johnson's 65-yard return with a five yard scoring pass to Eric McCoo. James Boyd returned a Tech fumble for a six-yard TD. McCoo scored again on a 41-yard jaunt. Omar Easy blocked a Bulldog punt at the 27 and Casey threw a 10-yard TD to Tony Stewart. The game got uglier for Tech. Casey tied Tony Sacca's five TD passing record against Georgia Tech I attended in 1991. McCoo had 131 rushing yards and three TDs. State led 43-7 at *halftime*. Penn State sent the Bulldogs back to the doghouse pounding them, 67-6.

I broke tradition with this one: With a 43-7 halftime score, a despondent wife, a seven year-old girl, and a five year-old boy on a hot, stifling, sun-blazed afternoon, we bailed early and headed for the hotel swimming pool. Based on what they put me through watching such a lop-sided contest, my obligation to see LA Tech was fulfilled!

Extra point: The "fun" didn't end there. Upon return to our mini-van in the hilly, grass parking lot, the right rear tire was flat. How appropriate to fix a flat after witnessing such a blow-out! St. Laurie and the kids sat drinking juices and eating snacks while they watched me change the tire. Watching me change a flat outside the stadium was definitely much more entertaining to them than watching the blow-out they had just witnessed inside Beaver Stadium! To achieve my ultimate Goal, sometimes I had to see the bad play *bad*.

Advanced Scouting
(60) Bowling Green at Temple
September 16, 2000

Philadelphia - Our family visited the Jersey shore this weekend to celebrate my father-in-law's birthday down in Tuckerton, NJ. After the festivities, I left with his grandson, Brian, to attend a night game at Franklin Field in Philly where Temple "hosted" Bowling Green. Conflicts with the Philadelphia Phillies' schedule at the Vet forced the Owls to use the University of Pennsylvania's home stadium built in 1895, oldest college stadium in America. Set on The Goal, the Falcons became my next addition.

Brian and I took our reserved seats at about the 20-yard line on the Temple side of the field. There I recognized a broad-shouldered, middle-aged guy wearing a white Temple sweatshirt and Temple baseball cap. What stood out right away were his big hands with huge knuckles and bent fingers as he exchanged greetings with several Owl fans in the section we sat in. The former Owl defensive lineman and member of the famous, New York Jets "Sack Exchange," Joe Klecko, joined the crowd that night to watch his son Dan start at defensive tackle for his alma mater. Later, Brian and I relocated to the upper deck to take in a great view of the city's skyline. We'd get a view of something better a little later on.

The Owls played Bowling Green in a very hard-hitting game. In this City of Brotherly Love, the home team featured an unusual brotherly starting combination, Jared and Jason Davis. A sophomore and a junior respectively, Jared handled Owl place-kicking duties standing in at 5'6" and all of 133 lbs. Jason played DE and LB at 6'2" and 230 lbs. It's pretty evident who dominated at the Davis's dinner table. You wonder how Jared developed such a strong leg – by kicking or by running!

The hitting on both sides and the action on the field was quite impressive for what turned out to be a pair of less than mediocre teams. Temple got out to a 7-0 lead in the first period on Tarnardo Sharps's 14-yard run. In the second, Devin Scott threw a 45-yard TD to Sean Dillard, and with 18 seconds left in the half, Jason McKie scored from the three to give TU a comfortable 21-0 lead over the Falcons. What Brian and I witnessed at halftime though was far more memorable and far from mediocre! Always an easy ticket with a struggling football program, no stadium on campus, and large venues to play at in the fourth largest city in America, Temple often offered additional entertainment at football games to attract students and local Philly sports fans. For this underwhelming match-up, they held a concert at halftime.

On a temporary stage set up in the east end of Franklin was a beautiful, blonde, female singer wearing a colorful, short dress, and black, knee-high boots. I peered though my binoculars as she performed some song as all the young kids in the stadium gathered to gyrate around the stage. Had I known who she was and that she was going to perform beforehand, our seats would have been right there to see as well as to join in. I never heard of her before and didn't know what song she was singing, but didn't care! I watched through binoculars from my 50-yard line seat high above. I figured Brian might know who she was. I asked, "Brian, have you ever heard of this *Jessica Simpson* before?"

"Oh yeah, Uncle Steve, she sings…" whatever. I didn't know the song, or care. At least Brian confirmed that she wasn't some local, fly-by-night songstress doing a one-night show for a loyal, local following. She *impressed* me! I predicted stardom for her right there. I got confirmation that this beautiful singer was on the way up the very next day when I told my seven-year old daughter that during the football game we attended, a Jessica Simpson concert broke out. She was impressed. "You've heard of her?" I asked.

Alex replied, "Yes. She sings…" whatever. Do I have an eye for talent or what? I'll never forget the day I discovered Jessica Simpson. Andy Sahm tossed a 7-yard TD to Jason Van Dam to cut the lead in the third, 21-7. Temple responded with ten more points, and the same combination for Bowling Green hooked up for a 23-yard TD. Final score: Temple 31 – BGSU 14 (not as memorable as halftime).

Extra point: Not only did Jessica impress with her musical talent at halftime that night, but she was recognized for football stardom longer than most of the players and coaches on Franklin Field's surface. She impacted one of the biggest events in all of football years later. Her relationship with Dallas Cowboy QB Tony Romo in 2008 supposedly affected his play in his team's loss to the eventual Super Bowl Champion New York Giants. Being a Giants fan, I *love* her! I still don't care what she sings. She brought down the Dallas Cowboys, and the Giants went on to win the NFL championship!

Snatched!

(61) Memphis at Army
September 23, 2000

West Point - Army Football offered a Family Fun Zone mini-plan featuring four discounted tickets for three home games. With my Goal now a vision, the 2000 Army mini-season ticket package conveniently included two teams on my "to-see" list - Memphis and Alabama-Birmingham. I gave away the third game in the package having already seen Boston College and because I was checking off Louisiana Tech at Penn State that particular weekend. Scheduling games was very strategic now. I focused to achieve The Goal.

This adventure to West Point turned into an extended family fun zone affair as I brought Eric, his favorite cousin Ben who just turned 6, and Ben's 10-year old brother, Matt. Matt was a veteran of tailgate tours. He served as my guinea pig several times to test the waters until Eric was game-ready, meaning out of diapers. Matt and I attended the last Princeton game ever played at Palmer Stadium before it met the wrecking ball. There, Matt spotted former Princeton safety Dean Cain whom he recognized as Superman from TV. Among his adventures with Uncle Steve, he jumped in front of the ESPN cameras during Game Day before Penn State-Ohio State in 1996.

At West Point, the boys tailgated on snacks and juices before we boarded the bus to Michie to watch Army's pre-game festivities. Disappointingly, rain clouds loomed overhead and prevented the Army skydivers from presenting the traditional game ball. The boys had been excited to see this. The skies remained overcast during the entire game.

The back-and-forth battle included a 62-yard TD run by the Tigers'

Sugar Sanders, a 72-yard punt return to tie by Army's Omari Thompson, a 23-yard fumble return by Cadet Anthony Miller for a score, and a 31-yard pass from Neil Suber to Jeremiah Bonds to give Memphis a 20-14 lead six minutes into the final period. Cadets and Tigers delivered some crunching hits throughout. Driving to overcome the six-point deficit with 4:50 left, Army's Curtis Zervic lofted a pass toward WR Bryan Bowdish in the end zone that could have given Army the lead, but Memphis safety Idrees Bashir swooped in front to snatch the pass from the jaws of victory with 100 yards of unobstructed green turf ahead of him. Bashir raced unscathed for a 100-yard interception return for a touchdown - a Michie Stadium record. A late safety for Army made the final score 26-16. Bashir, the future Indianapolis Colt, took the game from a pending Memphis defeat to assured victory, making it a memorable play for three young boys and me watching it all unfold from Army's Family Fun Zone.

Not your Father's Homecoming

(62) Illinois at Penn State
October 21, 2000

State College - Little known fact—the university responsible for the original Homecoming concept is the University of Illinois.[8] It just so happens that I added the Fighting Illini as my next team toward the Goal when they came rambling into State College under very unusual circumstances. The Lions' Homecoming "sacrifice" showed up with a winning record while this edition of Nittany Lions confronted the invited feast with three more losses than wins!

Traditionally, PSU's Homecoming game was always the toughest ticket of the season. It seemed like no matter how many seats they added to the stadium, they filled them. Aside from vague memories of a few fans holding up tickets along the south side of Beaver Stadium right before the start of a few games, I had never witnessed so many tickets blatantly available for sale – especially at Homecoming. They were always hard to come by, but not this year! Thanks to the Lions' lousy 2-5, 1-2 conference record before Illinois showed up, Penn State die-hards fanned stacks of tickets in the parking lot as soon as I parked my car. Usually, game program hawkers

8 University Archives' Student Life and Culture Archival Program, "Origin of the University of Illinois Homecoming," http://www.library.csi.cuny.edu/dept/history/lavender/footnote.hmtl, (2005)

strolled by to make their sale before you'd spend your next five bucks, but before they showed up today, fans with extra tickets desperately tried to unload them. I might have avoided this match-up as well had I seen the Illini play already, but the Goal is the Goal. I'd have to take one not for this team, but with this team.

Before the game, John Massimilla, Steve Ciesla, and I traipsed under the west side of Beaver Stadium with a front-row view to watch the visiting Illini take the field for pre-game warm-ups. John, ever the football-fashion maven, pointed out that Illinois socks with one blue and one orange band across the top reminding him of the sock six-packs mothers used to buy on sale when we were kids. He was right. They didn't look as "cool" now as they did when we were younger.

Despite the announced sell-out of 96,475, the alumni and students stayed away in droves. College football, unlike the pros, does not deduct "no-shows" from their announced attendance. Who could blame the alum or students for not showing up at this one? Empty seats abounded in the expanding stadium. Homecoming co-founder W. Elmer Ekblaw envisioned the homecoming football game as a festivity where students and alumni "could come into closer touch with one another."[9] Penn Staters must have found some other places away from the game to gather. This wasn't a typically good Penn State football team. This was not even your big brother's typical Penn State Homecoming, never mind your father's or grandfather's for that matter! Averaging 265.1 yards per game on total offense, they ranked 105th out of 114 1A teams. However, those that did refrain from using their Beaver Stadium Homecoming ticket that day could not have imagined what they would miss—on one particular play any way.

The Lions led 14-10 at halftime. PSU played its best football of the year and led 32-25 with just under six minutes left. What happened next was a play for the ages. After completing a 36-yard pass for a first down to the Illinois 39, Penn State QB Rashard Casey started to roll to his right looking to option the ball back. When the DE positioned himself to thwart a pitch-out, Casey completely reversed field. He faded back deeper while running all the way back to the near sideline where he looked like he would step out of bounds. Avoiding what looked assuredly like a big loss, Casey escaped two would-be tacklers near the sideline and reversed back across to the far side of the field once again. However, he found a seam and turned up field around right end at the original line of scrimmage. He raced up field for a dazzling 39-yard touchdown run. He ran three times that distance on

9 Ibid

that play for the final score of the game. For him it was a long home-coming via the scenic route! The 39-25 win gave Joe Paterno No. 320 for his long career, putting him in sole possession of second place in all-time collegiate wins, one ahead of legendary Pop Warner and only three now behind Paul "Bear" Bryant.

Extra point: Further fun Homecoming facts: Illinois students Clarence Foss Williams, class of 1910, and W. Elmer Ekblaw, class of 1912, are credited as the originators of Homecoming. Other schools previously featured alumni games, bringing back alum to play against the current varsity squads, but Homecoming inspired a new goal to gather alumni to attend a game rather than to play against them. The students' money-making proposal included the idea of holding a series of events on campus during the fall when underclassmen, seniors, and alumni could all gather without all the distractions present during the typical, commencement week activities. The first Homecoming took place on October 15, 1910 when Illinois' rival, the Maroons of the University of Chicago under Amos Alonzo Stagg, came to town. Ekblaw, also chief reporter for the campus newspaper, *The Daily Illini*, predicted "a particularly and distinctively Illinois institution which if successful will without doubt be followed by other universities."[10] Mr. Ekblaw was a man with great foresight at such a young age.

Rockets Sink Navy
(63) Toledo at Navy
October 28, 2000

Annapolis - I hadn't attended a Navy game in Annapolis since 1991 when the Mids lost to Air Force 44-6 in their 1,000th football game. This time, I looked forward to taking St. Laurie and the kids for our first family trip to a game at USNA. I planned an unusual, two-night stay in "Crabtown" so we could enjoy other activities in one of my favorite, college football towns. I decided that we should make the most of a family weekend along the Chesapeake to make up for the blow-out I anticipated. Since Toledo was the next notch in my proverbial gun, everybody was obligated to stay to the bitter end, or it wouldn't count! Leaving the Louisiana Tech game early was an aberration. With the Mids' season already spiraling out of control at 0-7, I figured this game might be over before it even started. The Toledo Rockets under Coach Gary Pinkel came in battle-tested sporting a 6-1 record with

10 Ibid

a season-opening 24-6 win at Penn State. I didn't anticipate a thrilling last minute victory for either team at Navy-Marine Corps Stadium.

Before the game, we checked out the sailboats and yachts in the harbor. The kids enjoyed some of the activities in the Billy the Kid Fun Zone inside the stadium. I took their picture with Navy mascot Bill the Goat and two handlers on the playing surface. Eric had a striking resemblance to one of the Midshipman - must have been the haircut. We spread a blanket on the grassy slope overlooking the field from the north end zone on a sunny but very windy afternoon. I anxiously hoped that the Mids would give the Rockets a tough test.

The Mids opened the game looking like they had a plan to win. They used a new, three-wideout formation to offset the strength of Toledo's defense, the second-stingiest in the nation yielding only 9.6 points per game. They followed their opening score recovering an onsides kick. Surprisingly, Navy led 14-0 before the Rockets even had the ball! They held on to a 14-13 halftime lead.

Navy coach Charlie Weatherbie probably outsmarted himself as his team attempted another onside kick into the wind to start the second half. Toledo took over at Navy's 45.

Tavares Bolden scored on a five-yard run and on the two-point conversion. The Rocket defense and strong winds played havoc with the Mids in the third period. Navy's next punt held up by the wind put Toledo at Navy's 28. Bolden took advantage with the wind at his back to pass 19 yards to Dontl Greene for the Rockets' next score. The wind held Williams' next punt up for only 24 yards, and TU started at Navy's 46. Three plays later, Chester Taylor broke off an 18-yard run finalizing the score, 35-14, for the Toledo win.

Extra Point: Loss or no loss, Annapolis is a great town to enjoy a family weekend. We savored a great seafood dinner downtown that evening, and spent Sunday morning touring the Yard after services at the Naval Academy Chapel. The Chesapeake Bay is picturesque. Preble Hall has got to be my favorite museum anywhere. It depicts the history of the U.S. Navy starting with John Paul Jones right up until today. Much of the history evolves around Navy grads who walked the same grounds you're visiting. The museum is a must-see for anyone visiting the Academy. A stop for lunch at the restaurant out on the city dock capped our family weekend in Annapolis. All the activities we enjoyed surrounding the game helped subdue the empty feeling of watching a struggling Navy football program after getting pounded by the Toledo Rockets.

Kids with Mids – Eric, Bill, and Alex pose with two Midshipmen Goat Handlers before the Navy-Toledo game.

Two-time, first-time, advance to the big-time!
(64) Middle Tennessee at (65) Connecticut
November 4, 2000

Storrs, Connecticut - In 2000, Division 1-A football welcomed several new programs into the fold. I'd seen the UConn Huskies play games since 1974 against the likes of Navy, Yale, Lehigh, Rhode Island, and Hampton when they played at the 1-AA level. Now I ventured to see them play as newcomers to 1A football against another team new to my eyes and to 1A football - the Middle Tennessee State Blue Raiders. MTSU had also jumped into the realm of "big-time" football recently albeit not with the momentum and fanfare of the Connecticut program. UConn had a national reputation as a basketball power house, and its football program was earmarked to join the Big East. The Blue Raiders would eventually join the fledging Sunbelt conference. I took 10-year old nephew Matt Wylie with me to add these two debutantes to The Goal. We drove three hours for what I promised him should be a fairly competitive football game. I lied.

By halftime, the Huskies had lost their bark and bite to trail by a stunning score of 52-7! Blue Raider Dwone Hicks gained 184 rushing yards and scored four TDs on only 17 carries. I figured that he was bound for stardom on Sundays. QB Mel Counts completed 17 of 21 passes for

221 yards and one TD. CB Kareem Bland returned an INT 70 yards for a first-half score. In short, the Raiders came to Storrs and made the UConn Huskies look like dog dirt. You know my rule now no matter what the score, but how do you keep a 10-year old interested in a game while hordes of "die-hards" leave the home team behind getting slaughtered, 52-7, at the half? It didn't phase my 10-year old guinea pig. He enjoyed the surroundings and fired off question after question after question. He also got very preoccupied with French Fries served in a large, dog bowl-type dish – something a real Husky could eat from. Despite Middle Tennessee mercifully posting the final at 66-17, Matt never begged if we could go. On the flip side, I started to wonder why I ever came up with this rule.

Extra point: Was this the right move for UConn? Rutgers, in a state more respected for its home-grown football talent, had not even come close to cracking the top of Big East football after ten years of conference play and twenty years at the 1A level. "If only we can keep the best players in New Jersey ..." What made UConn think that it could fare any better?

"There he is!" said one fan to another sitting near us as the remaining stragglers began to saunter away from the large, concrete bleacher known as Memorial Stadium. He pointed to some tall, lanky kid in a navy blue and white, Shelton (Connecticut) high school varsity jacket.

"I hear he's probably going to Purdue," remarked the guy next to him. Matt and I didn't know we were witnessing the prescription UConn football ordered to advance into big-time football. The kid was a highly-sought recruit named Dan Orlovsky. We'd see him in Storrs again. Regarding Dwone Hicks, he never made it to the next level. Wrong again!

Burnt Cookie

(66) Alabama- Birmingham at Army
November 18, 2000

West Point - My friend Les DiVite's Dad had passed away in recent years and my own mother was widowed for the second time eight years earlier. With the Family Fun Zone package at Army, Les and I brought our respective mothers, Barbara and Kathleen—known by her eleven grandchildren as "Grandma Cookie"—to enjoy a little tailgating at an Army game on a cold, sunny, November afternoon. My mother had told me that her first date with my Dad was to an Army-Columbia game back in the 50s. Army hosted the University of Alabama-Birmingham Blazers in the first game ever between the two this day. Both were now members of Conference-USA. This was the season's home finale for the Cadets who had struggled all season long. The Blazers arrived with a 6-4 record primping for a bowl bid.

After tailgating in the lot right inside the front gate close to the Thayer Hotel where we enjoyed hot-buttered rum, the four of us bussed up the hill to Michie. Tickets in hands, Les and I passed through our gate well ahead of the two grandmothers who each carried a couple of blankets to place over cold, aluminum bleacher seats. Deep in football conversation with Les, I suddenly heard the blood-curdling cry of "*Stephen*!" I turned quickly to see my mother clutching our blankets against her chest standing next to the security guard.

"He's getting fresh with me!"

The gate attendants, a man and a woman, stood looking at me with hands at their sides. Mrs. DiVite said nothing. Unlike my mother, I don't have eyes in back of my head. I didn't know if the guy was really getting fresh with my mother, or if she just took offense that he was searching for booze in her blankets. As far as I knew, we left our libations back in the car. Would Grandma cookie?...I don't think so. Security always checked blankets and bags going into Michie. I finally stepped forward and said, "Let's go!" Off we went without any further inspection.

Army (1-8, 1-5 in C-USA) trailed at halftime, 10-7. In the third, one play after the referee warned the Army band to stop playing when UAB had the ball, QB Jeff Aaron heaved a 63-yard scoring pass to a wide-open Leron Little to increase the Blazers' lead. UAB took a 24-7 lead in the fourth quarter following a 72-yard interception return by Wes Foss. Seasonal statistics showed that it was the sixth pass intercepted and returned for a TD against Army that season – fourth one in the fourth quarter a la Idrees Bashir of Memphis. After that, I ventured out to the concession stand to get four grilled chicken sandwiches and drinks. It was here that I learned how environmentally conscientious the Army is. They did not provide lids for the cups, straws for drinks, nor any small trays to carry cups in. What a hassle to carry food back to the seats. I had to go get Les to help me out. When we all finally unwrapped aluminum foil from our grilled chicken sandwiches, two of the chicken sandwiches were burnt! Grandma Cookie got pretty *pissed-off* to say the least. One was hers, of course. She made threatening remarks about the service at Michie Stadium, and she was right. I think she could have used some more hot-buttered rum back at our tailgate. UAB won 27-7 for its seventh win of the season. Army's season was now 1-9 with struggling Navy waiting to play in two weeks for their annual rivalry. UAB stayed home during bowl season despite their final record of 7-4.

Extra point: With my well-intentioned Goal now seriously underway thanks to a nice shot in the arm with the addition of eight new teams in the year 2000, I reached out to several media outlets and asked them to check out my new website www.collegefootballfan.com to see how they liked it and to introduce them to my unique Goal. *ESPN The Magazine* caught on and provided their analysis on their page entitled "*The Pulse: The Wired World of Sports*" in their October 2001 edition. Though they submarined my attempt at providing a tailgate party checklist, they admired the fact that I was already more than halfway to my lofty Goal.[11] As they say, any publicity is good publicity. However, it wasn't until after a few days of gloating over the small article that I noticed the photo of a hamburger bun with what looked like burnt chicken in between. What the…? I laughed my ass off! Of all the events I reported on during the 2000 season, they selected one snippet from one of my game reviews. Taken from the Army-UAB review, from which no editor pointed out my poor, late-night grammar, the line probably endeared itself to the publication's adolescent readership. Under a caption entitled "25 words (or less)," it read:

> *"Two of the four chicken sandwiches were badly burnt, which prompted Grandma Cookie to want to throw [them] back in the concessionaire's face!*
> *—A review of the chow at Army's Michie Stadium on collegefootballfan.com."* [12]

How many guys have had their mother written about in a national sports publication? Well, I have! The point being made was that despite the beautiful and festive setting West Point offers along with all its traditions on football Saturdays, disorganized parking, congested entry ways, lacking concessionary supplies, and poor food quality took away from the enjoyment of attending an Army football game. Grandma Cookie's quotation may have had some influence though. Since then, improvements have been noticed around the stadium, especially regarding the food service. The parking situation still stinks and tight security slows entry into games, but it's a necessity since 9/11. However, I think someone at West Point might have read Grandma Cookie's comment and did something about it. Ten years

11 "25 Words (or less)," ESPN The Magazine (29 October 2001): p 32.

12 Ibid

and two days since the day of this game, Cookie passed away. With a few friends and family members, she's enjoying better food and tailgating in a better place now.

Eli's Comin'! So are reviewable plays.
(67) Mississippi at Auburn
September 8, 2001

Auburn, Alabama - It had been 16 years since I visited Charlie and Lynda for an Auburn football game. With his excavating business, C.A. Murren & Sons, booming in the thriving Atlanta market, Charlie had access to some great Auburn seats through his suppliers of heavy construction equipment. C.A. Murren built several venues for the 1996 Olympic Games in Atlanta. In 2001, Charlie IV and Megan now followed the footsteps of their parents along the "Tiger Walk." Looking at the Auburn schedule before the season, I checked for SEC teams to add to The Goal. The Tigers hosted Ole Miss and Mississippi State. The Rebels provided the better opportunity to allow me to maximize the number of new teams to see and the best combination of games possible for each weekend. So I picked the Rebels' invasion of Jordan-Hare Stadium this season not just to add them, but to see QB Eli Manning, son of Archie and the younger brother of Peyton, perform. Watching Eli play against Auburn, in case he ever amounted to anything, I figured I could say that I at least attended his SEC debut.

For three quarters in front of a Tiger record crowd of 86,063, Auburn presented more obstacles than the supposed sophomore sensation could handle. Ole Miss never crossed the 50 on its first ten possessions. Rebel punter Cady Ridgeway didn't help matters much averaging only 32 yards on five punts. Auburn led 13-0 at halftime. In the third, the Tigers scored following an interception of a Manning pass. After that, Manning finally seemed to get the Rebels on the move. They thought they had six when Omar Rayford hauled in a long heave from Manning in the end zone, but officials signaled he didn't come down with a foot in the end zone. Instant replays later revealed Rayford caught it inbounds—but replay reviews didn't exist in 2001! The very next play, Auburn picked off Manning again. Casinious Moore ran it in for a 36-yard TD for his third TD of the day, and AU took a 27-0 lead. Eli didn't bail out though, and showed signs of leadership guiding Ole Miss back in the fourth to trail, 27-21. Eli could have possibly worked some more magic for a late score, but the Rebels roughed the punter late in the game and never got the ball back. Auburn preserved a 27-21 victory. Rayford's near-TD turned out to be a big play after all. Though Mississippi reeled off five straight victories at the end of the season, a final record of 7-4, 4-4 (SEC) was not enough to earn a bowl bid. As anticipated, much more about Eli would be heard during seasons to come.

Extra point: I had problems getting home from Atlanta to Newark the next day. On September 9, 2001, my Air Tran flight delayed and then engine problems turned my plane back to Atlanta to arrive home much later than expected. That turned out to be a mere inconvenience compared to what happened to four jetliners leaving Boston and Newark less than 36 hours later. Our world was about to change.

September 15, 2001 was the Saturday of the week that "sports stood still." All college football games were cancelled or postponed. My plan to watch California as my 68th team against Rutgers was postponed until the end of the season. After the cowardly events of 9/11, security at all sporting events took on new measures as we all became more wary when gathering in large crowds. Eerily, I recall the Virginia Tech-Rutgers game I attended with a bunch of friends in 1999. We saw Michael Vick and the Hokies defeat Rutgers that night 58-20 on their way to the national championship game. At one point though, a small, white, propeller plane with ID numbers blacked out underneath the wings and along the fuselage buzzed the stadium from behind us. Several minutes later, it returned from the opposite direction. From where I sat with a group of ten guys who got together for this one, the plane looked like it was heading right down toward us before it pulled up and flew straight overhead never to return again! Not until after the game did any of the other guys admit that they felt he same way I did - we were all ready to bail! The proximity to NYC, the covered up numbers, the threat to buzz a venue with a good sized crowd made me think about it again after 9/11. I never read anything about it in the papers the following day, but I still remembered it. I'll never forget how my heart raced as the plane approached us head-on! In retrospect, I still think it was one of those *bastards* from the Twin Towers attacks on some kind of a practice run.

Games resumed the weekend of September 22-23. Everything carried into a stadium was inspected thoroughly. At the UMass-Delaware game I attended that weekend, our country demonstrated a renewed spirit of cohesiveness and patriotism. The Fighting Blue Hen football team raced on to the field at Delaware Stadium with three American flags in the lead. Tributes were made to those who perished in the World Trade Center attack. Prayers were said. Travel and large gatherings are still under close scrutiny today and will probably be forever due to the attacks of 9/11. Proudly, we still haven't given in to the evil that terrorism brought to our country that day.

A whole, new world
(68) Washington at (69) UCLA
October 13, 2001

Pasadena, California - I booked a trip to Los Angeles in the spring of 2001 in anticipation of a great game between two teams out west. Despite trepidations now due to 9/11, I still carried out my plan to fly from Newark to LAX one month later to add two missing Pac-10 teams to my Goal—undefeated Washington visiting undefeated UCLA. My brother Chris and friends Jim Lewis and Jim Buckley comprised a foursome for my *Left Coast* tour.

This would be my first flying experience since the attacks of 9/11. The flight from Newark to Los Angeles turned out to be an awakening to a whole, new world. The experience indicated the world was undergoing some significant and scary changes.

Screening procedures to get to the plane were understandably more intense and comprehensive than ever before. I left early for the airport to compensate for two hours of processing. Security personnel checked IDs and scanned everyone from head to foot with electronic wands. Luggage was opened and searched, sometimes exposing travelers' under-garments for all to see. Guards chose some customers to go through more intense scrutiny than others. The atmosphere was tense. Pre-screening took longer than pre-9/11. Travelers were on edge. Reports indicated armed U.S. Air Marshals would be aboard certain planes. You eyed other people wondering if they were bad guys. Once through security, I waited in a chair near the gate—a little more relaxed now that I'd gotten through all the new, necessary but nerve-wracking rigmarole.

"Whose bag is this?" asked a security agent to no one in particular right in front of me. I and four others looked up from what we were reading, looked at one another, shrugged shoulders, and admitted it belonged to none of us. One guy said he saw some woman drop it off and then go down the other end of the terminal. Since no one among us claimed it, the guard made a quick call out on a hand-held radio. Another guard with a cart showed up in a New York minute. Security took no chances. They carefully loaded the bag on the cart and whisked it away. How could anyone be so stupid in light of what the country was trying to recover from? Or were terrorists still among us? You could feel the tension. Boarding passes and picture IDs had to be shown again to board and slowed the process.

I took my window seat somewhat drained from the new boarding process. I thought I could relax a little now aboard, but then an airline rep came through the cabin looking for a particular passenger. No one responded. This individual checked luggage and had a ticket, but never came aboard. The person's luggage made it on board though! We sat at the gate an extra twenty minutes while airline personnel rummaged through the cargo hold to find and remove the unaccompanied bags. I wondered if things like this always happened before and just weren't as scrutinized, or were people who hated us still trying to get us. I would be glad when the luggage was unloaded. I had three seats on the right side of the L1011 all to myself. I thought that I could actually take a nap on this flight, something I can rarely do on a plane, but I was ready to nod. However, the intensity of my flight was about to ratchet up more than a notch or two. A late passenger arrived and they let him on board. He was heading right to my row. Not only was he of Middle Eastern descent, he wore a turban! Sure enough, he took the aisle seat in my row. I couldn't sleep now! I'd have to keep my eye on this guy the entire five-hour plus flight. *No rest for the weary*. Seriously, how could I relax? He could be the nicest, most innocent guy in the world, but who knew? For me, the flight turned out to be even more intense after getting through airport security. This sucked!

What really miffed me is that this guy fell asleep shortly after take-off, and I couldn't. The stewardess brought out meals. At least I could eat. When I got served though, I was shocked! They provided me with a stainless steel fork—not plastic! Knives, metals or potential weapons of any kind were prohibited from being brought on board, but here they were providing anyone with a potential weapon right from the plane's galley. When he finally awoke from his long, pleasant slumber, the stewardess asked him if he would like some dinner. My adrenaline perked up. I was on my guard if this guy got hold of some real tableware. Thankfully, I evidently wasn't the only one watching. When they served him, he got plastic! What a relief. I felt a little better.

A few hours later on this cross-country flight, I had to get up, cross in front of the man sitting in my aisle, and make my way to the men's room. When I came back though, he wasn't in his seat! He was in mine – looking out over the Rockies. This was getting to be too much. What a crappy flight. I sat in his aisle seat keeping my eye on him. He finally noticed that I returned. He tried to make nice conversation, but instead, he reinforced my suspicions even more. Everything he said seemed friendly and tolerable until he gazed out over the Rockies again and said, "I'd like to drive over those someday, *if* I ever come back." - "If" with emphasis! What the *hell* was that supposed to mean? *If*? Was this guy busting my chops, or was he actually part of some kind of terrorist plot? Was I just on edge, or did he really mean he'd enjoy exploring the country to enjoy the sights. I sometimes think about doing that, too. It was the way this guy said it though. I didn't know what to think. We finally exchanged seats. I watched him out of the corner of my eye. I continued to keep my guard up making sure everyone aboard arrived safely. What a relief to finally get off that plane!

Because of airport security, my brother could not pick me up at LAX. Only commercial shuttles and taxis were allowed to pick up passengers, so our plan was for me to take a *Super Shuttle* van out to a hotel near his home. I relaxed a little more after my ordeal in the shuttle. I noted a high school game being played on the way through Long Beach. I saw the crowd dancing in celebration at the top of a small stadium. It got my mind off of that flight. It was good to be on the ground again. The ordeal made me appreciate even more the things we take for granted in this country - things like travel, visiting friends, family, different places, and enjoying sports! Sometimes we just don't realize how good we have it.

I stayed at my brother's that night and had dinner with him, his wife Jill, a UCLA grad, and their kids Emily and Nick. With Chris, I planned to attend the big showdown the next day between the Bruins and Huskies with the Emmy-award winning Jim Lewis and his fellow pundit Jim Buckley. I met Jim Buckley back in the '80s through the other Jim. Buckley, like Lewis, was a writer - for *Sports Illustrated* among other publications. We had the pleasure of meeting when he came to several of my big tailgate parties in the Meadowlands parking lot when both Jims lived and worked in New York City. A Cal grad, Jim Buckley now lived and worked back in his native California. He came down from Santa Barbara for the day. However, unlike previous games we attended together at Giants Stadium, this one would not be preceded by a big tailgate party. Instead, I attended my niece's soccer game the next morning while my brother coached. Now, I'm by no means a soccer fan of any kind, but I did get a "kick" out of my brother yelling, "*Attack! Attack!*" at a bunch of 8 year-old girls as if they were trained Dobermans!

Though we finally arrived for the featured game shortly before kickoff, our timing could not have been better for parking. For some reason, we were directed through and around Rose Bowl parking lots to a space in the first parking row adjacent to the famous stadium's north end. We literally parked in its shadows. Too bad we didn't have a tailgate plan. But if we did, we probably would have arrived earlier and not landed in such prime California real estate. We had to go through two security check points on long lines before entering the stadium. We took seats in the southwest corner of the end zone a few seats to the left of an ABC TV camera platform. This game was so big that Keith Jackson sat in the broadcast booth. Two Pac-10 powers met with 4-0 records - No. 7 UCLA and No. 10 Washington.

The Bruins offense blemished the Huskies' defensive reputation very quickly when RB DeShaun Foster put Washington's Wondame Davis flat on his back on the way to a quick 7-0 lead. Another Foster TD and a fumble-return TD gave UCLA a 21-0 lead with just over two minutes remaining in the first period. The game did not look competitive as hoped for, although Washington did get a late second-half score led by second-string QB Taylor Barton subbing for the injured starter, Cody Pickett.

To start the second half, Foster got his team back on track on his first play from scrimmage when he raced 64 yards before getting tackled at the Washington one. He scored from there. His most exciting jaunt of the game was yet to come. From his own 8-yard line late in the fourth right below us, he burst through the line toward the far end zone. He started to streak down the left sideline and then veered steadily to his right, outracing opponents all the way to the far right corner of the end zone for a 92-yard TD. Exhausted, he latched on to a sideline security guard until his teammates finally caught up with him. It was probably the longest and most exciting touchdown run I had ever witnessed. For him, it was a long, exhilarating, and exhausting run on that hot sunny, Southern California day – not the kind of weather I 'm used to watching a game in during mid-October. In the 35-14 UCLA victory, Foster finished with four TDs and a school-record of 301 rushing yards.

Extra point: The Jims, my brother, and I settled in after the game at a bar called *Pinocchio's* in Burbank for postgame libations. Foster's record-setting performance was memorable. The trip back home is a blur. It was a good trip, but like Foster's record-breaking performance, I'll never forget the flight on the way out to see UCLA host Washington. It introduced me to a whole new world that we live in today. Too bad for all of us.

Neither men nor boys: Toys from Troy
Troy (70) at Maryland
November 3, 2001

College Park - I returned to Maryland's Byrd Stadium for the first time in 22 years to see Coach Ralph Friedgen's surprising 7-1 Terrapins take on D1 newcomer Troy State, No. 70 in the annals of my history. Maryland, smarting from its first loss of the season a week earlier to Florida State, toyed with Troy right from the start. Marc Riley scored a 69-yard touchdown to get things going early in the first period. Next, Nick Novak booted his first of four FGs that day, and QB Shaun Hill opened up with two TD passes, one to Bruce Perry who also scored on a 10-yard run. The Terps dominated the toys of Troy racking up 509 offensive yards in the first half alone to take a commanding 34-0 lead. Hill threw for 228 yards and stalwart LB E.J. Henderson blocked a punt to turn things around quickly early in the game. The U of M defense applied pressure throughout sacking Brock Nutter eight times for 72 yards. Troy scored two TDs after Maryland led 44-0. The game was ugly. I sat high in the upper deck of Byrd looking at our nation's capitol out in the distance not believing what actually happened there on 9/11. The Terps toyed with the Trojans down on the turf below on their way to a 47-14 victory.

Extra point: Maryland finished 10-2, ranked 10th in the nation for quite an impressive one year turn around under "The Fridge". They were the first team to win the ACC outright other than Florida State since the Seminoles joined the conference in 1992. Troy State, coached by Auburn grad Larry Blakeney, finished its first D1 season at 7-4. Its biggest win came at Mississippi State. Besides it loss to Maryland, it earned the distinction of being the only team to lose to both teams in the 2002 BCS championship game, Miami (F) and Nebraska. Two Troy defenders had brighter futures ahead of them. Junior DE Osi Umenyiora and freshman DE DeMarcus Ware developed great reps on Sundays following their days at Troy. You never know where the pro teams will find such hidden gems.

No Shirt off His Back!
(71) Utah State at Connecticut
November 10, 2001

Storrs, Connecticut – This weekend, the family ventured up to Rhode Island for cousins Katie's and Kassie's combined birthday festivities. Of course, I conveniently planned to add another new team on my list since we were on the go. Utah State visited nearby UConn. I gained pardon from St. Laurie and other women in the family because this trip would be rather convenient compared to traveling out to Logan, Utah just to catch an Aggie game. By this time, I had enthusiastic yet pessimistic support among the extended family to actually pull off this feat. With Eric and me came my brother-in-law Gunther. Such a dedicated, fantasy football fan of pro football, final scores of any games meant nothing to him.

"Hey Gunther, the Packers just scored again - up, 14-0!" I informed him as he would return back into the room from doing something else as we'd watch.

"Who scored?" That's all that mattered to this fantasy fanatic who used to keep reams of statistics on green bar paper under his couch cushions to scout and select his players.

"How da heck do I know?" That was back in the last millennium. With the growing popularity of fantasy football, individual stats are reported up to the minute now.

With him came his 4-year old son, Blake. Anticipating the cold weather, his Mom bundled him up to enjoy his first 1A college football game with the rest of the boys in the family. Blake had already been in Uncle Steve's training program having tailgated at some University of Rhode Island and Princeton games. Also with us were cousins and college football veterans, Matt and Ben Wylie.

The Aggies and Huskies seemed to be an even match on paper with 2-5 and 2-6 records respectively. The Huskies struggled along in their second season of 1A ball just as Matt and I had seen them do in the previous season against Middle Tennessee. As a matter of fact, the recruit pointed out by the fan at the end of that previous UConn game who supposedly was off to Purdue, started this game at QB for his home state Huskies. Dan Orlovsky stayed locally to help develop the program in Storrs. His decision earned him the starting nod at UConn his freshman year. Utah State played Division 1A forever, but struggled with mediocrity most years. Two exciting skill players led their offensive attack. RB Emmit White led the nation in all-purpose yards with 201 yards per game. WR Kevin Curtis led the nation in yards per grab with 9.6 every time he caught the ball.

Our entourage took seats high atop UConn's Memorial Stadium on a cold day with a little snow flurry action in the mix – early for this time of year. Utah State moved the ball quite easily on its opening drive against the underlings. Orlovsky set UConn Frosh records the week before with 382 yards through the air and 3 TD passes in a 45-28 loss to Cincinnati, but his two INTs and two lost fumbles killed the Huskies chances in that game. The Aggies took advantage of his inexperience as did the Bearcats. USU led by halftime, 28-10. It looked like the benefit of adding another team to the Goal in Storrs was going to be another painful, first-game experience. Troy State, UCLA, Washington, UConn, Middle Tennessee, and Toledo recently came on board in disappointing blow-outs.

Concerned this would turn into another one-sided romp, we forged on. *The Goal! The Goal!* Utah State stretched its lead to 38-10. The weather got colder and our four, young boys grew bored while the remaining home team fans had nothing to cheer about. *Tough!* They had no choice but to stay until the bitter end or their parents would have to take up a collection to pay my airfare to Logan, Utah for an Aggies' home game! I thought about it anyway.

Other kids came by horsing around ran into our section. One wore only a T-shirt on his scrawny torso. Our boys stared wondering if they could get away with that. Gunther noticed the kid in the t-shirt and hollered, *"Hey, Kid! You cold?"* The skinny urchin turned to look directly at my brother-in-law probably waiting to get yelled at.

"No!" came back his terse reply.

Gunther wrapped his arms around himself and in a high-pitched voice feigned to shiver and chattered through his teeth, "Then give *me* your t-shirt! Because *I* am!" The kid paused, stared briefly, and then ran off. We all knew this was typical Gunther. He didn't.

The Huskies finally sparked some excitement when Orlovsky connected with Wes Timko for a 34-yard TD pass in the third. Emmett White of the Aggies stood on the sideline with his knee packed in ice. The Husky defense held. The offense responded when Orlovsky threw another TD pass to Cliff Hill to cut the lead, 38-24. With five minutes left, the Huskies rolled to another TD as Orlovsky plunged over from the one. Suddenly, the score was 38-31 with time left to score for either team. The home crowd got fired up. Our boys had something to cheer about now. Two struggling teams with dismal records played for the victory in sight.

When State got the ball back, the ice pack came off Emmett White's knee and he got back into the game. USU couldn't score, but they ate up the clock before turning it over to the Huskies on downs. UConn started to move the chains, but inexperience raised its ugly head when Orlovsky's low pass got picked off by DT Jorge Tapia who rumbled down to the Husky seven-yard line. Game over, but no blow-out!

UConn came up short with the help of costly Aggie penalties in its hard-fought comeback bid, 38-31. By the time the final gun sounded, the two teams had combined for 222 yards in penalties, but at least both teams showed fight right to the end after the Aggies got out to a 38-10 lead. The Husky comeback got our boys' minds off the cold and back into the game. Gunther's, too! He cared less what players put points on the board. Even he admitted that it just turned out to be a great football game. Almost got a free t-shirt, too!

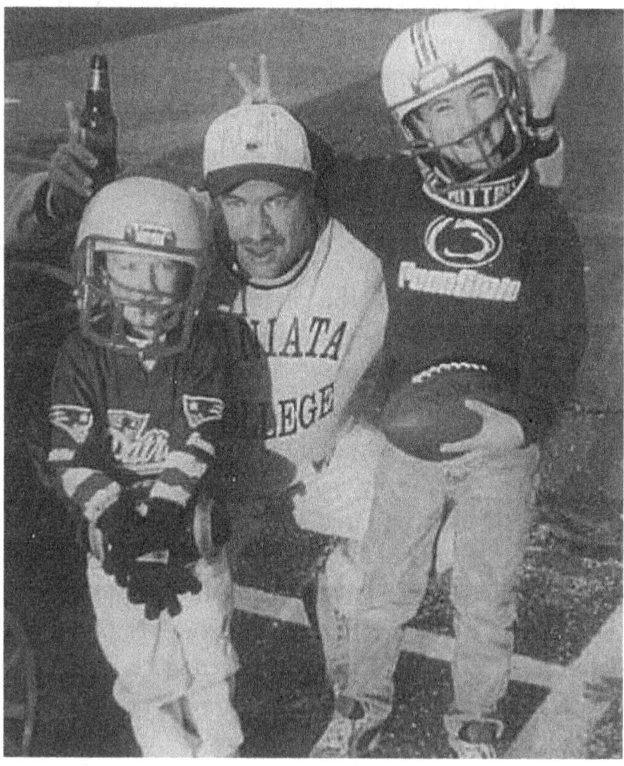

Cousins Blake Neumann and Eric Koreivo are suited up in case they're called into action at the UConn - Utah State game.

End of an Almost Imperfect Season
(72) California at Rutgers
November 23, 2001

New Brunswick, The Birthplace of College Football - Thanksgiving 2001 loomed bittersweet following the events of 9/11. We planned this year's dinner with St. Laurie's side of the family down at the Jersey shore. In previous odd-numbered years, I always attended playoff games at 1-AA Delaware or at D-3 Rowan that holiday weekend. This year, due to the postponements of September 15, the 0-10 California Golden Bears ventured all the way out to The Birthplace of College Football for an insignificant game against the 2-8 Scarlet Knights of Rutgers. Both teams looked to finish the season on a high note. The only significance for me was to finally attend a Cal game.

Unlike the game attended two weeks before in sub-freezing Storrs, the game on the banks of the Old Raritan was played on an unseasonably warm, balmy, short-sleeved, Friday afternoon. We took Eric's cousin Scott Bramhall, Brian's 8-year old brother. Not only were we basking in the warmth of the sun in the end zone bleachers in a game between golden and scarlet teams, but the boys enjoyed spoonfuls of frozen lemonade during what should have been hot chocolate season.

The Bear defense ranked 117th in the nation defending the pass, 104th in scoring defense, and 107th in total defense. They had surrendered 421 points for a new California season record. On the other sideline, RU established the lowest point output in school history - 109. Something had to give here: a record-setting inept defense against a record-setting inept offense. Maybe jet lag flying from California would give Rutgers the edge.

The 18,111 fans digesting Thanksgiving turkey showed up to watch two teams from 3,000 miles apart in a classic game of ineptitude. The Golden Bears enjoyed a 14-0 lead in the first on a Terrell Williams 37-yard run and a 40-yard TD pass from Kyle Boller to LaShaun Ward. Rutgers trailed 17-10 in the third closing the gap with a 15-yard TD pass from Ryan Cubit to TE L.J. Smith lending to false hopes that they would not lose to their winless visitor from a strange, far-off land. In the final 19:14, Rutgers played like... well, Rutgers. Mike Barr shanked a 21-yard punt. The Bears could only capitalize for three points with Mark Christian-Jensen's 39-yard FG with 6:48 left for a 20-10 lead. Junior QB Ted Trump subbed for Cubit to attempt to bring an anemic Rutgers offense to life. The Knights could only tally 41 more yards on offense. Trump threw an INT with 1:33 left. The

Bears sealed their only win of the season. In the end, the record-setting defense out-played the record-setting offense. Cal went back to Berkeley sending lame-duck, Head Coach Tom Holmoe out as a winner. The team carried him off on their shoulders – a celebration still yet to be practiced on the Banks of the Old Raritan.

Extra point: About the only memorable highlights were seeing future Baltimore Ravens' QB Kyle Boller throw a touchdown pass for Cal and future Philadelphia Eagle TE LJ Smith score on a reception for Rutgers. Enjoying frozen lemonade in the bleachers on a very warm day after Thanksgiving in New Jersey will be remembered even longer.

Beaver Tale

(73) Oregon State at Temple
September 5, 2002

Philadelphia - Schedules luckily fell into place to my advantage to start the 2002 season. Two teams from the Pac-10 that I hadn't seen yet would be within driving distance for a Thursday-Saturday doubleheader. Originally, both teams were scheduled on Saturday, September 7. With Philly and Boston in completely opposite directions from Byram Township, New Jersey, seeing both games on that Saturday would have been impossible. Eventually, the great schedule maker in TV land took pity on me (and more likely on his potential ratings) and saved me from an expensive trip out west. I couldn't have been luckier. Neither Oregon State nor Stanford comes east often to play football.

I left work early to take half a vacation day, and as a good employee should, I traveled with my new company-issued cell phone. Damned if it didn't ring when I parked my car in the lot on Chestnut Street not far from Franklin Field. Many people loved having these things so they could keep "in touch." To me, it felt more like a ball and chain shackled to my ankle. Instead of getting started before the game with a few brews at the New Deck Tavern on Sansom Street, I sat in the car and took care of some work issues.

After the calls I headed right over to Franklin where I hooked up with a former Juniata bud, Ned Ehrlich, now a true, Philadelphia lawyer. Ned and I always reminisced about our pre-season practices at Juniata, when as trainer and head student equipment manager, the Jewish kid drove the equipment van to take all the Catholic players to church in town on Sunday mornings. Ned's training career lasted for a brief time after college. I saw him on the field at the Meadowlands in August 1980 working with the training staff of the Philadelphia Eagles before their exhibition against the New York Jets. He later decided to forgo sports medicine in favor of a law career. Some of his experience put him in position to eventually negotiate individual player and union contracts. Ned met me this evening at the ancient Franklin Field. I appreciated having someone to enjoy the game with during my quick trip to Philly.

There wasn't much fanfare before this game. A first-time meeting between two schools 3,000 miles apart didn't stir much interest to pack the place. Temple football rarely stirred the masses in The City of Brotherly Love. Six-foot, six inch, OSU Soph QB Derek Anderson finished the game with 33 completions on 51 attempts for 286 yards and four TDs to outperform Owl QB Mike McGann who tossed three INTS and totaled only 99 passing yards. Steven Jackson added 117 rushing yards for the Beavers on 25 carries. Both Anderson and Jackson became quite recognizable in the pros about four years later. Anderson found fleeting fame in Cleveland, and Jackson moved on to play running back for St. Louis. Regretfully, Jessica Simpson didn't appear at Franklin Field this evening. I looked for her this time though! In the end, the Beavers slapped the Owls around and damned up their offense to hold it to 222 yards for a 35 –3 win.

Extra point: Oregon State was in the fold. Onward to Chestnut Hill.

Now that's what I call service!

(74) Stanford at Boston College
September 7, 2002

Chestnut Hill, Mass. - The second half of my Thursday-Saturday, Big East/ PAC 10 DH included not only the addition of the Stanford Cardinal to The Goal but also my first trip to Boston College's Alumni Stadium. The trip gave me a chance to catch up with my good friend Jack Hessler. We no longer did business together having both left our former companies, but we made it a point of staying in touch to at least exchange a "Merry Christmas!" every year to spite all the politically correct "Happy Holidays." I met him at his place in Foxboro on the way to catch a train to Boston's South Street Station to connect on the "T" to Chestnut Hill. I looked forward to a *bonus* of sorts at this game. I'd get to see BC senior TE Frank Misurelli, a former player from our local high school, Lenape Valley Regional, play today. I'd seen him play football and basketball at LVR.

Jack and I boarded the train in comfortable, double-decker cars equipped with skylights to travel quickly to Boston, or so we thought. The train pulled into Sharon, MA, where we abruptly sat, and sat, and sat, and... sat! An announcement finally came through. Power lines had fallen ahead of us and all trains along the line were delayed. The railroad people had no idea how long this could take. Great! They had no idea that I had to be at this game to see Stanford, my 74th team! Did they know they could now owe me an all-expense paid trip to Palo Alto? I sat stewing and cursing the idea that mass transit could really work in the U.S. while arrangements supposedly took shape for buses to pick us up at the previous station to transport us to South Street. When? Time was running out to be at Alumni Stadium for the 3:30 kickoff!

Hundreds of train riders lined up in the empty parking garage. Things did not look good. The line was long, and if buses showed up sporadically, this could be a long wait. I had no idea how long it would take to drive to South Street Station. I had no idea how often the trains connected to Chestnut Hill. If I couldn't see at least part of the first quarter, was I going to be able to count Stanford toward my Goal? Finally, four buses came barreling in and pulled up along the sidewalk. One came close to where Jack and I stood and we made sure that we were two of the first to get on the standing-only bus. We stood toward the back of as they packed in as many riders as possible. We rolled on to I-93 and sped along at 65 mph. You never see strap-hangers cruising along the interstates, but here we were. I still had no idea how we were even going to be close to see the first quarter no less the opening kickoff. Suddenly, a muffled shout came from the front of the crowded bus over the sound of a diesel engine. "Anybody back there going to the BC game?" As luck would have it, somebody up front also had a fixation to get to Alumni Stadium. I figured there must be a bunch on board with the same plan.

"Two back here!" I answered. A message relayed back to us to stay on board after everyone else got off at South Street. The driver agreed to drive us to BC's Alumni Stadium direct. What luck! I couldn't believe it. I still didn't know if we'd be there for kickoff, but at least we wouldn't have to wait for a rail connection. The bus doors opened at South Street and people filed out. In the end, there weren't a bunch of BC fans left on board clamoring to get to the game—just Jack, me, and two other guys. Luckily for us the other two guys got on last and were able to convince the driver. He just happened to live in the BC neighborhood, knew how to get there, and agreed to drive us. As bad as our luck had turned earlier, it got real good to make up for it. We rumbled past Fenway Park. We barreled along up hills and through nice, residential neighborhoods. Our new, best bus driver pulled right up to the main gate of Alumni, and four of us got off with profuse thanks. Jack and I got to our seats to watch the opening kick-off with seconds to spare. Sometimes things just fall into place even after things don't start out right. Thank you Mr. Boston Transit Authority bus driver from Chestnut Hill. The game turned out to be well worth his extra effort for us.

First impression once we grabbed ours seats as the game started: the Stanford mascot has got to be the worst in all of college sports! Slippery Rock has a rock, but a rock is hard. You can roll boulders over somebody. You can throw stones and people will get out of your way. The Stanford Cardinal? A tree? A Sequoia? Play football? It doesn't move unless someone or something chops it or blows it down! A tree prancing along the sideline - how stupid! At Auburn pep rallies, they entangle branches of stately trees with rolls of toilet paper at Toomer's Crossing. While they do it, cheerleaders dance! The trees don't.

In the first half, Frank Misurelli caught a pass for 34 yards, but damn the prancing trees! Stanford took a 27-17 lead on Michael Craven's 33-yard INT return heading into the fourth quarter. Bring on the lumberjacks! BC's Derrick Knight scored after a fumble recovery on a nine-yard scamper to cut the tree's lead down to three points. A little while later, Sando Sciortino's field goal tied the score. With 1:35 left to play, BC took over from its own 35. In four plays, the Eagles took it to Stanford's 12. With 36 seconds left, Derrick Knight took it through the middle for the TD and the final 34-27 margin in favor of 2-0 BC. Alumni Stadium erupted. "*Timber*!" The Eagles soared over the Trees.

Extra point: Jack and I returned via the T to South Street Station and made our return to Foxboro without incident. We got to the game with great last-minute heroics by our unknown bus driver. The Eagles beat the Cardinals the same way. Again, thank you for your outstanding effort Mr. Bus Driver! We couldn't have officially recorded team #74 that day without you.

Eagles avoid goose egg at Byrd
(75) Eastern Michigan at Maryland
September 21, 2002

College Park, Maryland - When this game appeared on the Terrapin's schedule, mixed emotions set in. I needed to see hapless Eastern Michigan to add as another new team. Was this game worth the four-hour drive to Byrd Stadium? The Eagles hadn't had a winning record in seven years. On top of the non-competitive nature of this contest, a 6 p.m. start probably meant an overnight stay somewhere. Would the cost of this trip be worth it? When, where, and who would the EMU Eagles ever play in a game of significance? Luckily for me, the starting time offered a chance to put together a day/night doubleheader. Navy hosted Northwestern that afternoon in what looked to be a potentially competitive game. Annapolis to College Park takes about half an hour. To see *two* games played so close together on the same day made the trip worthwhile. So, after watching a pretty entertaining 49-40 Northwestern win over Navy, I headed over to Maryland's Byrd Stadium without a game ticket.

I parked in the first empty lot I found on the MD campus for free, a rare opportunity at any big college game. I headed over to Byrd and walked past a lot where a kid with his mother offered me a $25 end-zone seat for $10. I couldn't refuse their generosity. The Maryland band dedicated their show to the U.S. Armed Forces, a perfect sequel having spent the day at a Navy game and leaving immediately afterward to catch the nightcap in College Park.

Never before had I seen a team less prepared for a football game than the Eagles of EMU! They didn't even bring any fans – not even a few green-clad cheerleaders. The "contest" turned into a Maryland highlight film. The Terps got things headed in the right direction after their 1-2 start to the season. All-America LB EJ Henderson was playing at full strength now after recovering from an injury. QB Scott McBrien was improving under the tutelage of HC Ralph Friedgen. He threw for 300 yards. TB Chris Downs filled in amply for the injured Bruce Perry and scored two TDs. Utilizing his speed for big plays, WR/returner Steve Suter was compiling a highlight film. He had a career night returning a kickoff 58 yards to set up one score and scored on a dazzling, 91-yard TD pass later. Leading 38-0 in the third, the "Fridge" pulled McBrien. EMU's Eric Klaban booted a 41-yard FG in the second half. Maryland conquered, 45-3 . . . and it wasn't that close! As expected, the very poor Eagles bided their time and mine to roll on toward

The Goal. I saw three teams score a total of 134 points that day. The Eagles kicked a late, meaningless field goal to avoid a shutout.

Extra point: This was the first of eight consecutive wins for Maryland before losing to Virginia to finish tied for second in the ACC and 10-3 overall. Under the "Fridge", the Terps won ten games for the second year in a row and won the Peach Bowl where they trounced Tennessee, 30-3. They finished ranked No. 13 in the USA/ESPN Coaches Poll. Henderson earned All-American honors including the Butkus award as the nation's top LB. As for the Eagles of EMU, they finished as the cellar dweller in the MAC's Western Division at 1-7, 3-9 overall. HC Jeff Woodruff eventually finished 8-26 during his three seasons there. The Eagles seem perennially in search of a new head coach. Between 1990 and 2010, they achieved just one winning season finishing 6-5 in 1995. They continue to look back.

Time and Now Tide

(76) Texas Christian at Army
October 12, 2002

West Point - The Texas Christian Horned Frogs arrived on the banks of the Hudson during a hard-driving, wind-swept, rain storm. Our tailgate plans got washed out, but St. Laurie, cousin Frank Scarpa, his wife Jessie, Dave Headden, and Charlie Roberts all showed up to brave the elements. Good thing I bought everyone's tickets in advance! The October rain felt cold and pelted our faces and rain gear, but TCU made the trip east so we were obliged. I intended to stay until the bitter end, come hell or *high water* - literally.

The weather wreaked havoc for both teams. Up 7-0, TCU fumbled away its next possession at the Army 37. The Cadets drove 63 yards with Carlton Jones running it in from the 20. Army's defense bent but didn't break on three occasions, allowing the Horned Frogs' Nick Browne to connect on three FGs. On a fourth possession, Ty Gunn rifled a 46-yard TD pass to Adrian Madise. Before the second period ended, a two-yard run by Army's Reggie Nevels kept Army in the game trailing 23-13. All the while, the rain drove hard and steady as the wind whipped around, but we were committed to the end. Well at least, *I was*. Frank, a rare, admissible Rutgers fan, and Jessie, who was with child at the time, decided enough was enough with the weather. St. Laurie, Dave, Charlie, and I remained steadfast. A driving rainstorm could not stop us from seeing the game in its entirety, or we all knew it wouldn't count toward the annals of The Goal!

Fumbles back and forth led to scores resulting in 32-27 TCU lead late in the third. But suddenly, we had a bigger problem than Army. A warning screamed over Michie Stadium's public address system, *"Attention all drivers parked by the South Docks! The Hudson has come up over its banks! Please move your cars from that location immediately!"* Guess where we parked?

Immediately? The fourth quarter was just beginning. It's a good, close game, and TCU can't count as the 76th team in the annals of history until time expires in the fourth quarter. I looked to cold, wet St. Laurie. She seemed to be looking for an excuse to leave a very good game. She took the keys and promised to meet us after the game. She had to catch the shuttle bus down to the South Docks first. I figured if we didn't meet her in the Thayer parking lot right after the game, we'd probably catch up with her somewhere downriver - like Hoboken, New Jersey! Okay, she gets points for this as the self-proclaimed, *Saint Laurie.*

Of course after she and many others left for the South Docks, Dave, Charlie, and I moved from our end zone seats to better sideline seats. We prepared to watch what we'd hope to be a down-to-the-wire battle. The rain subsided a bit, but the changing weather seemed to aid the Horned Frogs. A one-yard run by Reggie Holts and a 62-yard scoring jaunt by Donta Hobbs added up to a 46-27 TCU victory.

Extra point: Meanwhile, thanks to St. Laurie, the van was saved from the rising Hudson floodwaters at West Point. She met us in a lot near Thayer Hall. We took off our wet gear, had a few beers under the tailgate, and then headed home. Let the games continue - 76 down and 41 more to go (so I thought)! *"Time and tide wait for no man."* That's why St. Laurie intervened to save the van from the rising waters of the Hudson. The tide *had* to wait for me. I added another team to The Goal.

Angel in the desert

(77) Wyoming at (78) Nevada-Las Vegas
November 2, 2002

Las Vegas, Nevada - St. Laurie and I had never visited Las Vegas, but we always wanted to. Checking out possible games to see in 2002, I said, "Honey, I've got enough frequent flyer miles saved up and can get a good deal on a hotel. My mother can come and watch the kids. Why don't we plan a long weekend in Vegas?"

"Why, so we can see a football game?" Ah, she knows me so well! But she had always wanted to go to Vegas, so she was willing to tolerate a few hours of my favorite pastime in order to hit "The Strip." With Wyoming in town to play UNLV, I could kill two teams with one ticket though I didn't buy any in advance.

My research indicated we wouldn't need a rental car. We arrived at the Holiday Inn within a short distance of *The Strip* on Friday night. The hotel offered limo service to and from the airport. UNLV's Sam Boyd Stadium wasn't far from where we stayed—or so I thought. I also found public bus transportation could take us close by the stadium—again, so I thought. On Friday night, we hit The Strip. We went to Caesar's Palace where I could play a few college tickets using my "expertise." We felt excited to be here. Game time was 5 p.m. on Saturday, so we did more touring and a little bit of gambling the next morning. In the afternoon, we ate dinner early at a steak place near a bus stop on the way out to Sam Boyd Stadium.

We caught the public transit bus. By my calculations from the Vegas map in my road atlas, I was sure where we could get off to walk a short distance. I pointed out the Thurgood Avenue sign to the bus driver to be sure it led to Sam Boyd. She looked at me and just nodded. Things were going good. We'd have plenty of time to get there to buy tickets, have a few beers, and settle into our seats. We started to walk down Thurgood with housing developments of fairly new concrete homes on both sides surrounded by concrete walls. The road turned. No stadium came into sight, but it couldn't be that far. It must be behind one of these developments, I thought. Ahead of us lay an expanse of homes and buildings set in a valley. Where the heck was this stadium?

Eventually, a gray-haired resident came through the entrance of one of the concrete complexes and walked toward us. I asked him if he knew where the heck Sam Boyd Stadium was. He turned and pointed out to the distant valley ahead of us.

"You see that bright red building right in the middle there? That's Sam Boyd Stadium." He had to be kidding! It had to be five miles away. It didn't look that far in the atlas. Maybe I got off the bus at the wrong street, or maybe I didn't realize that the map of Nevada wasn't the same scale as smallish New Jersey. The scale must have been off! I thought it would be much closer. St. Laurie smirked, sighed, and shook her head. She already complained her feet were starting to hurt. I tried to figure out if I could bend my own rules to be sure this game would count if I didn't end up there until the second quarter. We tramped on. Not only was I not going to hear the end of this, no way we were going to get there on time for the opening kickoff on foot! I picked up the pace with my saintly wife trailing behind. Time and pride were now on the line. Unexpectedly, a white mini-van, or I should say a *white knight*, pulled up from behind heading in our direction. A dark-haired, mustachioed guy hollered at us from the shoulder on the opposite side of the street. "Hey, you need tickets for the game?" I couldn't believe it! This was some kind of positive sign that someone upstairs wanted me to accomplish this Goal. St. Laurie must have said a prayer, and God sent us an angel! On a more worldly level, my professional, negotiating skills kicked in right away.

"I'll make a deal with you," I said. "You give us a ride to the stadium and I'll buy your tickets at face value."

"Get in!" We climbed in. St. Laurie sat in the back next to the baby in the seat. He said, "My wife couldn't make it! Only five miles away, but I have to watch the kids so I can't go to the game. They're good seats in the end zone right behind the goal post. It's a good stadium to watch a game in." If this wasn't divine intervention, I didn't know what was. I couldn't thank this guy enough. We bought the tickets, and he dropped us off at the main gate. We walked through the parking lot and to our seats. The teams ran onto the field as we sat. St. Laurie's feet didn't hurt anymore. I saved some face, got good seats, had a great story to tell, and the two teams could officially count toward The Goal. It couldn't get any better than this. Of course, it could turn out to be a great ball game, but that would be asking for too much. At this point, who cared? I was saved!

As for the game, it was an offensive showcase. UNLV led 35-21 . . . at the half. In the third, Wyoming put up the only seven on the board to trail 35-28 heading into the final period. UNLV scored again to go up by fourteen. Wyoming made it closer in the fourth quarter (and it was getting downright cold . . . isn't this the desert?) retaliating with a TD, but missed the extra point. With 2:27 left in the game from their fourteen, Wyoming took over again. During the drive, QB Corey Bramlett converted a pass on fourth and five from his own 33 into a first down with a 14-yard completion to Dustin Pleasant. With no time left on the clock, Bramlett connected with Scottie Vines in the end zone below us to close the score, 42-40. And yes, with a little Vegas luck, Bramlett ran it in for the two-point conversion. Overtime! *Jackpot!*

Even St. Laurie commented, "This is really a great game! It was worth the trip!" *Two* miracles in one night were just totally beyond my comprehension. On top of this, *I* was cold. I couldn't imagine how *she* tolerated the declining temperatures.

Wyoming got the ball first in OT and chose to play on our end of Sam Boyd. They scored on a run on the fourth play. This could have been the ultimate game if not for the next play. Freshman Scott Parker missed the extra point - wide left! On the Rebel's first offensive play, Jason Thompson passed to FB Steve Costa for a 25-yard TD. Dillon Pieffer did not miss the extra point for UNLV. The Rebels triumphed in a game that even thrilled St. Laurie, 49-48!

Extra Point: We saw two teams with losing records (UNLV 4-5, Wyoming 2-7) each play in their most exciting game of the season. Of course after the game, it was now dark and cold. We had no idea how we were going to get back to our hotel. No buses could be found. Walking was out of the question. A limo driver approached us. For $75, he would take us back. Seventy-five bucks? I hesitated and thought to check other options, but with St. Laurie's immediate *blessing*, it was a good deal. After the ordeal to get to the game, we couldn't believe how quickly he got us back. It was the best $75 we spent all weekend. However, I'll never forget the time the Angel in the Desert rescued me from several fatal blows—missing a game and lifelong humiliation! Moreover, I knew now that someone watching over me wanted me to get this done even more than St. Laurie did!

Over in a Golden Flash

(79) Kent State at Connecticut
November 9, 2002

Storrs, Connecticut - "What goes around comes around" as the old saying goes. Connecticut competed in its third season of 1A football, and on this particular day the Kent Golden Flashes showed up at Storrs to not only become my 79th team, but to provide the competition in the last football game ever to be played at UConn's 50-year old, Memorial Stadium. Over the years, the old block of concrete provided me opportunities to see the Huskies play "small school" football as well add some major college football teams I needed to see to achieve my objective. This would be the Huskies' send-off before moving their games to 40,000-seat Rentschler Field, 30 miles east in East Hartford. I went by myself, disappointed a few friends from back in our early tailgating days at the Meadowlands couldn't make it. Adding a new team, attending the farewell to an old stadium, seeing a couple of local boys, the Atieh brothers from Boonton, make good playing for Kent State, and watching a possible NCAA record-breaker, QB Josh Cribbs, offered opportunities to enjoy another "insignificant" game between the 3-6 Huskies and the 3-6 Golden Flashes. But it was over in a less-than-a-Golden-Flash: To start the game, UConn QB Dan Orlovsky tossed a five-yard TD pass to Wes Timko. The Huskies' Dwaun Black blocked a punt and Cathlyn Clarke returned it for a 31-yard TD. DB Roy Hopkins intercepted a Josh Cribbs pass and returned it to the Kent eight. Orlovsky scored from the one. Then in the second period, UConn's freshman RB Terry Caulley put on a show. He tallied four TDs in the second quarter alone, three on the ground and the fourth on a 35-yard pass play. By half time, the Huskies led Kent State, 49-0! Caulley ran for 175 yards in the second. Cribbs, who was striving to be the first player ever to gain over one thousand yards *both* passing and rushing for more than two seasons, got hurt, but was unimpressive even before his injury. Kent put together three scores in the fourth against UConn guys who hadn't played all season. Another school bit the dust, but more significantly, the UConn team, annihilated only two years ago by Middle Tennessee, 66 – 10, now became the annihilator. Final score: Huskies 63 – Golden Flashes 21. It was over way before the final score.

End runs and Enron

(80) Hawaii at (81) Rice
November 16, 2002

Houston - Back in 2000, after I analyzed how many 1A teams I'd seen and the possibility of seeing the rest, I brazenly approached St. Laurie with a bold idea: we'd finish The Goal together with the final game in Hawaii to see the Rainbow Warriors play! We honeymooned there, and we'd both love to go back. As The Goal progressed though, reality set in. The cost to go back was one thing, but on the other hand, I knew there was no way St. Laurie would take a fall vacation to Hawaii with the kids at school or winding down into the holiday season - no way we could pull this off. In the meantime, I contacted my former Juniata College roommate, Todd Kulp. A decade earlier at a class reunion, Todd and I exchanged pieces of paper with phone numbers. When I eventually pulled mine out to call, the paper tucked in my wallet had *my* number on it! Did I mention we met at our reunion? There was alcohol. The Internet hadn't arrived yet. We eventually caught up through the Juniata College website.

Todd was a graduate of Central Bucks West in Doylestown, Pennsylvania, a high school football powerhouse, but Todd never played a down of football. He dabbled in business and politics. Todd planned a presidential, political campaign on campus at Juniata. One night, he invited me to go to the airport with him to pick up the main speaker, Pat Paulsen, the *"Rowan and Martin's Laugh-in"* comedian-turned-presidential candidate. Besides seeing President Gerald Ford and Bill Clinton at Army-Navy games, that's the closest I've come to meeting someone with presidential aspirations.

After graduation from Juniata, Todd attended the University of Texas to earn his MBA and settled permanently in the Lone Star State. I contacted him there when I saw a double-dip of new teams: Hawaii at Rice. Of course, St. Laurie asked what happened to finishing The Goal in Hawaii. I told her the Goal may be achievable earlier than expected and that we'd never be able to break away to Hawaii while the kids were in school. *"Excuses! Excuses!"* she replied. She knew more than I that the reasons I gave rang true.

I met Todd for dinner with a bunch of his co-workers at a Houston restaurant Friday night before the game. We drank and they told typical office war stories. I didn't know the characters personally, but I could relate to many similar circumstances where I worked. They worked for an oil rig platform company—one of the biggest builders of such in the world. Todd worked in Finance. When he and I talked one on one to catch up later on, he told me how his career path led through scandalous Enron where unscrupulous accounting practices led to bankruptcy in 2001 and in jail time for its shady management. He worked with the main culprits convicted – Jeffrey Skilling, Anthony Fastow, and Kenneth Lay - but he departed long before all the allegations took place. He sensed trouble early and conferred his words of wisdom that told him to move on. He said, "I've worked for mean people who are smart and dumb people who are nice, but I promised myself never to work for *mean* people who are *dumb* again!" Words to live by – Todd avoided a bad situation and moved on to better things, so I thought.

Talk about dumb. The next day we went out for Mexican lunch and went back to his place to watch games. We loafed. We weren't far from Rice Stadium. USA Today indicated the game kicked off at 3 pm. However, I didn't realize all the starting times were set in the Eastern Time zone! Thinking we had plenty of time to check things out before the game, we showed up shortly before two. The game was about to start! Kickoff commenced at 2 pm CST. Luckily, we didn't have to battle a large crowd. Only 19,174 showed up. We got there in a nick of time.

This game presented a couple of firsts. This was my first all-WAC game and my first game in football-crazed Texas. Rice isn't the most traditional of football programs in the Lone Star, but the game offered some points of interest. For instance, the game program boasted of Rice's propensity to lead the nation in player graduation rates. Thirty-one players graduated the previous spring and earned Rice the Academic Achievement Award presented by USA Today and the NCAA. Also, Rice Stadium hosted Super Bowl VIII. I envisioned fellow Boonton High alum Jim Kiick and FB Larry Csonka punishing defenders once again that day as the Dolphins defeated the Vikings, 24-7.

Hawaii took a 14-10 lead at halftime. At the intermission, I realized I came all the way out from Jersey to see a performance by "the MOB" - the Soprano-free *Marching Owl Band*, that is. They looked more like an Ivy League band dressed in dark blazers, ties, sunglasses, and baseball caps than the big, traditional, brass marching bands of the South. They sounded much better than the Ivies though. They played *real* instruments.

The second half showed off Hawaii's offensive firepower programmed by Head Coach June Jones and led by eventual record-setting QB Tommy Chang. Chang spread passes effectively among receivers to rack up 369 passing yards. Two consecutive drives in the third resulted in TD passes of eight yards to Jeremiah Cockheran and 17 yards to Britton Komine overcoming the Warriors' deficit to take a 23-14 lead. Rice's Marcus Battle took his only handoff of the game and ran for a 60-yard TD that pulled Rice to within 23-21. The Warriors' Justin Ayat converted a 21-yard FG to conclude the third quarter scoring.

The Warriors took a 33-21 lead on Thero Mitchell's three-yard TD run with 7:50 left. Rice steadfastly stuck to the ground game under former Air Force coach Ken Hatfield with quarterback Kyle Herm at the controls until the final period of play. Herm's replacement, Greg Henderson, tossed a 54-yard TD to Battle to cut the Rainbows' lead to 33-28, but further drives stalled and Hawaii enjoyed a long, happy flight home with its fifth consecutive win to go 8-2 overall and 7-1 in the WAC. For Rice, it was their season finale to finish 4-7 and 1-5 in the conference. Maybe they should have gotten the ball more often to Marcus Battle today and all season long.

Two-point conversion: I pulled the end around on St. Laurie by seeing Hawaii play in Houston instead of finishing The Goal in Honolulu, but once the kids finish college and *if* we have any money left over, maybe we'll take that trip back to Hawaii. Of course, I'll have to check the Rainbow Warriors' schedule in advance first. Maybe we can stay two Saturdays, or maybe they'll play on a Saturday and the following Thursday or Friday. St. Laurie will understand. She knows the methods of my madness all too well now!

As for Todd's end run on Enron, he got out of there and was now working for Transocean, the world's largest offshore drilling contractor, based in Houston. In April 2010, everyone became familiar with the Transocean Deepwater Horizon oil rig that exploded in the Gulf of Mexico off Louisiana leaking oil into the gulf. I hope my end run to take St. Laurie to Hawaii is more successful than Todd's end run around his former employer. Todd's had an interesting career to say the least.

Shipshewanna, Indiana
(82) Washington State at Notre Dame
September 6, 2003

South Bend, Indiana – The Washington State Cougars play far from New Jersey. What chance existed that they'd ever come out east to play? When I saw them slated to open in South Bend against Notre Dame, the gears started turning. How could I work this out? Don DiVite, Les's brother, told me once that the lubricant distribution company he worked for in central Jersey advertised heavily in some big-time, national college-football game programs. Previously, Don managed to get all of us tickets to the Big East basketball tournament and NCAA opening-round games at The Meadowlands. When I asked him about the possibilities of working out ND-WSU tickets, he knew he couldn't go, but he contacted some people to come up with tickets for Les and me. Bingo! We booked a long weekend and a ten-hour drive to see the Irish host the Cougars to notch the newest team in my belt play at one of the most revered venues in all of college football. Call it the luck of my Irish ancestors. This was the first time these two teams would face each other on the gridiron.

By the time we got tickets, hotel rooms around South Bend were no longer available. Searching the Internet, I came up with a discount hotel deal in Shipshewanna, Indiana, 42 miles east of South Bend. We left early Friday morning anticipating the slight possibility of getting to Notre Dame in time for the traditional Friday night Irish pep rally. We arrived a little later than anticipated and drove right to the hotel. Despite the distance from South Bend, it turned out to be a pretty good place to stay. Had we brought our wives, they probably could have enjoyed the place with its shops, flea markets, and restaurants. We also learned that the Amish thrived in towns beyond Lancaster, Pennsylvania. Buggies pulled by trotting horses moved hastily along the main roads. Friendly people on board waved to us, figuring we came to spend money *there*. Hungry, we decided to delay South Bend and have dinner right down the street at the Blue Gate Restaurant. It offered great prices for all-you-can eat Amish dinners. For dessert, we ate home-made Amish pies. More Amish than Irish, nothing in town indicated that we were within a one-hour drive of the most prominent of schools in college football. Instead, banners welcomed a rodeo to town! Les and I needed a fix of Irish spirit after dinner, so we drove west to South Bend.

We thought we'd catch something happening on campus, but aside from women's soccer, nothing else stirred. Soccer did nothing for us. We drove around until we came to some bustling spot on a corner. The parking lot was packed and the lights shined at the *Linebacker Inn*—just what we were looking for! Like the lot, the joint was packed and hopping. For a three-buck cover charge, you at least get one, cold beer. All the beers served there came nice and cold. ND fans partied loud and celebrated the anticipation of another successful season under Coach Ty Willingham, his second at South Bend. They talked Irish football. The spirit of Notre Dame football filled the air!

A group of Washington State fans came in. Some were so big we were sure they played for the Cougars in recent years. Being the Cougars first venture to Notre Dame, they had no idea what to expect, so they probably brought along some protection—like last year's offensive line. Rock music blared on the juke box while fans danced where they could find room. About every fourth song though, the jukebox went from party music to "*The Notre Dame Victory March!*" Of course, all the Irish fans joined in on the song. Les and I definitely found the right place to get in on a little Friday night, Irish spirit. We didn't stay until closing as we had to shuttle back to Shipshewanna to come back to enjoy more Irish pre-game festivities the next morning.

Les and I headed to South Bend early to savor the Notre Dame pre-game traditions. We toured the Convocation Center with all the Irish stuff to buy, see, and experience. Former RB Allen Pinkett joined other former Irish football captains to sign autographs. We took our pictures in a rotunda where you stand in the middle of a surrounding photograph of a kick-off between the Irish and Stanford. I bought Eric a gold towel inscribed with the famous, Irish, locker-room inscription, *"Play like a champion today!"* I think it's a great message about living life daily. It still hangs in Eric's room. We grabbed sausage sandwiches before heading over to listen to the *Band of the Fighting Irish* getting the fans primed before the game. At the final Kickoff Classic played the previous season, Frank Rafferty, Les, and I watched the Irish defeat Maryland, 22-0. Frank's biggest disappointment—Notre Dame didn't bring the band! I called Frank on his cell phone so he could hear it live. I didn't want let the Irishman miss out on this. The Irish band led the parade to Notre Dame Stadium. Along the way, we witnessed a Notre Dame tradition featuring a "drill" by the Irish Guard—students dressed in tall, bearskin caps and kilts who march out in front of the band. During this drill, fans go nose-to-nose and scream in the faces of a Guard trying to instigate a reaction. The young, tall uniformed Irish Guards didn't flinch in their traditional fashion to the red-faced, beer-breathed, middle-aged alum.

In 1980, when I visited Notre Dame Stadium to witness the start of "The Bold Experiment," the venerable venue held 59,075. Now keeping in line with the growth, popularity, and growing budgetary demands, the stadium held 80,795. ND's famous stadium ranked now as the 15th largest in the country. If they could add more seats, they'd continue to fill them. Les and I found our section in the south end zone and kept walking down the steps with our eyes on *Touchdown Jesus!* right before us. The seats Don got us were in row 6 just to the left of the goal post. They provided prime views for some significant plays to be seen.

Unfortunately for the Irish, they bumbled, stumbled, and fumbled during the first half, and the hard-hitting Cougars took advantage taking a 19-3 halftime lead. During the halftime festivities, Notre Dame introduced former team captains from throughout their historic decades. In the locker room, Tyrone Willingham was surely performing his rendition of a Knute Rockne pep talk! If ever the Irish offense needed a fire lit under it, this was the time. A die-hard Irish fan from Ontario, Canada, wondered aloud if the Irish offense had even practiced since last season. Throughout the game, Carlyle Holiday's passes were floaters ripe for the picking. Despite 21 completions, Holiday garnered only 134 yards through the air. Many thrown were of the "dangerous" variety.

All the halftime inspiration took a while to work, however, and it wasn't until late in the third quarter, trailing 19-9, that ND started rolling. A fumble gave them field position to close with Holiday's pass to Raheem McKnight, 19-16. Holiday was injured on ND's next possession, and

Frosh QB Brady Quinn entered the game to the delighted cheers of the ND faithful. Despite Holiday's supposed quick recovery, Willingham left Quinn in for the entire series. Julius Jones scampered the final 22 yards around right end to pay-dirt and the first ND lead of the day, 23-19, with 5:03 left in the game. They added a field goal, but left Wazu too much time on the clock. The Cougars scored with a minute left on a stunning, diving, bobbling catch by WR Sammy Moore to our right in our end zone to tie it, 26-26. Overtime at ND...perfect! It turned out to be a memorable game adding Washington State at a season opener in South Bend.

The Cougars selected our end of the stadium away from the ND band and student section. State's Drew Dunning misfired with one of his patented line drive kicks that went wide left from the 34-yard line. The Irish took over. From our prime seats, Nick Setta's kick started wide right, but curved in through the uprights! The Irish were 1-0 after an exciting, hard-fought, comeback game, 29-26, under a bright, blue September sky in South Bend, Indiana. Games like this kept me pursuing this crazy Goal week after week. Not only did I watch my 83rd team, we saw a great college football game, my fourth in overtime! Les and I attended mass at Notre Dame Cathedral with a thousand others right after the game. Hours later, we drove back to Shipshewanna.

Extra point: The morning before we headed to South Bend on game day, I got up early to do my usual two-mile walk. I walked extra far this morning because Shipshewanna doesn't offer the hilly climbs of northern New Jersey. What was funny though, I realized that the horses pulling buggies with the Amish on board ran quick paces with strides reminding me of trotters seen at the Meadowlands and at Freehold Raceway. On my walk that morning, I watched some trotters training at a nearby practice track. It made me realize that the fastest must earn the right to race, and the losers pull Amish buggies! I wondered if the Amish play the horses.

We're glad we stayed in Shipshewanna. We'll have to go back there some day to check out the rodeo. Then we'll head over to South Bend for some more Irish spirit!

Still rockin'!
(83) Texas Tech at North Carolina State
September 20, 2003

Raleigh, North Carolina – The Red Raiders ventured east so I flew down to Raleigh to stay with transplanted Penn Stater, Joe Massimilla, John's brother. Last time we left Joe, now a dad with two young sons, he swore at Greg Hardman and me for our snoring contest in his apartment back at State College the night after the PSU-Iowa game in 1983 – something about no sleep and having to study. Joe had plans with his boys this particular day, but Bill and Katyna Esoda, good friends of his a few doors down, saved me their extra ticket for the Texas Tech game and invited me to join them to see my next addition take on their beloved Wolfpack.

Phil Rivers started at QB for NC State and had an arsenal of offensive weapons. Red Raider Head Coach Mike Leach never learned the meaning of "off tackle" or "end around", maybe "draw play". His QB B.J. Symonds arrived in Raleigh as the nation's total offense leader. In 2002, State triumphed over Tech, 51-48. I hoped for a similar score this year in Raleigh.

Bill and Katyna picked me up at Joe's and we headed to Carter-Finley Stadium where I savored lasting impressions of a great time there in 1998. Would this experience be as good? First, Bill and Katyna presented me with a red NCS golf shirt to wear to the game! Next, I learned that State takes care of its fans. On a blistering day for a noon kickoff, each seat came with a scarlet *Howl Towel*, a cardboard fan on a stick, and two discount coupons for Coca-Cola products. Somebody already polished off a dozen two-ounce bottles of Southern Comfort strewn under the seats in front of us. No full ones remained. I checked, but I understood that they weren't offered as part of the promotional package.

Major renovations and expansion had taken place since my visit five years earlier. The enclosed stadium made the atmosphere even more raucous than the energetic night I remembered against Syracuse. What a great place to watch a game!

Despite major yardage racked up by Tech in the first half, State dominated, 21-0. The Wolfpack throttled its Big 12 foe with a balanced offense, a flexible defense, and aggressive special teams play. The high-powered but scoreless Red Raider offense managed to move from its own 20 to State's 8-yard line with 25 seconds left. However, a 25-yard FG by PK Keith *Toogood* - no good!

Bill and Katyna beat the stadium crowd out before halftime to take a short walk back to serve up lunch to members of the hungry, NC State swimming team. I stood in long lines on the way out of the seating area on this hot, sun-drenched Saturday. At least I got some shade from the sweltering heat!

State RB T.A. McClendon rambled for 67 yards on one play in the first series of the third quarter to put the ball at the Tech one. RB Josh Brown went in on the next play to put a nail in the Raider coffin to lead, 28-0. One of Tech's patented long drives finally paid off as the next 80-yard drive ended in a 3-yard TD run by RB Johnnie Mack. Though trailing 28-7 in the third, there was still a feeling that with a few breaks, the Red Raiders could get right back in this game with its high-powered offense. Bang! NC State fumbled on the kick-off return. Tech seemed poised to click at the Pack 22. A heavy rush by State pushed Tech back into a fourth and twelve-yard situation. Symons set up in the pocket, broke loose, rushed up field, passed the first down marker, and fumbled! A block in the back after the recovery gave State the ball at its own six. This seemed to be the final nail necessary to seal the Raiders coffin, but the Pack had a few more. A 37-yard pass to WR Jerricho Cotchery and pass interference in the end zone were key plays before Josh Brown scored his second TD from two yards away. The Pack was in control, 35-7, with 3:13 left in the third period.

Both teams scored touchdowns on long drives in the fourth. The Pack continued to score just like the previous season's shoot-out. Tech padded stats with its first team offense and used the clock against second and third team defenders to make the score seem somewhat respectable. Despite 586 passing yards by slinging B.J. Symonds, who fired the ball 63 times, Rivers finished more efficiently completing18 of 22 for 257 yards in a 49-21 victory. Over all, it was an old-fashioned ass-whipping with some miscalculated coaching decisions by Tech's Mike Leach. He deferred some easy first-half field goals to get points on the board to possibly build momentum for his team.

Instead, the Raiders came up empty, but that was their style. State's defense rose to the occasion in tough situations.

Two point conversion: The week after my trip to Raleigh, Tech visited Ole Miss to play the type of game I expected against NC State. They beat the Rebels and Eli Manning, 49-45. Rivers and Manning, the two QBs the Raiders faced back-to-back would be traded for each other in the first round of the subsequent NFL draft between the Chargers and Giants. As for B.J. Symonds and his 586 passing yards...

I tailgated with the Esodas and friends after the game. Once again,

NC State proved to have a fun, partying, football atmosphere despite their strong association as an ACC basketball school. In the Esoda's tradition, they asked me sign the underside of their tailgate canopy as did all their guests. I wrote: "Collegefootballfan.com: Texas Tech #84, but NC State rocks!" Carter-Finley is a great, energetic stadium to watch a game. I will always look forward to going back there (2009 - South Carolina 7 NC State 3).

Baking in Beantown

(84) Ball State at Boston College
September 27, 2003

Chestnut Hill, Mass. - The Ball State Cardinals arrived to play Boston College a year later than when I originally planned to see them. In 2002, the Cardinals visited the UConn Huskies in Storrs, Connecticut. Instead of just heading up, I found out the night before that all tickets to Memorial Stadium sold out due to Parents Weekend. I probably should have gone figuring I could find at least one ticket among the 16,000 concrete bleacher seats. Instead, I stayed locally and took Eric and his cousins to see Princeton defeat Columbia that evening, 44-16. Regretfully, I missed a good game in Storrs. The Cardinals beat the Huskies in a close one, 24-21.

This year, the Cardinals would visit Chestnut Hill. As fate would have it, BC also hosted the Cardinals on their Parents Weekend, another tough ticket. This time I didn't let that deter me from adding Ball State to the annals of my history. I called the Ball State ticket office for three seats in the visitors' section of Alumni Field. I called up my buddy Jack Hessler in Foxboro. Eight-year old Eric and I would meet him there to give the "T" another shot to get us to Alumni Stadium. This time, no wires fell across the tracks, and mass transit ran on time to let us see both squads with 2-2 records match up on what would be another overwhelmingly hot September afternoon.

Before the game, we made time to check out colonial Boston. We followed Patriot Path for a little while. On the cloudy, overcast morning, we stopped in Quincy Market for sandwiches and "chowda" that really hit the spot. We toured past the site of the Boston Massacre, the original city hall, gravesites of Ben Franklin's parents, and that of Patriot and Brew master, Sam Adams, all before catching the next train to the game. Parking spaces are few at Boston College which doesn't bode well for impromptu tailgating.

Spaces are reserved. Against Stanford, Jack and I noted tailgaters parked on the varsity baseball field adjacent to Alumni Field. I envisioned the grounds crew must do a bang-up job up there after snowy winters with little time to prepare in the spring. Last year's tough winter must have been worse than usual because the clay infield was roped off this year. Jack mentioned that a friend of his, a long-time season ticket holder, cancelled his seats this year when told that his space was no longer available. I guess he either used to park on the infield or else he got bumped by some big donor who had a space there and got relocated to another spot somewhere on the cramped campus.

Security didn't have any issues with us carrying food and water into the stadium on what was turning out to be a blistering hot, sunny afternoon. Most venues don't allow fans to bring stuff in forcing you have to buy theirs. We beat the crowd and got in with everything in plain sight as we strolled through the gate.

We sat under the intense sun with the few Ball State fans that showed up in the section on the twenty behind the visitors' bench at Alumni Stadium. Jack couldn't take the sun and left to get into the shade before the first half ended. Shade under the stands was welcomed at halftime in Boston just as it was the previous weekend in Raleigh, NC, but probably even more so! Today was a *scorcher.*

Greg Toal and Derrick McKnight each scored a TD on the ground in the first half for the Purple Eagles. Cardinal QB Talmedge Hill ran for one TD and passed for another in the first half, but two botched punting attempts by Ball State in the first half resulted in two more BC touchdowns to give the Eagles a 28-16 advantage at halftime.

Q3 started off with a bang, literally! McKnight got clocked on the return by ubiquitous LB Lorenzo Scott and turned the ball over to BSU. Taking over at BC's eight, Dante Ridgeway slanted across the middle from the spread formation and scored his second TD of the day on a pass from Hill. It seemed like State was ready to challenge Boston College for the rest of the game trailing, 28-23. But in the signature words of Lee Corso, *"Not so fast, my friend!"* Instead, the Eagles took off exploding for 25 consecutive points. They drove 81 yards to score on a one-yard play action pass from Quinton Porter to wide-open TE Sean Ryan. Porter and Ryan went for seconds on the two-point conversion. BC forced BSU to punt on its next series, and with many second team defenders on the field, Ball State yielded a 24-yard FG by Sando Sciortino at the end of Q3. BC widened its lead, 39-23.

The host team struck quickly at the beginning of the final period. Cardinal WR Ryan Hahaj didn't challenge Eagle CB Jazzmen Williams for a "wounded duck" thrown by Hill, and Williams returned the ball 40 yards to the BSU nine yard line. Porter found Ryan wide open again from two yards out on play action. The Eagles were flying high, doubling the Cardinal output, 46-23. QB Paul Peterson led the Eagles on their next series down the field, and RB Horace Dodd would finish the drive with his second TD of the game, a 1-yard TD run, to make it 53-23. BSU TE Mike Steinhaus put the last points of the day on the board for the final score of 53-29. Ball State was in my book.

Extra point: We left Alumni via the T, half-baked by the sun. We hung around Quincy Market again and replenished with drinks and pizza in the shade at *Ned Devine's*. We watched street entertainment and saw converted military ducks take tourists in and out of Boston Harbor. We walked past upscale hotels and saw work remaining on the "big dig." We traveled through two centuries of history before and after the game. Boston offers a historic, sight-seeing tour for any college football fan on the way to and from a Boston College game in Chestnut Hill. Be careful though, under a hot sun on a September afternoon, you can get baked, fried, or re-fried. They don't call it *Beantown* for nothing.

Am I really *here*?
(85) UL-Monroe at (86) UL-Lafayette
October 11, 2003

Lafayette, Louisiana - As John McGrath aptly pointed out in his article, *"College Football's Superfan"*, about my website in the 2005 edition of *Lindy's* pre-season publications: "Sometimes it's heaven, watching college football games between big-time heavyweights. And sometimes you make a U-turn and drive a few miles down a highway, and find out it's even better."[13] That's basically what happened when I determined it was too big a risk to travel to Dallas in 2003 for the Red River Shootout - the perennial war waged at the Texas State Fairgrounds between Texas and Oklahoma. My former Juniata roommate and Texas MBA, Todd Kulp, tried to get tickets for the annual Red River Rivalry, but to no avail. Rather than take a chance and not find a ticket or go pay some outrageous scalper price, I decided to hold my cards and look for the next "best" match-up that weekend. No other

13 "College Football's Superfan," *Lindy's 2005 Pre-season* (2005): p. 20.

glamorous match-ups benefiting The Goal were scheduled that weekend. So to come up with two new teams to meet my criteria, logistical analysis helped determine my final decision. I could use frequent flier miles, so I decided my best strategy was to opt for a game between two teams yet to be added who were quite a distance. My internet search indicated that some of the highest airfares from Newark's Liberty Airport to other parts of the country included flights to Louisiana. On a previous business trip to Lafayette, I recalled seeing signs to UL-Lafayette, home of the Ragin' Cajuns, not far from my hotel close to the airport. A free airline ticket, no need for a rental car, a cheap hotel, and some good old Cajun' cooking nearby set my sights on what seemed to be one of the worst college football match-ups this side of the new millennium. The week before, in a game I referred to on my site as the "Battle at the Bottom of the Barrel," ESPN.com coined it as its "Pillow Fight of the Week." Undaunted, I flew to Lafayette, Louisiana to see the Ragin' Cajuns (0-6) host the Indians of UL-Monroe (0-6) for not only the basement of the Sun Belt Conference, but for a game to determine which team was the worst in all of Division-1A college football! Both teams were necessary to reach The Goal - perfect for my purpose.

I just *love* Louisiana. People there start with *Mardi Gras* in New Orleans and party throughout the state for the rest of the year. They even have Margarita drive-thrus! Walking up to the visitor's side of Cajun Field about 40 minutes prior to kick-off was like walking through a ghost town. On the home side though, I found a lively parking lot entertained by a rock band hosting hundreds of Cajun tailgate homecoming parties. In the middle sat a Budweiser beer wagon, an oasis of refreshment after a three-mile walk with no immediate tailgate plans. A Ragin'Cajun cook-off took place for Homecoming festivities. They know how to eat, drink, and party all year long in Louisiana. The Ragin' Cajun Marching Band performed and marched into Cajun Field before I bought a ticket on the home side, but I could choose to sit anywhere I wanted to among a Homecoming crowd of 13,540.

After the Monroe Indians completed a pass on the first play from scrimmage, I laughed, shook my head, and said, "I can't believe I'm really *here*!" Two 0-6 teams - I could have been watching Texas play Oklahoma. As for this setting, the personality of today's game took shape around me. Ragin Cajun QB Eric Rekieta heard the calls and saw the facetious signs, "Rekieta for Heisman!" After an early Monroe touchdown, the two teams demonstrated why they were ranked at the very bottom of 1A football. During the next six series, both teams generally went backwards because of poor blocking, delays of game, and motion penalties. Both teams generally began each series with a first and 15 or more. Even the person running the electronic scoreboard at Cajun Field felt frustration or a chance at sarcasm. The result of a Monroe punt from the six-yard line on fourth and long prompted the scoreboard message, "Nice play!" That's as good as it got.

By the end of the first half No. 116 UL-M led No. 117 UL-L, 28-14. During halftime, Lafayette-Louisiana (formerly SW Louisiana) introduced a distinguished alumnus - Cy Young Award Winner and former NY Yankee Ron "Gator" Guidry, also known as "Louisiana Lightning." I wondered if Guidry was somehow paying attention to the Yankee-Red Sox playoff game going on while attending his alma mater's homecoming festivities. Hmmm? Two 0-6 college teams or a "classic" Major League playoff series? It had to be a tough call for the Gator.

UL-L tied the score with a one-yard run following a long pass by "Heisman candidate" Rekieta to Fred Stamps (198 yards) and on a 64-yard TD pass between the same combination early in the third. The Ragin' Cajuns were challenging in the second half. Monroe took back the lead, 35-28, when substitute QB Dan DaPrato ran 45 yards to the UL-L five to set up a one-yard TD plunge by Jason Schule. Around that time, the loudest cheer of the day came from the combined stands of Cajun and Indian fans when LSU was announced on the short end of the score against Florida. Louisianans couldn't have been happier at Cajun Field! Call it jealousy or lack of respect, but there's pure Ragin' Cajun and "Injun" hatred in Louisiana for the SEC's Tigers. Two girls wore the shirts with the message, "If you don't support the Cajuns, move to Baton Rouge!"

After several non-scoring series for both teams, Monroe scored again to go up 42-28 on Kevin Payne's 2-yard TD among his 148 yards. It wasn't over! Rekieta retaliated leading a pair of scoring drives culminating with TD passes to TE Josh Joerg and to Bill Sampy. Lafayette tied Monroe at 42-42 with 5:23 left. "I can't believe I'm really *here*!" At that point, a young, UL-Lafayette coed ran down behind me from the exhilarated, student section so she could converse on her cell phone with someone who was evidently on the way to pick her up. With the score knotted at 42, she intensely shouted into her phone.

"It's the fourth quarter. We just scored. It's 42-42. There's 4:17 left. This is *serious*! I have a *dollar* on this game!" That's the kind of fan loyalty that makes college football a great game. I would've thrown in another dollar to make it twice as serious for her, but she bolted back to her seat. On a third and 14 on their ensuing series, the Indians ran a double reverse option pass to Mack Vincent who hauled it in at the Lafayette 34. With 1:46 left, Tyler Kuecker (supposedly pronounced "kicker") booted a 31-yarder which gave the Indians the game-winner. Wow! What an exciting game. The 1-6 Indians congratulated their vanquished foe, knelt to pray with them, and then sprinted to their contingency of fans who celebrated like it was the national championship. LSU be damned! "I can't believe I'm *really here*!"

Extra point: Despite the ineptitudes on both sides rated as the two worst in 1A by ESPN.com the prior week, it was a hard-fought, exciting, memorable game played between equally talented teams played in a spirited, competitive game at the Cajun homecoming. My timing worked out better than I could imagine. The annual Red River Shoot-out between Texas and Oklahoma ended in a Sooner rout, 65-13. Instead, I got to enjoy a memorable 45-42 game. Though at the opposite end of the spectrum, it allowed me to add two new teams instead of one, and even better, neither 0-6 team got blown out. I'd save a Sooner game for a later date. Rekieta ended up with 474 passing yards and four TD passes, but eventually, no Heisman. As I said all along that day, "I can't believe I'm really *here*!" However, I'm glad I was! *"What better way to spend an autumn afternoon?"*

Toe beats Heels by a foot

(87) Arizona State at North Carolina
October 18, 2003

Chapel Hill, NC - I drove further than usual to catch my last remaining Pac-10 team. The Arizona State Sun Devils traveled east to face the North Carolina Tar Heels. The rematch of the previous year's UNC 38-35 victory in the desert provided me with an opportunity to see a game played in Chapel Hill for the first time.

During my drive, it sounded like followers of 1-5 North Carolina had already written off football season. A local radio sports program on a station referred to the *"Voice of the Tar Heels"* already talked basketball. There was cause for excitement though because Roy Williams was on his way from Kansas to take over the Tar Heel basketball program. However, the sportscaster lost control of his senses when he dedicated a song saying, "*'Love Train'* - with no love to the Wildcats!" *Wildcats?* I knew what he meant. Someone needed to remind him that today's football game was against the *Arizona State Sun Devils*! A b-ball game versus the *Arizona Wildcats* would follow a few months from now.

Before the game, I walked the campus and checked out UNC's Kenan Football Center. The museum featured trophies and historic displays. I never realized until then that UNC led the NCAA with the all-time number of leading 1,000-yard rushers. Southern Cal always comes to mind as "Tailback U", not North Carolina. Festivities for today's game included honoring former UNC running back Charlie "Choo-Choo" Justice, an All-American from the late 40s who played in two Sugar Bowls and one Cotton Bowl for the Tar Heels. Twice, he finished second in the Heisman balloting. His number "22" was emblazoned on the field at both 22 yard lines in Carolina blue. The UNC band honored him with a song written about him in his hey-day entitled, *"All the way, Choo-Choo!"* Charlie Justice passed away the night before this honorarium at the age of 79.

The game started off competitively, but the officiating crew created controversies from the start with horrible calls, no calls, and even a "re-call"! Questionable calls mounted, but mostly against the visitors. ASU tallied 16 flags for 153 yards while Carolina had only three for 22. Visiting teams normally warranted crews from their conferences, but supposedly because of distance, an ACC crew officiated - hard to believe in this day and age. One example of a bad call came on a UNC possession when QB Darian Durant got called for intentional grounding. He clearly ran beyond the tackle position and threw to receivers in an area when he tossed it out of bounds. Everyone at Kenan understood the rule except for the refs. After a long discussion amongst this bumbling crew, the umpire waved off the flag and hollered," No foul!" In unison, you heard the NC crowd respond, *"No shit!"*

The score stood deadlocked 14-14 in the second period until ASU's Jess Ainsworth booted a 21-yard FG. The Sun Devils recovered a misplayed punt at the Tar Heel 12 with 1:38 left. One first down, one offside penalty, and six time-outs later, Ainsworth booted a 24-yard FG to extend the ASU lead, 20-14.

Trailing 27-17 later in the game, one Tar Heel fan blurted out, "Bring on basketball season!" His football team didn't give up though. On the next play, Durant completed a 63-yard pass play to my favorite name ever in college football, Jawarski Pollock! Now the Heels trailed 27-24.

Arizona State missed a 32-yard FG to start the last quarter, and UNC took over from its own 20. With the aid of a questionable interference call, the Heels had first and ten at the ASU 20. On the final play of the 15-play series, Durant showed good patience as he rolled to his right and waited a split second to connect with TB Jacques Lewis at the right goal line pylon for a 1-yard TD pass. Carolina took the lead, 31-27, with 7:43 remaining. Game over? Wrong. The teams traded punts until Sun Devil Daryl Lightfoot returned a punt 28 yards to put his team on their 39 with only 36 seconds to play. A 42-yard pass to Derek Hagan eventually put the Sun Devils at the five with six ticks left. Andrew Walter spiked the ball to reset the clock at three. With no time remaining, Walter fired to Skyler Fulton who dragged his toe about one foot in-bounds at the back of the end zone for the game-winning TD, 33-31! The Wildcats, er...Sun Devils, sprinted en masse to their cheering fans on the far end of the field where the State contingent started their chant, "A-S-U! A-S-U! A-S-U!" The Heels were beaten with no time left. They hung their heads. Their fans fell silent, and together, UNC's collective thoughts turned: "Bring on basketball season."

Extra point: Anybody have the Devils giving three? With no PAT attempt, the final score: ASU 33–UNC 31. This turned out to be the second of seven consecutive games I attended where the final score was not settled until the last play of the game!

Do over!

(88) Akron at Connecticut
October 25, 2003

East Hartford, Connecticut - I call this a "do-over" because I'd seen the Akron Zips play before against Rhode Island in the opening round of the 1986 1-AA play-offs in a very memorable 38-28 loss. However, note the extra "A" in 1AA. That game did not count in my endeavor to see every 1A team play. Akron was now a full-fledged member of the Mid-American Conference. In addition to *re-certifying* Akron toward The Goal, I got to watch the Huskies play at their new facility, Rentschler Field - "the Rent" for short. Season tickets sold out in the 42,000-seat stadium for its inaugural season. I had the foresight to contact Akron to buy tickets and sit in the visitor's section filled with players' families. Unfamiliar with the new stadium, I ended up parking quite a distance away following the designated traffic pattern. The main lots are former runways of the Pratt-Whitney airplane engine factory adjacent to the stadium.

Both teams came in with identical 5-3 records. UConn's offense averaged 486 yards per game compared to Akron's 485.9. On paper, the game couldn't be more even. Leading 28-21 to start the second half, the Zips scored on their first possession when Jason Swiger converted on a 53-yard

FG attempt just clearing the crossbar to take a 31-21 lead. UConn scored on a TD pass to cut the lead to three when Dan Orlovsky tossed an 8-yarder to TE Tim Lassen. An Akron field goal made it 34-28. Unbelievably, Husky fans began to leave their seats. Traffic concerns? Post-game, homecoming festivities? Doubts about UConn coming back? The real question was how could anybody leave an exciting, close game with nearly 11 minutes left? Sure enough, about two minutes later, Orlovsky connected with WR O'Neil Wilson for a six-yard TD pass to finally take the UConn lead.

Akron wasn't about to zip up their pouches and hop away! On the Zip's next possession, they took back the lead with Swiger's leg, 37-35. Exciting game! Well-played! Lots of action! Result in the balance! Still over four minutes to score. The Huskies played hard to win, but the fickle fans continued to leave. How could they have seen enough? This didn't make any sense. Connecticut got the ball back on its 45 with 1:32 left on the clock. At the Akron 41, UConn had a fourth and 10. Orlovsky threw to WR Shawn Feldeisen near the sideline for an 11-yard gain. UConn "fans" listened to radio coverage on their way out of the converted runway parking lots. On third and 10, Orlovsky connected again to set up at the 19. With 37 ticks left, he completed to Feldeisen at the six and ran downfield to spike the ball to stop the clock. An illegal substitution moved the Huskies back to the eleven. With five seconds left, Matt Nuzie came out on the field. His kick went up. It was good! No time remained. The Huskies celebrated with their remaining fans for their sixth win of the season - a hard-fought, well-played 38-37 win. For the Akron fans that remained sitting near me, it was a tough loss, but for me, it turned out to be an exciting and worthwhile *do-over*!

Extra point: For the third week in a row, I saw a game decided by seven points or less with the last two contests decided on the very last play. Prior to the aforementioned Arizona State win over UNC, Wisconsin defeated Penn State, 30-23. The Lions got to the Badger 15-yard line on a "Hail Mary" pass as time expired. A week after UConn's win over Akron on the final play, PSU fell to Ohio State, 21-20, as David Kimball's 60-yard FG fell just short as time expired. Next, Yale tied Princeton, 17-17, on Alvin Cowan's 22-yard TD pass with no time left. Yale took a 27-24 lead in the second OT on John Troost's 26-yard FG. On Princeton's next series, the ball was fumbled away on a pass completion near the goal line to end the game. Pitt defeated Virginia Tech, 31-28, when FB Lousaka Polite barreled over defenders for a TD with 47 seconds left to remain in first place in the Big East. Finally, in a D-3 playoff game, Montclair State advanced defeating Allegheny College, 20-19, blocking a 36-yard Gator FG attempt with no time left in the game. The 2003 season was my best ever for last minute excitement!

Fathers and daughters
(89) Northern Illinois at Maryland
September 4, 2004

College Park - Maryland hosted my first of three consecutive games featuring Mid-American Conference teams needed toward The Goal to start the 2004 season. However, Northern Illinois posed much more of a challenge than Eastern Michigan did last time I saw a MAC team at Byrd Stadium. The Huskies of Northern Illinois not only finished 10-2 the year before, they returned QB Josh Haldi who accounted for 2,544 passing yards and 25 TDs. His return gave hope to NIU for another successful season.

I had my eyes on this opener for another reason as well. One Juniata College buddy, Daryl Reigel, had his 18-year old daughter, Whitney, enrolled at UMD. She'd been recruited for the Terps' softball team. Whit, as her family often refers to her, experienced tailgating many years previously with us at The Meadowlands as a tot. Daryl brought her by to meet all our JC cohorts as we tailgated before a Navy-Notre Dame game. Of course, he couldn't stay long to join in the festivities. It was an early sign to all of us that our lives would be changing drastically.

The Terps already announced their first four games had sold out. But Daryl had been in contact with Whit, and as an athlete, she had an "in" on how we could get seats. Outside of Byrd, I found Daryl, Kim, and their three daughters. Whitney, whom I hadn't seen since she sweated it out playing high school basketball the year before had already entered the rigors of college sports training. Kim told me she was ecstatic that all the recruiting twists and turns for her daughter were over. And she was only talking about college softball. It's hard to imagine what football is like! Whitney took us to the ticket window right before the game where unused tickets allocated to Terrapin players became available to the general public. She had the inside scoop since one of her upper-class roommates dated a football player. Later, Daryl confided in me that he had concerns about that. His recollection of college football players when he went to Juniata was that they were "horny and crazy"! I don't know how or where he got that impression. Whitney's roommate's boyfriend started at offensive tackle for the Terps. We checked the game program. The boyfriend stood 6'5" and weighed 308 lbs. Daryl gasped, "How do you stop something like that?"

We got great seats just a few rows up and to the right of Maryland's bench. The band paraded around on the stadium track. The Terps charged out from the Gosset Football Team House past the bronze Terrapin. Norman "Boomer" Esiason strolled along the sideline in front of us with his kids to watch his alma mater play and greet some well-wishers. Excitement filled the air with 51,830 fans basically hovering over us in the season opener.

The Terps got an early break - literally. Starting NIU QB Josh Haldi went out with a foot injury. However, Maryland's QB Joel Statham botched a pair of laterals in the backfield that cost him a turnover and a safety on the second and third possessions of the game. Maryland led 10-2 after a tough half. On the second half kickoff, NIU return man Don Sheldon hesitated in the end zone before bringing it out to around the 25 where Maryland stripped him of the ball and recovered at the Northern Illinois 24. RB Josh Allen went to work this time with his final carry resulting in a one-yard TD run up the middle. The Terps now seemed in control early in the second half, 17-2.

It was 23-12 early in the fourth when Statham dropped back to pass, but DE Ken West forced a fumble with a solid hit from behind. LB Jason Hawkins scooped up the loose pigskin and rambled 85 yards unchallenged for a Husky TD. On a two-point conversion, sub QB Phil Horvath connected with wide-open WR Sam Hurd on a slant pattern to close the gap, 23-20. The home crowd felt nervous, but Maryland held on defensively to win with the three-point margin. This MAC team challenged the Terps.

Extra point: I looked forward to my next game to add another college team. I left Daryl with four years ahead of him to try to figure out how to stop 300-lb linemen from pursuing his daughter in college. I hoped he would figure it out and let me know before my daughter goes to college in 2011!

Dumped on!

(90) Western Michigan at Virginia Tech

September 11, 2004

Blacksburg, Virginia - For the second week in a row, I sought to notch another Mid American Conference team to my growing list with high hopes to see of one of those upset specials like the ones recorded by MAC teams over some big time programs the season before. WMU was poised to challenge under new Head Coach Bill Cubit, formerly offensive coordinator seen at Rutgers. With him came his son, Ryan, whom I'd seen start at QB for RU in a win against hapless Navy and in a loss to winless Cal. In this game, he'd step into the role replacing starter Blayne Baggett who left the game injured early as did starting RB Trivon Riley. The Broncos' receiving corps consisted of two good ones in juniors Greg Jennings at wide receiver and Tony Scheffler at tight end.

The Hokies home opener started as a solemn occasion as Virginia Tech's Corps of Cadets (ROTC) honored alumnus Lt. Tim Price, a 2001 graduate, who lost his life in action in Iraq only a few days prior to this game played on 9/11. A moment of silence was observed. It gives one pause to reflect that the guys over there come from all walks of life from all around this country to put their lives on the line for peace and freedom against terrorism. The somber occasion was marked by the Corps marching on before the game with musical accompaniment by its drum corps, the "Highty Tighties," and it ended on a high note with the awesome display of a loud and majestic flyover of a B-52H Stratofortess.

Flanker Eddie Royal scored on the Hokies first play from scrimmage on an 11-yard reverse. Cedric Humes rumbled in from the 21 for the next TD. TB Justin Hamilton punched it in from the one, and Bryan Randall threw his first of two TD passes in the game to Royal on a 35-yarder. It was "only" 28-0 at the half. Several series into the second half, it was evident that the Broncos were not ready to make any great comeback effort. WMU's offense was anemic, and their defense wasn't so hot either as Tech Freshman QB Sean Glennon threw two TDs after replacing Randall. I was committed to stay, of course. Getting bored while sitting in seat No. 1 on the end of row H in section 103 of the south end zone witnessing the pending decimation, excitement loomed, but it wasn't on the field.

PLOP! A platter of nachos landed directly into my lap—cheese, salsa, peppers, and chopped meat! A genteel grandmother on the way down the stairs with a snack for her grandkids was jostled by some VA Tech ROTC on his way up who bumped into her arm and disposed of her hot platter into my lap. She apologized profusely and offered the wad of napkins she had. Luckily she only got the left leg and missed the new pair of binoculars dangling from my neck. I cleaned up my shorts as best I could, but it put a further damper on any note-taking in what was a boring game any way. The accident initiated a conversation with one Hokie fan as we watched the rest of the game together, a happy victory for him after four straight losses, and a disappointment to soiled-and-spoiled me after having seen so many good games during the previous season. It was a letdown after a long drive to Blacksburg to see such a crushing blow-out. How much can be said about a team beaten by the widest margin of victory I'd ever seen? Virginia Tech, coming off an opening loss to USC in the Black Coaches Association Classic, dominated Western Michigan on offense, on defense, on special teams, with second teams, and every imaginable way. The Hokies broke these Broncos, 63-0!

The carnage continued as the nacho cheese and chili sauce dried on my shorts during the fourth period. Western Michigan became the 90th team toward The Goal, and the streak of good, close games seen since last September after Chestnut Hill came to an end. A clunker was due and this was it. To get to this crazy Goal, sometimes somebody has to get dumped on once in a while. However, I never expected it to be me.

Extra points: WMU finished the season a dreadful 1-10, but the following season, the Cubits led them to a 7-4 season, the Broncos' first winning record in four years. They were non-entities in this game at Lane Stadium, but Tony Scheffler and Greg Jennings both got drafted in 2006 by the Denver Broncos and the Green Bay Packers respectively. Jennings played a key role in the Packers' drive to Super Bowl VL.

Only the Beginning

(91) Central Florida at Penn State
September 18, 2004

State College - Eleven year-old Alex and I left New Jersey heading west to State College late because of her Friday night dance at school. Storm clouds overtook clear skies by the time we reached the half-way point to State College as remnants of Hurricane Ivan made their way up the east coast. Lucky Alex—she slept. For me, the drive was an intense, white-knuckler! Despite elements limiting driving vision, tractor trailers sped by me bumper-to-bumper in the fast lane, and I wasn't going slowly! I didn't feel relief until we got to the hotel a few intense hours later.

Before the game, Alex and I met up with Jimmy and Elizabeth "Biffy" Malayter, fellow, former Boonton Bombers. The Malayters fell in love with State College when their daughter, Erin, attended Penn State. Tyler, their son, attended PSU as a junior this year. Not only did Jimmy and Biffy become Nittany Lion season ticket holders and avid tailgaters, they bought a house in State College so Tyler could live in it. They planned to move in permanently after his graduation and to settle into the area for the long haul. It's an idea I always keep in mind. If I can ever afford to retire, I don't want to live in a retirement community with a bunch of old people. I want to live near a university where the action is—sports, cultural events, festivals, concerts, restaurants, bars, beautiful, young women (just to look at), and a little reprieve during the summer followed by a fall of Saturday afternoon tailgate parties before some big games! Basketball season follows football. Baseball arrives and then it's time for a summer break again. The four seasons are so well defined in college. Sounds like a great life plan to me!

Inside the stadium, Central Florida football warmed up for the game. Their Golden Knight mascot reminded me of a golden "Marvin Martian" from the old Warner Brothers cartoon shows. UCF's new head coach, George O'Leary, watched his players prep for their third game of the season after his very brief, off-season stint with Notre Dame and several years as an assistant in the NFL. The Knights sported a 0-2 record.

The sun burst out by game time. St. Laurie called right before to warn us about a mud slide near the Delaware Water Gap on the Pennsylvania side that backed up Route 80 east-bound for miles. We'd have to consider a different way home later. The announced crowd of 101,715 consisted of many pre-game sales that turned up as no-shows. The combination of weather, parking limitations, and the quality of the two teams playing (PSU 1-1) caused many Nittany Lion fans to be pleased they missed this one. The Lions led 21-6 at halftime in a pretty ugly game. At intermission, they paused to honor the 45th anniversary of the 1959 Penn State Liberty Bowl team. *Forty-fifth?* The Lions were stretching things a bit here to get fans in to see a lousy team play in their newly expanded stadium.

Amid a swirl of bizarre plays, one PSU fan nearby wished aloud, "Snap it over his head!" on a UCF punt. The ball slipped through the UCF punter's fingers and through the back of the end zone for a safety. The Lions led, 23-10. The punter expressed disbelief with his arms out and palms up as he ran toward the bench. That must have convinced O'Leary to kick from the tee rather than punt it on the subsequent free kick. For me, it turned out to be the second week of watching an inept MAC team play a traditional football power. Despite the result, however, I came away knowing that Penn State would not fit that latter description this season. PSU won, 37-13.

My impression turned into reality as the Nittany Lions lost their next six games. They won their last two to finish 4-7. Rumblings around Penn

State said 78 year-old Joe must go! As for the Golden Knights, this result continued a trend for the entire season. The game would turn out to be their third of eleven losses in 2004. George O'Leary's return to college football ended with the Knights bringing up the rear of 1A football at 0-11.

Two-point conversion: Alex and I took a long way home after the game, avoiding delays but passing cresting rivers, flooded trailer parks, and drowning cows!

In 2005, his second year, O'Leary coached the Golden Knights to an 8-5 season finishing with a 49-48 loss to Nevada in the Hawaii Bowl. Good coaching can turn a college program around quickly to respectability.

The author caught up with these Penn State die-hards who dress this way for every Nittany Lion game at the 2007 Valero Alamo Bowl where PSU defeated Texas A&M, 24-17.

Undefeated and BCS-bound, not!
(92) Arkansas at Auburn
October 16, 2004

Auburn - I contacted Charlie Murren to see if he had an "in" this season to attend the Arkansas-Auburn game. The Razorbacks remained one of my two SEC teams left - this year Arkansas, maybe next year, Mississippi State. Boy! Did Charlie have an *in*.

Every family wants their kids to achieve beyond what they've done. I remember my first trips to Auburn to stay with Charlie at his Magnolia dorm. Back then, Lynda, his future wife, worked in one of the school's cafeterias. Now, their two daughters attended Auburn. Laura, a freshman, didn't live in a dorm much better than Charlie's, but as far as convenience, she had a great location allowing us to tailgate close to Jordan-Hare Stadium right in front of her apartment. Charlie backed up his truck loaded down with tailgate trimmings and furnishings right up the front door of Laura's first-floor apartment to set up our tailgate, convenient with running water and a private bathroom. Megan, a junior, outdid her Mom as far as college employment. Majoring in journalism, she worked for the P.R. staff of the Auburn Tiger football program. She worked the press box during games charting and distributing stats to the working press. Basically, she worked for Tommy Tuberville, knew all the players, kept game stats, and even wrote a featured article in that day's edition of *Auburn Football Illustrated*. Talk about an in! It only got better.

We arrived at Auburn early to meet with Megan before the game. Once we set up the tailgate on Laura's front lawn, Charlie and I ambled over to Jordan-Hare. Charlie was as excited as I was and proud, too! Megan arranged to meet with us before the game to take us on a tour of the stadium press box. This was big! After 25 years of attending games, this was our first opportunity to view the field from the perch of pundits. Megan greeted us with hugs and press passes. We took the elevator up to press row. She showed us how the press lives compared to us true fans among the huddled masses. We passed a bunch of the media guys seated at tables enjoying a free buffet in a lounge well-protected from the elements. We checked out their covered, unobstructed view of the entire playing field. Tables provided plenty of elbow room and wiring for electronic hook-ups stood ready for their observations for the entire sports world to read and hear. We strolled by a radio booth and popped into the CBS-TV broadcast booth. Vern

Lundquist and Todd Blackledge hadn't arrived yet, but Charlie and I were ready to fill in just in case.

The game itself featured a number of players who would soon be watched by NFL writers, too. The home team struck quickly on a reverse flea-flicker 1:10 into the game. Jason Campbell hooked up with Davin Arrmashodu for a 67-yard TD pass. The Tigers extended the lead, 10-0, on John Vaughn's 27-yard FG. Auburn made it 17-0 before the quarter ended on a 30-yard scoring strike from Campbell to TE Courtney Taylor. The Tigers drove 53 yards on their next possession culminated by Ronnie Brown's one-yard TD plunge. RB Carnell "Cadillac" Williams did the damage this time as he took it over from two yards after another long Tiger scoring drive. Houston Nutt's Razorbacks finished the half with an 80-yard scoring drive of their own when Matt Jones tossed a 19-yard TD pass to Chris Baker. Auburn led in a 30-6 rout.

Led by future Redskin QB Jason Campbell, the fourth-ranked Auburn Tigers went on to a 38-20 win. RBs Ronnie Brown (Dolphins) and Carnell "Cadillac" Williams (Buccaneers) ran for 103 and 75 yards respectively while each recorded a TD. Matt Jones, the Arkansas QB and only returning starter on offense for the Hogs, got drafted as wide receiver by the Jacksonville Jaguars. Megan provided me with my own personal stat sheet fresh from press row to have all the info I needed for this week's Game Review on www.collegefootballfan.com.

Extra point: The final of 38-20 wasn't as close as it sounds. Campbell watched from the sidelines by the fourth. However, even though this turned out to be one of 13 wins for Auburn against no defeats, the big news for the season was that the Tigers got left out of the BCS championship game - a game that was supposed to end all the controversies regarding the national title. It didn't! USC whipped Oklahoma for the national championship, 55-19. Auburn defeated Virginia Tech in the Sugar Bowl, 16-13, to remain undefeated at No. 2. Don't get me started now on how a playoff system could work for college football and why. That's another book! Arkansas fans, for you the story gets better. Read on!

Business Trip
Arkansas at (93) Mississippi State
November 20, 2004

Starkville, Mississippi - My employer operated a production facility outside of Jackson, Mississippi. I planned some meetings with staff and suppliers there in mid-November. As luck would have it (no…really!), the Mississippi State Bulldogs hosted Arkansas that weekend in Starkville, MS, a two-hour drive north of Jackson. I saved the company airfare by scheduling my return flight on Sunday. I took care of my hotel, rental car, and meals over the weekend. My 93rd team fell into my lap earlier than expected. I'd finish up the SEC this weekend. I was slightly disappointed they played the Razorbacks that weekend because I'd already only seen Arkansas play five weeks earlier. I take them as they come though. Besides, the two conference foes with sub-par 4-5 and 3-6 records respectively might be indicative of a pretty competitive game.

In the spirit of SEC football, I ate breakfast at a local *Chick-fil-a*. We don't have any in Jersey that I know of. Besides, the fast food chain was the proud sponsor of the Peach Bowl. The drive to Starkville was easy along flat, state highways of Mississippi. I found parking close to MSU's baseball stadium, a pretty neat-looking little ballpark, launching pad of several well-known major league players.

I toured the campus, checked out the tailgating, and bought a ticket from a guy outside Wade Davis Stadium looking to unload an extra. I sat on the Arkansas side next to the visitors' section filled with red-clad Razorback fans. Their cheerleaders stretched, tumbled, and performed 20 rows below me. I sat among very friendly but frustrated MSU Bulldog fans. One asked me where I got my ticket from since I was sitting in a friend's seat. I told him where I got it and segued quickly into how the pursuit of the Goal brought me to Starkville. He was fascinated. He and fellow MSU fans opened up on how disappointed they they'd become with their program. They hoped for better days and asked about my recent experiences. We enjoyed talking football.

One big play turned around the entire game. In Q3, Mississippi State took possession at its own 42 trailing, 17-14. Stopped at the Razorbacks' 20, Keith Andrews came in to tie the score with a field goal. What seemed automatic became the turning point of the game. Thud! His kick was low, blocked, and deflected directly into the hands of Pierre Brown who found himself in a perfect position to catch the deflected ball over his shoulder.

He raced 76 yards for an Arkansas touchdown. It was a 10-point swing that averted a 17-17 tie, and gave the Razorbacks a 24-14 lead as the third period ended. Gimpy but game QB Matt Jones, the future Jaguars wide receiver, led Arkansas to a 24-21 win.

Extra point: A questionable call by the side judge before the end of the half thwarted a last minute Bulldog scoring drive that launched MSU Head Coach Sylvester Croom into his Joe Paterno imitation. Angrily shaking a finger at them, he chased the officials all the way to their locker room at the opposite end of the field from the team locker rooms before heading back. TE Eric Butler was clearly knocked out of bounds where he intended to get out which should have stopped the clock, but the official signaled to keep the clock running with :25 remaining. Mississippi State had to burn its final time-out of the half. It was a critical momentum killer for the Bulldogs. But, no complaints from me about adding the Bulldogs. I met some great fans at Mississippi State and thoroughly enjoyed a fun, football afternoon. I considered this one a very successful business trip!

Didn't get a good night's sleep?
(94) Boise State at Georgia
September 3, 2005

Athens, Georgia - I looked forward to 2005 with great anticipation. Over 14 weekends, the schedule I planned offered me opportunities to add 12 new teams I hadn't seen yet. It also included several new venues including a significant one at which to open the season. Good old Charlie Murren III came through again. My unexpected trip to see Mississippi State the previous year completed the SEC for me. So instead of heading out to an Auburn game, Charlie came up with tickets through one of his managers at work. Gary Smith, a Georgia grad and season ticket holder, came up with six tickets for UGA's opener to allow us to see the next team toward The Goal, the Boise State Broncos. Not only for me, but for Charlie and Lynda and their son Danny who lived about 30 miles away from Athens, it presented the first chance to see a game "between the hedges" at historic Sanford Stadium, second largest campus venue I got to visit. I do have to say that it also turned out to be the loudest!

What a great start to the season for me personally. Both schools ranked in everybody's Top 25 preseason polls. The hometown Dawgs were experienced and deep. Boise State boasted a high-powered offense led by

Heisman hopeful QB Jared Zabransky. On top of the great match-up and new venue to start the season, Eric now age 10, joined me for his first trip to fly to a game with me. He couldn't wait! In addition to the game and the flight, we got a baseball bonus—Charlie met us at the airport late Friday afternoon and we drove directly to Turner Field the see the Braves host the Cincinnati Reds.

The next day, Charlie and Lynda set up one of their great tailgate spreads in a parking lot under shade trees at the corner of Lumpkin and Dougherty in Athens. We took seats in the upper deck to watch warm-ups and pre-game festivities. The stadium reverberated already. We got ready to watch a very competitive game, so I had hoped.

On his first pass from scrimmage, Zabransky rolled right and threw an interception right into the hands of MLB Tony Taylor. Two minutes and three seconds into the "contest", DJ Shockley completed the short 37-yard drive with a 14-yard TD run. Unchallenged, Zabransky's next pass ended up in the hands of LB Dannel Ellerbe. The Dawgs started at the BSU 38, and Shockley zipped the ball to SE Kenneth Harris for a 40-yard TD pass. Zabransky fumbled at the UGA 20 on his next series to thwart any offensive threat by the Broncos in the first quarter. On the next offensive series, he overthrew a pass directly into the waiting hands of Rover back Tra Battle who took it to the BSU 41. The Boise QB faced little or no pressure on any of his errant passes. Brandon Coutu put up three from the 43 yards out for a 17-0 Georgia lead. FS Greg Blue would be the next recipient of a misguided Zabransky pass. Danny Murren noted that Zabransky could only complete passes to the players in the *red* jerseys! Later, in the shotgun formation, the snap hit an unwitting Zabransky in the shoulder pad. The Dawgs recovered his fumble at the Boise 20 with :48 remaining in the half. Eric blurted, "This is sad!" Boy was he right! Georgia's Danny Ware snuck out of the backfield on the next play for a 20-yard scoring strike from Shockley. Georgia took a 24-0 lead before the half.

Boise Coach Dan Hawkins finally pulled Zabransky. What a horrible 2005 debut for a player who had such a brilliant sophomore season and was picked as a potential Heisman candidate. Sorry to say that I cannot remember a poorer individual performance. All I could think of were those clever *Holiday Inn* commercials: "Didn't get a good night's sleep?" Lowlights of Zabransky's performance this day would be perfect for one of those ads.

The first-half score also sent Charlie and Lynda off to explore downtown Athens for the rest of the game. Gary, Georgia grad, fan, and host, stuck around with us. The shoppers didn't miss anything. UGA was up 45-7 after three quarters, and it ended up 48-13. The game was a sour disappointment. We witnessed a clunker to start the season.

Zabransky should have stayed at a Holiday Inn. He evidently didn't get a good night's sleep. We slept better. We stayed at the Murrens' house.

Baskett Catches
(95) New Mexico at (96) Missouri
September 10, 2005

Columbia, Missouri - For my employer at this time, my purchasing responsibilities included two facilities in the state of Missouri. Between St. Joseph and Springfield sat Columbia, home of the University of Missouri. I managed to schedule project meetings at both sites on Thursday and Friday. I extended my stay through the weekend (again being the company man I am, I saved the firm money on airfare with a Saturday stay and took care of my own expenses). The Missouri Tigers hosted the New Mexico Lobos Saturday at 6 p.m. Conveniently, I just happened to need to see both on my drive toward The Goal!

In Springfield, I talked with colleagues at work who graduated from Mizzou who highly recommended *Harpo's* as the place to go before and after the game. Another got in contact with someone they knew who might have an extra ticket. It's always great to enjoy a game with someone who's a fan of either team in the game, especially since I show up "neutral" in some cases. By Friday, my Saturday plan fell into place.

Slated for a 6 pm kickoff, I drove off to discover Missouri wine country on Saturday morning. Not a connoisseur by any stretch, I had no idea that the Show-me State produced wines. The locals told me some tasted pretty good and before California took over as the nation's leading wine producer, Missouri pleased the pallets of many. St. Laurie loved red wines, so while I had the time I did some shopping. She didn't favor ball caps, t-shirts, or plastic stadium cups (I know, I know...hard to believe, right?), but I figured a few bottles of wine would be greatly appreciated. I proved to be right!

After my cultural tour, I drove to *Harpo's*. The place was packed with Tiger fans. Cold, jumbo beers went down easily while big screens showed Marshall at Kansas State and TCU's upset of Oklahoma. The waitresses looked great and Harpo's hopped! A nice feature they offered there for those that catch a buzz before the game is that you can catch a bus to the game!

It ran regularly from various stops in downtown to Memorial Stadium before and after. Rather than take the bus though, I decided to take in more culture with a walk through Columbia to the game about a mile away. Not exactly sure where I would meet my Tiger tailgate host, Tom Richardson, I wandered the parking lots and pulled out the cell phone twice to hone in on my unknown destination. I found Tom and friends for a great tailgate. The food was worth waiting for while I resisted at Harpo's—good sandwiches, beans, and apple cobbler! Meeting Tom for the first time, we shared some personal football histories. He reminisced about attending the 1969 Orange Bowl when Penn State defeated Mizzou, 10-3. I remembered staying up late as a kid to watch that one the night before going back to school after holiday break. What made The Goal the most fun was meeting fans in different parts of the country who rooted avidly for their teams no matter what their recent history. I always enjoy the atmosphere of experiencing a college football game at a new locale. Tom's wife couldn't make this game, so I got to sit with him and his group of Missouri Tiger die-hards.

To finish the scoring in an exciting third quarter of play from the Mizzou 41, UNM's DonTrell Moore took the hand-off, ran right, dropped back, and hurled a long pass to an open Hank Baskett for his second TD of the day to tie the score at 28-28. In the fourth, New Mexico QB Kole McKamey hooked up with Baskett again on a 47-yard pass play to the Tiger seven-yard line before the signal-caller ran the option to the right and the Lobos retook the lead, 35-28. Mizzou knotted the score at 35-35 when Brad Smith connected over the middle with Chase Coffman on a 13-yard TD pass. McKamey scrambled for 12 yards on third and eleven to his own 32 to keep the next Lobo drive alive. A 22-yard pass to Baskett got the Lobos into field goal range where Kenny Byrd put it through the uprights from 40 yards to take a 38-35 lead with 4:26 left. Smith's next pass was intercepted down the right sideline by Gabriel Fulbright for his second pick of the night. At the 2:01 mark in the fourth, UNM sealed the game with a perfectly executed, nine-yard "alley oop" pass from McKamey to Baskett, who leapt high above the defense for the final TD to complete the 45-35 score. We attended a fun game to add these two new teams to my personal record book.

Extra point: Missouri QB Brad Smith was an offensive force to be reckoned with, but three turnovers by the Tigers (1-1), two in key situations, made the difference in the final outcome. Smith put on a show throwing for 248 yards and one TD among nine different receivers while rushing for 165 yards and 3 TDs. He was tough to bring down – slithering, sliding, and running past defenders on first and second contacts. However, one of his two interceptions and a questionable fumble resulted in scores for the visitors from New Mexico. The Mizzou loss overshadowed Smith's record breaking night as he set both the career passing yardage mark and the career rushing yardage mark for the Tigers. He's been a multi-purpose threat for the New York Jets since. Hank Baskett signed on with the Minnesota Vikings before moving on to play for the Eagles and Colts.

Deflated victory
(97) Baylor at Army
September 17, 2005

West Point - I caught a big break toward The Goal in 2005 when Army opted out of Conference-USA. The program sought more flexibility in its scheduling to play more teams at their talent level and to add some more traditional games as well. The timing worked out great for me. Before 2005, Army scheduled a few new teams for me to see with their C-USA affiliation. This year, their new status as an Independent provided me with three new teams to see on their slate. Baylor, Iowa State and Arkansas State would all play Army at West Point.

The Baylor Bears showed up first. On a hot, sunny Saturday, I brought the entire family for a little tailgating, football, and supposed quality time. We took our seats in the Family Fun Zone in the northern end zone at Michie. The cost of adding the Baylor Bears to the Goal eventually bored the family (again). The Cadets and Bears played a dull game on a hot day. People left early, and my kids stretched out on the bleachers watching the Bears play one for dear old Dad.

Baylor took the opening kick-off and scored three points on a 39-yard FG by Ryan Havens. A 40-yard Shawn Bell pass set Havens up for his second FG from 27. Halfway through the second period, Joe Riley put Army on the board with a 49-yard boot. Army fans nearby were astounded that he converted from that distance. With seconds left in the half, Bell connected with Paul Mosley out of the backfield on a 7-yard TD pass. Army got Riley into position for a 56-yard FG, but it was asking too much as the ball fell too short and too wide as time expired to end the half. Halftime marked a tribute to late Heisman Trophy winner Glenn Davis, "Mr. Outside," who passed away the previous March. His "41" decorated both 20-yard lines.

Flowers and a portrait of the three-time All-American (1944-1946) were presented to his widow, son, and daughter.

Trailing 13-3 with five minutes remaining, Army lost what little momentum it had when QB Zac Dahman's pass attempt on first down was tipped and fell on to the chest of S Maurice Linguist who was laying flat on his back! Baylor took advantage and scored on a seven-yard end around as Dominque Ziegler took it around the left side. The Bears were up 20-3. Taking over from its own 40, Army's Dahman passed on each down to get this team downfield. With 45 seconds remaining, Corey Anderson hauled in a 10-yard pass to close out the score at 20-10 in favor of Baylor.

Extra point: The best and only real entertainment occurred as we watched the new Plebe class use some tactics they must have already learned in Field Tactics 101. Overzealous but a little bored during their first home game, they absconded with the six Baylor flags. A frontal assault to carry away "Judge" the Bear, the big, inflated Baylor mascot, provided a diversion as the Baylor cheerleaders came to his defense, but one plebe snuck up from behind and pulled his plug. He deflated big Judge with a sneak attack from the rear to quickly deflate green and gold Judge into a heap of vinyl. The Baylor student still stood inside the inflated pant legs with the upper torso draped over him. It had to be hot in there! The attacker from the rear escaped. No arrests were seen. Extra duty for punishment? Maybe. The Corps had two more home games I'd attend to come up with new ideas to harass visitors. At least the plebes showed that they could put their newly-learned, basic strategies to use during the Bears' "deflated" victory over Army, 20-10.

Long distance double-header

(98) Iowa State at Army
September 23, 2005

West Point - Six days after Army's loss to Baylor, I traveled back to West Point with Charlie Roberts to see Army host its second consecutive Big 12 team, Iowa State. This weekend turned out to be my first long-range, double-header. Earlier, my friend Rich Williams called to tell me that he and his wife Laurie had two free Southwest Airline tickets that they had to use by the end of September. The other "Saint Laurie" started a new job coaching high school field hockey near their new home in central Pennsylvania and had no time to travel anywhere. So Rich and I checked schedules for September 24. Our best option entailed flying to Chicago Saturday morning and driving to Evanston to watch re-invigorated Penn State play at Northwestern. The tough part—I obligated myself to see Iowa State play at Army at West Point that Friday night. I had team No. 98 right where I needed them. The killer was that we had to catch a flight out of Philly early the next morning! It takes over three hours to drive straight from West Point to Philly.

Charlie and I bought a pair of tickets in the parking lot before catching the bus to Michie. You could hear a helicopter in the night sky and eventually saw the yellow canopies on their descents as they approached the stadium. Four sky divers landed on Blaik Field with the ceremonial game balls. Two jumpers nailed the 50-yard line. The Corps donned fatigues this night for inspiration. No Iowa State flags were captured, no ISU cheerleaders were confronted, and no mascot was sneak-attacked like Baylor's Bear, so orders must have been passed down to Plebes to cease and desist harassing visitors. Whatever bird mascot that was on the ISU sideline, it never had any feathers plucked. The 2-0 Cyclones visited Army with wins over Illinois State and Iowa, earning enough votes to show up as the No. 22-ranked team in the nation.

In less than a week, HC Bobby Ross made some significant improvements for Army. Army led in the fourth causing State to go for broke on a fourth and 19 to stay in the game. Cadet DE Craig Cameron tackled QB Brent Mayer for a loss to supposedly take the ball over on downs, but a late flag flew at the Army tackler for an unseen face-mask call against Army to give new life to the visitors. Bobby Ross fumed and chewed out the refs to no avail! His tirade continued after the Cyclones took advantage and tied the score, 21-21, on Ryan Kock's four-yard run. The Cyclones scored again on a three-yard TD by Kock for a 28-21 lead, but they still had their hands full. On fourth down and three at the Cyclone 26 with 38 seconds remaining in the game, Army came up short on a draw play to give the ball back to ISU at the 24. Using three time-outs remaining, Army forced ISU to punt consuming only 9 seconds on three downs. They took over on their own 48. Dahman dropped back to pass, but ISU sacked him to end the game. The controversial win stood. Iowa State defeated an improving Army team with the help of a very bad call. ISU looked like a very over-rated 3-0 team. The Cyclones lost their next three contests including their game against Baylor who had not impressed against Army the week before. They finished the season unranked at 7-5 to confirm our assessment.

It took over an hour to get out of the parking lot because of typical traffic mismanagement at West Point. Didn't they know I had places to go, things to do, some sleep to get, a plane to catch, etc, etc? We didn't get rolling until 12:30 a.m. I got home, kissed the sleeping wife good night at two, woke up at five, kissed the sleeping wife good-bye, drove to Philly airport over two hours away for an 8:30 a.m. flight, met Rich, got through the slow security check, ran to the gate, boarded as the last two passengers, slept a little on the flight to Chicago, got to Midway at 9:30 Central time, picked up the rental car, and proceeded to look for Northwestern's Ryan Field in Evanston for the 11 a.m. Northwestern-PSU kickoff. We still needed tickets. Sometimes, it takes extra effort to *see 'em all*!

Extra point: We ended up paying $10 per ticket from some locals and missed just a few plays. We saw a classic game as PSU defeated a good Wildcat team, 38-35, in the final minutes of play on their way to the BCS Orange Bowl. At the conclusion, we even took a shot at driving up to Camp Randall to see the Wisconsin play Michigan for a 6 pm kickoff! We sat for two hours on an interstate in Chicago before scuttling that mission, so we headed to downtown Chicago and had a great time. At *Harry Caray's*, we ate and drank while watching college football and pro baseball on all the screens. We joined in with Harry's clientele singing their traditional, "*Take me out to the Ball Game*!" Later, we watched more football over at *Mother Hubbard's*. They asked what games we wanted on the big screen, and they put on whatever we wanted. After *Hubbard's*, we walked a few blocks over to the *Chicago Blue's Club* featuring the *Charlie Love Blues Band* and Nellie Travis. Fantastic! I want to party in Chicago again.

Back at *Caray's*, it was while I was in the head when I overheard a guy only a few feet away ask the men's room attendant if he knew what Army did that weekend. Army? He had come to the right place. After finishing my business, I burst forth from behind the john door and exclaimed, "I was there! Lost a tough one, 28-21! Got screwed!" He stood in disbelief, not at the result, but that someone sitting in the latrine on a late Saturday afternoon in Chicago only a few feet away could claim that he attended the game that he was interested in at West Point less than 24 hours ago. How does that happen? If he believed me or not, who knows? I could have told him about the Penn State-Northwestern game as well, and if it wasn't for lousy Chicago traffic, I'd be at the Michigan-Wisconsin game this very moment. I love college football!

UNJ-Durham Fans?
(99) Utah at North Carolina
October 1, 2005

Chapel Hill - Like Arizona State the year before, the Utah Utes ventured east to Chapel Hill to put them within the limits of my eight-hour driving range. This time, St. Laurie came along to visit with my good friend and former work colleague, Mary Jean Shannon. She and husband Bruce, along with their kids Tyler and Grace, now lived in Cary, not far from Chapel Hill. MJ and I teamed up together on many business projects. She and Bruce "bled orange." They met at UT in Knoxville, and their kids will have no choice. I always held PSU's bowl wins versus Tennessee over Mary Jean's head when I had to keep her in check at work. It had been about five years since we last worked together, but we kept in touch about kids and football, particularly about my Goal and her Vols! She and Bruce had other plans that Saturday, but welcomed us to come down to stay Friday night. They made a great dinner for us while Tyler and Grace proudly performed their renditions of "*Rocky Top!*"

On Saturday morning, St. Laurie and I parted, looking forward to visiting the Shannons again some time. We headed to the game where I found convenient parking at the Chapel Hill Museum. A student we met on Franklin Street was nice enough to give us a personal tour of the campus on our way over to the stadium. When it came up in conversation that we were from New Jersey, he looked me square in the eye and seriously asked, "Oh, so you're *Duke* fans?" Puzzled, I told him no, and as a matter of fact to the contrary, we were Navy fans. Navy played Duke at Durham that afternoon. I had initially hoped that I could have made this a double-header Saturday, and if both games didn't share the same kickoff time, we'd be seeing that game as well and rooting for the Mids. However, my priority was to watch UNC host my 99th team, Utah. Duke fans? Surprisingly, he explained Carolina considers Duke "the University of New Jersey at Durham" since so many Duke students from our home state matriculate there. I'd never heard that before.

We still needed tickets. We walked past a tailgate lot filled with Carolina Sky Blue regulars. A middle-aged, North Carolina die-hard stood on the outskirts with a pair of tickets in the air. I'd been in his position before. Your friends can't show. You've got a pair. The game's not in big demand, but you'd like to get a few bucks back. I always felt that I'd like somebody else to use my extras to at least enjoy the game. We worked out a quick deal. We got tickets in the upper deck, and he got a few bucks before he went back to enjoy his tailgate! We sat with him later.

Utah visited Chapel Hill just one year after its greatest football season ever, a 12-0 finish and a final No. 4 ranking. The Utes trounced UNC in Salt Lake the previous year, 46-14, recording 699 yards in total offense. I hoped this year's game would be more competitive, especially with coaching and quarterback changes at Utah. After 2004, Head Coach Urban Meyer left for Florida, and QB Alex Smith was drafted by the San Francisco 49ers.

Utah was definitely not the same team this year. In fact, they gave up a 95-yard kickoff return to start the game! Brandon Tate cut to his left and through a big hole to win one lucky UNC fan a new Honda in a contest UNC offered weekly if the opening kick or second half-off goes for a Tar Heel touchdown. A pretty slow first half followed, but UNC led 10-7. We had great seats in the upper deck of Kenan Stadium on a blazing hot afternoon. St. Laurie sought shade with many others behind the stands during the half time show. Fresh-squeezed lemonade refreshed.

What a difference a year makes. After allowing the Utes to dominate on offense in last season's 46-16 loss, Carolina's defense stepped up to hold this year's version of Utes to 378 total yards and forced *five* turnovers. Carolina led 17-14 when Matt Baker started the final stanza with a 40-yard pass to Mike Mason to get to the Utes' one-yard line. Barrington Edwards went in from one to extend the Tar Heel lead, but Utah's Dan Beardall converted a 35-yard FG to whittle the margin to 24-17. Utah took the ball back on their 44 to start a drive for at least a tie, but on third and fourteen, LB Tommy Richardson recovered Brian Johnson's fumble at the Heels' 19. Gaining only one yard, UNC punter Dave Woolridge held the Utes in check again by holding them to no return yards among his five punts on the day. He averaged 39.8 per boot and hanged them high to force fair catches. Utah's Quinto Ganther fumbled on the ensuing drive, and Richardson recovered again for the Heels on his team's 49-yard line. Seven plays later, WR Jesse Holley caught a tipped Baker pass on the right side and sped across and up the left side to the end zone for six. The home team took a 31-17 lead with 5:11 left on the clock, and the previous year's embarrassment was avenged. Fumble recoveries by LB Tommy Richardson and big pass plays from Matt Baker in the final period sealed the game for the Heels. Even if I was a Duke fan, I'd be impressed!

Two-point conversion: UNC replaced Coach John Bunting at the end of the 5-6 season with former Miami Hurricane and Cleveland Brown Head Coach Butch Davis.

One of the biggest cheers at Kenan came late in the game when the scoreboard indicated that Navy beat Duke, 28-21. Even though the Duke football program has been down for many years, it's still NC's primary rival, enflamed by the two schools' basketball traditions and a mere nine miles between campuses. We'll watch for future double-header opportunities between these two venues, especially if Duke ever gets better. Maybe the University of New Jersey at Durham should consider "if only we can get the best players from Jersey..." Never mind!

The century mark + one
(100) Ohio U. at (101) Buffalo
October 29, 2005

Amherst, New York – No. 100 versus No. 101 should have been something special to mark the momentous occasion of hitting the century mark of the Goal. Had anyone else even gotten this far in the annals of college football?

The drive up to Buffalo took six hours, but it was interesting on a gorgeous, cool, fall day. Snow already covered the peaks of the Pocono Mountains. Route 17 passes through the small town of Appalchin, NY, site of the first, big Mafia bust. You travel through the beautiful Finger Lakes region generally along the Susquehanna River. I recommend the pizza at *Picnic Pizza* past Corning on the way up.

When teams struggle, it's economical for my purpose. Parking at UB cost $5, a program costs a buck, and a ticket to sit anywhere, $15. The cost to see two new teams in one shot along with the price of gas, a cheap hotel room, and a bar bill at *Hooter's—priceless*. Not many people buy Buffalo Bulls tickets to begin with, so no extras were available out in the parking lots.

The last time I watched Frank Solich coach a team, the competitors in that game were headliners. His Nebraska Cornhuskers visited Penn State in front of 110,753 where the Lions wrecked Nebraska, 40-7. Solich didn't lose many for NU, but losses like that one redirected his career to the University of Ohio. Now on the beautiful campus of SUNY Buffalo, I watched him stand alone at midfield as his Bobcats loosened up in front of 5,814 fans who trickled into the barren 30,000-seat stadium. I saw D2

East Stroudsburg do battle at West Chester the Saturday night before in front of a comparable number in a driving rainstorm! Today was a gorgeous, cool, fall day. Ohio got off to a quick start to lead 13-0 early. They made it seem as if this game would be a laugher. The Bobcats led the Bulls 20-0 at halftime.

The end of the halftime festivities marked a first for me among 288 games over 26 years. The Bulls lined up at midfield and Head Coach Jim Hohfer had them run wind sprints to the end zone and back several times. Not having been to a Bulls' game before, I wasn't sure if this was typical, a punishment, or something to get the Bulls blood boiling. A comment in the men's room at the half was overheard, "Jim Hohfer has to be the worst coach ever." From my experience, I could substitute a few other names from among others I'd seen.

Something stirred the Bulls up in the second half. They charged onto the scoreboard to finally challenge closing the score, 27-20. Both teams now played like they meant it! Buffalo was back in the game. The Bobcats had to get back some points. On a third and seven pass from their own 23, Ohio fell short by a foot and was forced to punt. The ball bounced down around the UB 43, but before the play was over, one overzealous Bull turned and slammed down an Ohio player about 25 yards away from the ball - right in front of an official! In a game marred by 29 penalties thrown by flag-happy referees who overturned three rulings and flagged Ohio for two sideline infractions, the ubiquitous yellow flag came out. The Bulls were set back fifteen yards for what I deemed as the "Bonehead Play of the Year". Now the refs even got to *eject* one Bull player. Hohfer threw his headset and raged at his offender! UB momentum waned. On the very next play, Drew Willy's pitch to Steven King was mishandled. Ohio recovered the ball at the Buffalo 24. The Bobcats got six points back at the fourteen when Austen Everson connected on a TD pass to Dion Byrum. In front of a few close friends, relatives, and me, the Bobcats battled to a 34-20 win that put them in a four-way tie for first in the MAC's East Division.

The Bulls had the ball when the clock ran out, and I left the game with two thoughts in mind: I had a long ride home ahead of me, and boy, was I glad this one was over! The whistle-blowing and flag throwing resulted in a four hour game that was hard to enjoy. Surprisingly, this game even included TV timeouts! Who was watching? It certainly wasn't pretty, but I had the satisfaction that these two teams were in the fold and that I didn't incur the misery of having to watch both get blown out by *powerhouses* that scheduled them for easy wins.

Extra point: One of two loud, brazen, drunken Bull fans - the only two die-hards the Bulls really had - drew the loudest cheer of the day from the paltry crowd when he saw the head coach of the Bulls basketball team.

"Reggie Witherspoon!" he shouted and pointed at the coach. "*Big* basketball season, Reggie! *Big!*" Fans down in North Carolina weren't the only ones looking forward to round ball during football season.

It's too bad the Bulls struggle because the UB setting is a nice place to watch a game. In 1983, I watched Nebraska QB Turner Gill beat Penn State at The Meadowlands, 44-6. In 2006 when Buffalo played Ohio again, both squads were under coaches with Cornhusker connections – Gill and Solich. As for Jim Hohfer, he showed up on my schedule again in 2010 as offensive coordinator for the FCS runner-up, the Fightin' Blue Hens of Delaware. His team did not run any sprints after halftime festivities. They defeated Lehigh and Georgia Southern in both games I attended before falling to Eastern Washington in the national championship

Out on the nut farm

(102) San Jose at (103) Fresno State
November 5, 2005

Fresno, California - My future brother-in-law, Frank Lorito, not only lived in the same town as me now, but he also grew up as a kid in Boonton. We traded stories about events and people we both knew having lived in both small towns. Frank's sister, Marie, who I didn't know, graduated from Boonton High School my freshman year. From Frank, I learned Marie moved out to Fresno, California 30 years earlier with her husband Sam who started a farm. The wheels of my mind started turning, "If he's going to marry my sister..."

It got better! Marie's son Frankie just graduated from Fresno State. Best yet, my new-to-be-cousin Frankie had season tickets for Bulldog football! His Uncle Frank had *never* visited his sister and her family in Fresno because he feared flying. I worked to convince Frank that he could overcome this fear of flying and that he should do it by visiting his sister in California. He was way overdue to get out there. To show him the kind of brother-in-law I would be, I'd help by going to Fresno with him, especially if we could work out something in the fall, and particularly on the weekend of November 5. I'd keep it open just for him. That's the kind of guy I am.

Also, it just so happened that the Fresno State Bulldogs hosted the San

Jose State Spartans that Saturday. These two teams would probably never make it out to Jersey, much less the east coast. Since I'd seen neither, this seemed like the perfect opportunity to add these two teams to get this thing done and visit my new relatives. *Finally,* Frank realized how much he missed his sister. We were on our way, but on separate flights. He "toughed" it out on his own. I was proud of him flying solo, but I would get out there to show my support. He arrived in Fresno a day before I did.

A few days prior to departure, my site Collegefootballfan.com, took on more hits and e-mails than usual. A Fresno fan who managed a Bulldog website made note of my history and upcoming trip out to Fresno. Thanks to his mention, radio station KMJ580's *Dog Talk Show* contacted me to set up an interview before Saturday night's game. They'd call me on my cell while tailgating with my long-lost Chimienti cousins and their Bulldog friends. It turned out to be a larger tailgate than I expected.

The Chimienti homestead sat like an oasis in the middle of flat fertile farmland. Trees, a swimming pool, and vineyards surrounded it. Sam converted most of his farmland to grow almond trees to meet the demands of the growing market. Frank and I toured the land with him to see the intricate irrigation system and see first hand the methods to get rid of pesky ground squirrels. It reminded me of Bill Murray's war with the groundhog in "Caddyshack." Picking off the little varmints with a rifle firing down rows of almond trees seemed the most challenging. New technology, similar to Murray's, took a lot of the challenge away.

We stopped in Sam's workshop, filled with equipment for planting, maintaining, and harvesting almonds and citrus. He told us how he knew nothing about farming when he moved out from Jersey 30 years ago. When he started growing almonds, he faced other challenges. At first he used to shake the branches of trees with sticks while the nuts fell on to mats lying below. He realized that this wasn't going to work if he ever wanted to turn almonds into cash. He invested in machines with long steel bars with cushions on the end that wrapped around the almond tree trunks. The arms vibrated at high speeds shaking off all the nuts so quickly that the trees sent up thick clouds of white smoke.

Frank and I witnessed a dose of difficulties farmers face when Sam stopped by his office to check his mail. He received a letter doubling the cost of his beehives needed for pollination of the almond trees. Bees were unexplainably dying off by the millions throughout the country, reducing supply and raising costs for farmers, but also threatening the longevity and supply of certain food crops. Frank and I were getting an education out on the nut farm. As a matter of fact, Sam helped us to better understand the distinctive regions of the state of California. He broke it down. He explained, "Fruits in the north, flakes in the south, and nuts in the middle!"

On to football—I figured the game would be a blowout unless the Bulldogs took the Spartans lightly, and they had good reason to. Co-WAC leader Boise State would visit Fresno the following Thursday. Two Saturdays after this game, the Bulldogs would travel to the L.A. Coliseum to match up against the No.1 Trojans of USC, part of Coach Pat Hill's mantra, "Anybody, anytime, anywhere!" He offered his dogs big bones to chew on.

Speaking of chewing, what a tailgate! It's a good thing I convinced Frank to get out and visit his sister. Despite living and farming in Fresno for 30 years and sending a son to Fresno State, Sam and Marie had never been to an FSU football game! They hadn't realized what they were missing. Cousin Frankie invited us all to party with some of his fraternity brothers at *Zuber Realty's* tailgate party. They had a large area cordoned off next to a company truck that brought in all the tables, chairs, grills, and buffet supplies needed for a large gathering. A Mexican-style buffet was set up with servers piling up chili, rice, beans, and other good stuff on our plates. It was first-class all the way! Margaritas and pitchers of beer were available for all us Fresno fans, old and new. Frankie's buddies were intrigued by my Goal. I was having a good time with the nuts from the middle until I had to excuse myself for my KMJ580 moment of fame.

Frank, Marie, Frankie, and others crammed into cars nearby to tune in. The call came through. I was on the air! The hosts asked typical questions about who I'd seen, what teams remained, how I got to this game, and some of my travel experiences. Near the end, when one of them thought they would trap me into some form of shame, I caught him off-guard! "So basically what you do is travel around the country, go to games, and eat for free!"

"And drink!" I unabashedly replied. When I get together with friends, old or new, near or far, it's a party, especially at a football game! I'm not allowed to carry a cooler on a plane, but I make the effort to bring beer or something with me. At least I get around to visiting friends, old and new, who I rarely get the chance to be with otherwise in these times when everyone is constantly busy. Going to games around the country gave me great experiences to do this on many great occasions.

The No. 22-ranked Fresno State Bulldogs did not, after all, look past their "defenseless" WAC rival to its next two games. FSU's Paul Pinegar threw for 368 yards and three TDs and ran for one. Wendell Mathis rushed for 105 yards. For San Jose, Yonus Davis ran for 136 yards, but TB Al Guidry broke off a 30-yard touchdown run to avert a Bulldog shut-out. FSU proceeded to bash the San Jose State Spartans, 45-7. For me, it was the second time I'd seen a team coached by Dick Tomey, credited for building Arizona's Desert Swarm defense, get its butt kicked (PSU 41-Arizona 7).

Extra point: Turned out I was wrong about Fresno's travel plans. The Bulldogs came to Jersey to open the 2008 season against Rutgers in New Brunswick, and we went and saw Fresno win again, 24-7. I'm definitely glad I didn't wait until then. I thoroughly enjoyed experiencing a Bulldog game while visiting my extended family out on the nut farm!

The Big Tailgate Party
(104) Arkansas State at Army
November 19, 2005

West Point - Midget football, soccer, and all other kids' fall sports activities basically ended in our area the weekend before Army's final home game at Michie in 2005. With this in mind, I planned this year's "Big Tailgate Party". A busload of friends and family came not only to revive a tradition I hosted many years ago at The Meadowlands, but to take advantage of Army's schedule to see another new team, the Arkansas State Indians.

Tailgating couldn't have been better. We packed 53 adults and kids on to our *Lakeland Bus* with all kinds of coolers and extra clothes. Our driver got us there in good time and we got a prime spot for tailgating in the big bus lot right inside the gate near the campus ski slope. We set up tables and chairs for the array of food and drinks. The Bloody Marys were perfect, and everyone who tried my famous (infamous?) hot-buttered rum loved it. The kids had a wide-open lot to play football in. St. Laurie, more dedicated to tailgating than to watching football, stayed in the parking lot during the game so we didn't have to put everything away. The weather was clear, sunny, and in the 40s—perfect football weather in November.

Our seats were in rows E and F behind the goal post in the north end zone. Most of the kids we brought stood along the end zone wall near the miniature tank that Cadets ride on around the field. The only times they came back into the stands was when the kicking teams set up for extra points and field goals. They high-fived the Army Mule mascot, talked to the cadets on the tank, and even went to take a closer look at Army's female cheerleaders. Some guests questioned if the girls were actually cadets. They were surprised by the attractiveness of our future Army officers. They might want to make some enlist, but definitely not Megan Ward's son, Colin. He met a friend of a friend attending West Point, and sat among the Cadets in the stands. Megan insisted that that's the closest her son will ever get to being "in" the Army.

Army, on a three-game winning streak, got off to a fast start. Carlton Jones rushed for 187 yards and the game's first 2 TDs to spot the Black Knights a 14-0 lead. The defense played solid against the Indians. It was 28-3 by the half. My tailgaters were disappointed by the Army halftime show in which young girls danced to tunes played by the Army dance band. "Where's the marching music?" demanded my sister Amy, Frank Lorito's future wife. We convinced her earlier to have her picture taken with shirtless boys with letters painted on their chests to spell out "ARMY." We had the picture taken with three, leaving out "R" to spell "AMY." Frank later discovered the phone camera he used was out of memory. He lost a cherished moment. Too bad we didn't have a MARY with us. The real halftime entertainment started when the kickers returned to warm up. Michie Stadium is one of the few that has no nets behind the goal posts, so it's a free-for-all to catch any balls kicked into the stands. Roy McDonald came up with one that he thought was going out over his head until the ball thudded into his chest - a tailgate-party highlight.

The second half was mostly more of the same as Army dominated. Jones added more rushing yards to his total and Scott Wesley capped a fourth period drive with a 1-yard TD plunge. Army won, 38-10. We hung around to watch the Cadet celebration. One kid, Kenny Costa, was told by Cadets nearby that he could run on to the field with them after the game. When the Cadets swarmed the goal posts afterwards, Kenny and the others were smart enough to stay out of the way. The Cadets, dressed in combat fatigues, ran on to the field to take down the goal post directly in front of us. It took a while before they could muster enough weight for the goal to crack before it fell. "Is it supposed to crack that way?" inquired "kick-returner" Roy McDonald. The fans, the team, and the Corps waited for the goal post to come crashing down to sing the Army Alma Mater. After that, the sections of goal posts were dispensed of in the Lusk Reservoir adjacent to the stadium. Quite a celebration for a team with only four wins, but four *consecutive* was the most for Army since 1996, and the streak had them confident and gearing up for the grand finale against Navy in two weeks.

Extra point: At least I watched the Cadets win one of the four games I saw them play during the 2005 season. It helped make a memorable tailgate party for a lot of friends and kids attending an Army game at West Point for their first time. I attended the 2005 Army-Navy game in Philly as my fourth Black Knight game of the season: Navy 42 – Army 23.

Brain-freeze at Yukon…er, UConn

(105) South Florida at Connecticut
November 26, 2005

East Hartford - Originally, I had planned to see the South Florida Bulls travel to Syracuse to watch them play the suddenly hapless Orangemen in the Carrier Dome. I hadn't been to SU since 1999, but I decided since the family Thanksgiving would be in Rhode Island, I'd save the Bulls and see a the more competitive game against the Yukon …er, UConn Huskies the Saturday after. Not only did the Huskies present more of a challenge for USF, but the Bulls, in their first year of Big East Conference play, ventured into East Hartford leading the conference with a surprising 4-1 record. A win here and a subsequent victory against WVU meant not only the Big East title, but a BCS bowl bid! Jim Leavitt's five-year old program had much at stake in this game against the Huskies.

Coming to East Hartford presented the team from South Florida with weather their players probably never encountered before. Unfamiliar sub-freezing temperatures as the sun went down resulted in a combination of dropped balls, bone-chilling hits, and "brain-freeze" that affected the final outcome.

Trailing quickly 7-0 after FB Lou Allen's 60-yard TD run for UConn, the Bulls had to call two time-outs to adjust to the noisy crowd of 40,000. Several players went down with stingers never felt in the sunny climes of Tampa Bay. To make matters worse, the USF QB Pat Julmiste's frozen hands mishandled a snap and UConn scored on a safety. Julmiste eventually warmed up and threw a nice pass deep to the left corner of the end zone where S.J. Green outran the Husky coverage for a 31-yard TD pass to trail, 9-7. The Huskies' Darius Butler returned the ensuing kickoff for a 90-yard TD to give the Huskies a 15-7 halftime lead. Usually reliable Matt Nuzie missed the extra point.

Kyle Bronson nailed a 42-yard FG for the Bulls in the third, the only points of the quarter. With UConn ahead, 15-10, with 2:53 remaining in the game, low temperatures caused "brain freeze" on both sidelines. UConn had the ball on its own 39. USF called time out to stop the clock. On a day when UConn's punter Chris Pavasaris shanked several punts, he needed all the help he could get. After the time-out, the play clock started to tick off 25 seconds. The game clock would not start until the next play started. UConn seemed content to let the play clock run out to take a five-yard penalty, but no time came off the game clock! What was UConn thinking? With inept punting throughout the game, they dug a deeper hole for their punter while taking no time off the game clock! Pavasaris's punt went for 10 yards. The Bulls took over at the UC 44. USF now controlled the football with 2:36 remaining. Plenty of time remained to put together a 44-yard drive and eat up the clock to leave little opportunity for a potential Husky comeback.

South Florida even had two timeouts left. However, those Yukon temperatures caused even deeper "brain freeze" on the USF sideline than on the Connecticut sideline. Instead of handing the ball to Andre Hall, the nation's fourth leading rusher coming into the game, and possibly setting up some play-action passes off that, head coach Jim Levitt went for it all on the first play. Not only was it a poor decision, it was a poorly-executed pass. Husky CB Tyvon Branch had plenty of time to get under a high - arching throw in the end zone. Touchback – Huskies! They held on to win, 15 – 10.

Extra point: The upset derailed a pretty good USF season. They took themselves right out of the conference title and big bowl payoff on that hurried call that turned out to be the final offensive play for the Bulls. The UConn defense was stingy, but the strategy to overcome it seemed inappropriate due to brain-freeze on the South Florida sideline. They don't call them the Yukon…er, UConn Huskies for nothing!

Mr. San Diego State!

(106) Texas- El Paso at (107) San Diego State
August 31, 2006

San Diego - Several years before the 2006 season, I read a *Sports Illustrated* article about a San Diego State fan by the name of Tom Ables who had attended almost every Aztec game since 1946! I decided that if I ever went out there to watch the Aztecs play, I would have to meet him. SDSU seldom ventured out to play games on the east coast. They play from Hawaii to the Rocky Mountains and sometimes foray into the Midwest. When the 2006 SDSU slate became final, the Aztecs announced their season home-opener against Texas-El Paso. Perfect! I needed both teams.

I contacted San Diego State by e-mail to see if I could get in touch with their greatest fan when I came out to see them play. They forwarded my message to Tom and he contacted me the very next day. He enjoyed hearing about my quest to see every team play. He also said that he had 22 season tickets for his family, and if any weren't being used, my brother Chris and I were invited as his guests. Of course, going to a Thursday night opener in California also opened up the opportunity for me to attend a game on Saturday. As I would be staying with Chris in Long Beach, I could join him and Jill, a UCLA grad, along with their kids Emily and Nick, who'd never been to a Bruins game at the Rose Bowl before. On Saturday, UCLA would host Utah for my left-coast weekend double-header.

In San Diego, Chris and I kicked off the season having the honor and privilege of sitting with Tom, who cheered his Aztecs on in person for the 646th time. We shared a great time exchanging stories and rooting for Tom's Aztecs. For instance, I'd seen coaching legends Paul "Bear" Bryant, Joe Paterno, Bobby Bowden, and Harold "Tubby" Raymond. Tom's history went back even further. In one of his early SDSU games covering for the school paper as a student, his team played the University of the Pacific, coached by none other than Amos Alonzo Stagg. Talk about a great connection to college football history! Tom still writes articles for the program Aztec Game Day. Under "*Looking Back*" in this game's edition, he gave a history of all the head coaching debuts at San Diego State. Chuck Long, former Oklahoma offensive coordinator and former Iowa Hawkeye QB I'd seen against Penn State, made his head coaching debut for the Aztecs in this game. In an editor's note, it stated Tom had seen 645 games in 61 seasons. He missed a trip to Cal Poly in 1964, but has been to 475 Aztec games in a row since! He also missed the 1951 trek to the Pineapple Bowl in Hawaii because he couldn't afford it.

Denny Fallon, president of the SDSU Alumni Association and rabid Aztec fan, of course, stopped by to welcome my brother and me and presented me with "vintage" Aztec sportswear featuring "Monty," as in Montezuma, the Aztec chieftain.

During halftime, we conversed with Tom about some of the stadiums where I'd like to attend games in the future. He provided us with his insights to the ones he'd been to: Wisconsin's Camp Randall—"Great atmosphere!" Ohio State's Ohio Stadium—"Loved the stadium and the fans there." After a 16-13 loss, the Buckeye fans gave his Aztecs a standing ovation. The Big House at Michigan—unimpressed. His wife, Nancy, veteran of 411 games as of this date, says that the one place she will not go to is Laramie,

Wyoming. "Too cold!" Tom told how the Aztecs almost didn't make it to the game there on October 6, 1984, because the team traveled through a blizzard to get there. Wyoming pushed for a no-show forfeit while the Aztecs were traveling through treacherous weather. SDSU showed up an hour late, and they went on to defeat the Cowboys , 24-21, when the Aztecs kicked a field goal straight into the jaws of the blizzard to break a 21-21 tie just as time ran out to end the game.

As for action on the field this evening, UTEP was led by Jordan Palmer, brother of former USC star Carson. He led them to a 14-3 lead at the half. Tyler Campbell, son of Pro Hall of Famer Earl, returned the ball for SDSU to start the second half. Things didn't look good for the Aztecs trailing 27-3 in the third quarter. A quarterback switch and a couple of big plays by the Aztecs defense helped SDSU get back into it. With 4:38 remaining, the Miners were up, 34-24, and there was no sign of quitting from Tom's Aztecs. Starting the next drive, the replacement, Darren Mougey, completed four straight passes to bring State to the UTEP 10. The Aztecs settled for Garrett Palmer's 34-yard FG. With 1:59 left in the game trailing 34-27, their onside kick went out of bounds. The Miners took over, but the suspense didn't end there. UTEP Coach Mike Price decided to hand off to a runner three times rather than take a knee to avoid risking a fumble back to the Aztecs. "Didn't he ever hear of The Miracle at the Meadowlands?" I asked Tom.

He smiled and said, "Herman Edwards played for San Diego State!"

There was no miracle at Qualcomm today as time expired for a final of 34-27 in favor of the Miners. SDSU fans told me they often have to look for a silver lining. Tom Ables said that he was proud that his team never quit. We think he had every right to feel that way. Take it from the guy who just attended his 646th Aztec game.

Extra point: In 2010, Tom, accompanied by his son Ken, went back to Laramie, Wyoming to attend his 700th Aztec game. A week later at halftime against Colorado State at Qualcomm, San Diego State presented Tom (with Nancy at his side) the ball from that game commemorating his record. He proudly displays it in his office at the company he owns, Venture, where he still works today. By the end of the season, Tom was up to game 705 and planning for the 2011 San Diego State season. I hope to catch up with him again some time.

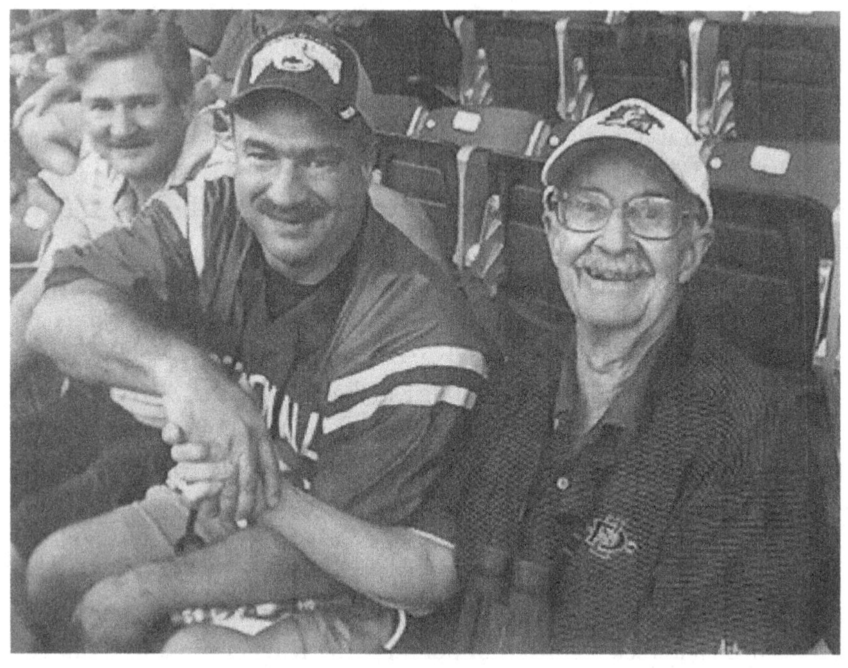

The author and his brother Chris (left) meet Mr. San Diego State, Tom Ables, at the Aztec – UTEP Miner game. Tom heads into the 2011 season looking forward to attending his 706th Aztec football game.

Hey, Ralphie... Girl?
(108) Colorado State vs. (109) Colorado
September 9, 2006

Denver - In 2005, when Lindy's pre-season football publication did a nice article about my pursuit of The Goal, an illustration depicted me as "Super Fan" in a funny cartoon checking off my list. The list accurately depicted teams I had and had not seen. The article gave me some new notoriety. My Web site www.collegefootballfan.com picked up more hits, and I received more e-mails.

One in particular came from Dave Plati, Sports Information Director at the University of Colorado. Dave noticed that I'd never seen his Golden Buffaloes or the Colorado State Rams play. He extended me an invitation to attend the 2005 game known as the Rocky Mountain Showdown between the two rivals, played annually at Denver's Invesco Field at Mile High Stadium. I had to decline his benevolent offer. I had already committed to add Boise

State against the Georgia Bulldogs that day. Dave left the invitation open for a future encounter. I penned in the intrastate rivalry for 2006. With air miles saved up, I took St. Laurie on our first visit ever to Boulder, Colorado. Dave sent me a media guide, parking pass, complimentary tickets, and a sideline pass to meet and even run on the field with Ralphie IV, Colorado's famed bison who charges on to the football field leading the team before each game. I couldn't thank Dave enough for this great opportunity!

On Friday, my wife and I toured the beautiful Boulder campus. We visited brown-bricked Folsom Stadium, the bookstore, and other facilities. The campus seemed quaint for a big university. We didn't catch up with Dave since he was busy with media activities that day, but one of the nice things that he did that I didn't know about was to inform the media of my attendance. A blurb in the papers mentioned me and The Goal before I visited Colorado. CSTV contacted me for an interview to be held supposedly during halftime. I couldn't imagine my mug on TV being interviewed at a college football game!

St. Laurie and I arrived early at Invesco and found our seats in the front row at the 20-yard line to the left of the CU bench. Wearing my blue Collegefootballfan.com jersey given to me by St. Laurie for Christmas the year before (the front of my jersey has the number "119" on front for all the teams in 1-A football. Above the number, it reads, "SEE THEM ALL"). I was greeted by several fans who had read the article which at the time I knew nothing about. Several shook hands with me and stated that it was something that they would love to do. They wished me luck. Comments like theirs inspired me to write this book to share these stories with fans like them.

With sideline passes, St. Laurie and I passed though security checks leading down through Invesco to the playing field level. We walked along the end zone to the Colorado sideline. We ventured over to meet Ralphie IV and her handlers and to take some pictures. Ralphie stared at my blue jersey, probably trying to figure out how I fit in among black, gold, and green. I'm glad I didn't wear my red one.

St. Laurie and I got to talk to one of her handlers, Taylor "Bubba" Leary. The political science major started his second season "escorting" Ralphie IV on to the field. Handlers try out every year. Taylor planned to do so again his senior year. They were already training Ralphie V for 2007, as Ralphie IV in her tenth season, started to get a little too mean and ornery in her old age. You could see her swinging her horns close to the nearest handlers when she ran out in the second half. The training entails running her down the length of the field and right into her trailer. Taylor said Ralphie appreciates the run just to get away from the maddening crowd. Females are chosen as mascots because they are smaller than the bulls. As big as Ralphie is though, it was the lone Colorado State Ram handler who got tripped and dragged a little by the Ram mascot toward the end of the game. Mascot handlers can take some knocks on the field during the season.

Just being along the sideline on the field near players running drills thrilled me to be there right before a big game. Today, I got to absorb the atmosphere surrounding the field with all the game preparation going on before us. I spied a couple of CU staffers nearby to ask how I might be able to catch up with Dave Plati to thank him. He was up in the press box. They had read about me, and we talked for a while before one of them said, "By the way, my wife would love your jersey. When I first read it, it looks like it says, 'SEE THE MALL.'" I requested "SEE 'EM ALL." However, *K&N Sporting Goods,* owned by Frank Rafferty who loves the Notre Dame marching band, couldn't come up with an apostrophe for a contraction. That frustrated me originally, but now I grew more concerned that people might think I'm a living ad for 119 shopping malls!

I was invited to run out on the field with Ralphie IV and her handlers, but I got cold feet mainly because I didn't feel right about running out in front of all those CU fans that'd never gotten a chance to do this. Here I was, only a first-timer at a CU game, and at the big intrastate rivalry. Did I deserve to do this? Now that I've accomplished The Goal though, I would do it if I had the chance again.

With Bernard Jackson as the unexpected starting QB for the Buffs, at the three, he started right and reversed left to score six. State responded with a 27-yard pass from Caleb Hanie to Johnny Walker to get to the Buffs' three. Hanie optioned right from there to take it in standing up unscathed. The two teams played to a 7-7 first-quarter tie. Kicks and punts really travel well at Mile High. CU's Matt Di Lallo boomed a 71-yard punt to put CSU back on their 15. On that series, State fumbled and CB Terrence Wheatley recovered for the Buffaloes on the Ram 26. The Rams would not yield, however, and CU's All-America PK and captain , Mason Crosby, put three on the board from 41 yards out. Hanie (20 of 23 for 233 yards) was on target to Walker and Brett Willis to lead his offense down to the Colorado three. With play action, he connected to Kory Sperry. At the end of the first half, the Rams held a 14-10 edge.

At the beginning of the third quarter, CSTV's sideline reporter, Ann Marie, came over to invite me down for an interview about The Goal. With my pre-game sideline pass to meet Ralphie, I worked my way back up to the main concourse, through security to elevators to take me down to the playing field. I found my way to the entrance to the field at about the 50 right behind the CU bench. Things had gotten intense there. I was only a few feet behind the CU defense huddled with their coaches. There was pad-pounding and shouting going on. It felt great to be there. The intensity of big-time, college football electrified me!

I spotted Ann Marie about 20 yards to my right and went to meet her. The game continued. The crowd roared. I thought the cheers were for me (not really!). Fans focused intensely on the action—definitely a great perspective for a first-timer on the field in front of 65,701. Ann Marie introduced me to the camera crew and told me what she would ask. We worked our way to the north end zone to our left as CU was driving that way. I walked past St. Laurie. She laughed. Ann Marie and I stood together waiting for a break in the action. Meantime, she asked me to check her teeth for chocolate stains. No! She passed inspection. It struck me that she has very good teeth.

After Colorado's Mason Crosby missed a field goal, the red camera light suddenly flashed at us! Ann Marie quickly introduced me to CSTV Land as a "True college football fan" whose Goal was to see all 119 teams play. She hit me with her first question, "Why do you want to do this?" I could see we were going to be pressed for time, so I left my three-page speech in my pocket. I told her I had always enjoyed college football, loved the action on the field, and got caught up in the spirit of the games like the one here.

"How many teams does this game make?" I told here that these were No. 108 and No. 109 with ten left to go after this one.

"What teams are left?" she asked. As I was about to answer, she held up her hand as she listened to her headset. Action was continuing on the field behind us, but I didn't know what was going on. The red light went back on. She asked again.

"Oklahoma. Oklahoma State, Kansas State, and a few Sun Belt teams," I said. "I'll finish up next year with Idaho and Nevada." Presumably pressed for time, I refrained from telling her about my upcoming double header with Tulsa at Navy and FIU at Maryland. I figured everyone else was anxious to get back to the action on the field with a close game at hand. I'm sure there would have been more time if a blowout was taking place, but that's not something I'd want, especially after traveling 1,600 miles. I always root for a close, memorable game. She signed off, and I thanked her for my two minutes of television fame. I told her that maybe I would see her at some other game in the future, and I proceeded back to my front row seat. With coverage to 70 million households, someone must have seen it on CSTV. Back home though, I knew everyone was watching Notre Dame play Penn State The third quarter ended with Colorado State still leading, 14-10. As did the fourth . . . game over.

Two-point conversion: Hey, I got on TV! Maybe some day I can meet Ralphie V!

In a hurry!
(110) Tulsa at Navy
September 23, 2006

Annapolis - The state of Maryland offered another opportunity to take advantage of an Annapolis-College Park, day/night double-header. This time, both games featured one team to add to my madness. In Annapolis, the Golden Hurricane of Tulsa ventured to Navy-Marines Corps Memorial Stadium. I wouldn't have much chance to savor the experience afterward. Maryland and Florida International (No. 111) kicked off at 6 p.m. at Byrd Stadium.

Navy-Marine Corps Stadium had been upgraded proudly since I last visited in 2002. Class Memorials and dedication plaques now adorned the walls of the stadium. Monuments paid tribute to the graduates of USNA and to its football alum of the past. Every American, college football fan should take the time to visit this stadium. It is truly a monument to our men and women who have served in the Navy and Marine Corps. The wall on the hill overlooking Jack Stephens Field displays many plaques dedicated by corporations and individuals. At least two come from traditional Navy football opponents. Boston College dedicated one to their graduates who served in the Navy and the Marine Corps. Notre Dame also dedicated theirs to "foes on the field," even though the Irish never played at Navy-Marine Corps Memorial Stadium. The 31,604 in attendance at today's game gave a standing ovation to a special group this afternoon. Wounded soldiers from Walter Reed Army Medical Center came to watch the game.

After a scoreless first quarter, each team scored once in the second – Navy on a 26-yard run by Flanker Shun White and Tulsa on a 34-yard pass from Paul Smith to Ryan Bugg. At the half, the Navy D&B Corps played music from the movie "Top Gun" to commemorate the Navy's official announcement on Friday retiring F14 Tomcat fighter jets, the aircraft flown in the movie. Of course, the Corps finished the show with their always-stirring renditions of "*Anchors Aweigh*" and "*The Marine Corps Hymn*".

Navy drove to the six-yard line to open the third. QB Brian Hampton fought for the final yard, which went under review, for Navy's second TD of the day. Tulsa responded with an effective drive of its own. Coach Steve Kragthorpe called for a pass on fourth and goal at the USNA seven where Smith connected with TE Ted Curtis on a criss-cross pattern. Curtis hurdled CB Jeremy McGowan, who made no attempt to wrap his arms as he had on his previous hit to stop Smith, into the end zone for a 7-yard scoring play. Tulsa and Navy remained tied 14-14 after three. In the fourth, Matt Harmon's 39-yard FG for Navy was followed by Jarod Tracy's 29-yard field goal to tie it 17-17 at the end of regulation. This turned out to be Navy's first overtime period ever. USNA remained one of only two teams that had not yet played OT in 1A football.

On Tulsa's first possession, Smith connected with Bugg at the six. On the next play, Donnie Johnson gathered it in from Smith to put Tulsa on the board. Tracy's kick made it 24-17 for Tulsa's first lead of the game. Navy scored even quicker. Hampton completed his longest pass of the day from the 25 at the back of the end zone where OJ Washington caught it with one foot close to the end line. The play went under review. It stood! I pondered how late I would arrive in College Park to see Florida International qualify as my 111th team. Visions of a 51-48 OT final danced in my mind. Would I have to figure a different time and place to add FIU? Much to my surprise and to my chagrin, Tulsa DB Nick Graham's rush from outside put those thoughts to rest when I heard the ball thud twice –first when he blocked it and the secondly when the ball hit the ground. *Thud- Thud!* It spun on the ground in the end zone right in front of me from my seat on the grassy hill. The block of Harmon's point-after won the game for the Golden Hurricane, 24-23.

Extra point: Not waiting to hear "*Navy Blue and Gold*", I beat a substantial part of the crowd to the buses to satellite parking to head on to College Park. A couple of fans recognized me from my brief interview during the Colorado-CSU game on CSTV. Someone had actually seen me! Nolan and his wife, Nebraska grads, talked about having a similar goal to get to all the stadiums. We compared college football anecdotes. Good luck to him in his quest. It's not easy seeing all the teams no less a game at every 1-A venue. Maybe I'll see him at a game in the future. In the meantime, a kickoff beckoned me to Byrd Stadium!

He should know by now!
(111) Florida International at Maryland
September 23, 2006

College Park - Despite the overtime at Navy, I still had time to make it to Maryland, get a ticket ($5), buy a program, and eat two hot dogs before the 6 p.m. kickoff between Terps and the Florida International Panthers. *Yes,* two new teams in two games in one day!

In the first period, a screen pass from Maryland's Sam Hollenbach to Josh Allen at the Panther 14-yard line was perfectly timed for a score when FIU blitzed. FIU countered in the same period. TE Sam Smith shook one tackler on a short pass and rambled downfield unscathed for an 89-yard touchdown. Hollenbach connected with Isaiah Williams for a five-yard TD pass with :10 left in the half for a 14-7 Terrapin lead.

In the fourth, the Panthers' A'mod Ned burst up the middle and outraced two Terp defenders until they caught him from behind at the five-yard line after a 52-yard jaunt. FIU settled for Dustin Rivest's 27-yard FG to cut the Terp lead, 14-10, with supposedly plenty of time left for either team to score. However, with only over a minute left in the game, the "big play" Panthers took over at their own 20. On fourth and four with 43 ticks remaining, FIU spent its second time-out. The Panthers didn't seem to have a passing game plan to get the ball out of bounds to stop the clock. A six-yard completion got the first down. They were still 68 yards away from a TD with :35 remaining. Josh Padrick spiked the ball to stop the clock on first down. He completed another six-yard pass over the middle. They spent their final time-out with :18 left, 62 yards away. What was FIU thinking? What was Head Coach Don Strock's plan? He must have learned something from Don Shula and from Bob Griese all those years on the bench with the Dolphins! On third and four, Padrick heaved a long pass to Chandler Williams for a 53-yard gain to the Terp nine. One second remained! FIU rushed down field for one more play. The officials spotted the ball. FIU snapped. Padrick fired toward the end zone. Maryland safety Chris Varner intercepted at the two. He fell on the ball to seal Maryland's third victory of the season. Maryland walked away with an unimpressive 14-10 win. The final score was definitely not indicative of a well-played, hard-hitting game. Instead, I watched two lethargic teams play to get a game over without any sense of urgency to win. Neither team played hard, and in the case of FIU, smart, to win.

Extra point: What was most disturbing about FIU, a team coached by former NFL quarterback Don Strock, was that they had no clue how to get the ball near the sidelines to manage the clock when they needed to drive for a final score. If they could have controlled the clock and saved a timeout or two, there could have been a different result! FIU finished the season 0-12. This game and a fight that erupted a few games later against Miami indicated the former second-string NFL QB had no control over the Panthers. He was fired at the end of the season. Years of NFL bench-warming evidently did not prepare him to coach at the collegiate level. He should have at least known something about clock management under pressure in a tight game. He evidently didn't pay much attention to his mentor and teammate in the pros that were pretty good at it.

Honorary Pony on The Boulevard

Tulsa at (112) Southern Methodist
November 18, 2006

Dallas - Originally, I planned to see SMU play at East Carolina trying to hook up with my old Syracuse buddy Bernie Olszyk. He relocated to Williamsburg, Virginia in anticipation of his approaching retirement. However, plans changed that week as Bernardo's work duties called him away. I didn't feel like going all the way to Greenville, NC by myself. Did I panic? Of course not! I re-checked the SMU schedule and noted a golden opportunity I initially didn't notice. The Mustangs hosted the Tulsa Golden Hurricane at 2 p.m. on November 18. Not only that, but 40 miles north in Denton, Texas, the Mean Green of North Texas State hosted Howard Schnellenberger's Florida Atlantic Owls that evening. This presented must-see football action. That Saturday in Texas offered the chance to add *three* new teams in one day! I booked a flight, a couple of cheap hotels, and I headed to the Lone Star State for what I referred to on my site as my "Texas Two-Step to See Three!"

I headed over to SMU late Saturday morning to check out the campus and the pre-game happenings. I found a side street off campus figuring it looked like a direct route for a quick getaway heading north to Denton on I-35 North after the game. I could see lights and flags over Gerard J. Ford Stadium a few blocks from where I parked. Some construction blocked a direct path, and I walked along a street that led to the middle of campus. I ventured to an intersection of a tree-lined street with a wide, green-grass median. No traffic passed by, but people gathered on both sides of the street to tailgate. I turned left toward the stadium when I spotted a beer wagon with a fresh- tapped CO_2 system. What timing! No line formed yet, so I ventured over. Beers were $5 a pop. Oh well, I figured I'd get one and see what else "The Boulevard" of the SMU campus had to offer. I fell into the perfect trap! Brian Bischoff of the SMU Mustang Club approached me. The club offered $5 a beer, but if I chose to join the Mustang Club for a nominal fee, I could get all the beer and wings I could handle, two tickets to the game, and a ticket for this evening's basketball home-opener against Dayton. He made me an offer I couldn't refuse! With Matt Doherty, formerly of Notre Dame and UNC, now the new head basketball coach at SMU, the last part of the offer was tempting, but my mission already lay ahead of me this evening.

Brian introduced me to other club members Chip Hiemenz '06, Jamie, and Jeremy among others. Chip worked for SMU's office of Development and Alumni Affairs. The beer wagon was equipped with three TV monitors to keep up with action around the country. In front of the Natorium across the street, the *PitPops* provided music. I met Jared Romo, QB of last year's Mustangs, who led them past the No. 22 ranked TCU Horned Frogs, SMU's first win over a ranked team in many years. All nice guys, the fan turn-out disappointed these die-hards after last week's tough homecoming loss to Houston. For their sakes, I hoped that the Ponies would get their bowl after their long, dry spell following the NCAA's death penalty in 1986.

Figuring beers cost five bucks each, I drank my $25 worth before the game to be sure my two tickets were free! The game hadn't started yet, I ate wings, and I wouldn't be driving for at least four more hours after watching a game. Life on The Boulevard is great on Saturdays before games. The guys enjoyed hearing about my exploits, and I enjoyed getting updates about the SMU program. I thanked them for their great hospitality and headed into Gerard J. Ford Stadium. They gave me directions on how to get to Denton quickly. They also recommended watching the Mean Green from a beer pavilion at Fouts Field, but also warned me about a particular annoyance I'd find there.

Tulsa scored just about every time it had the ball in the first half. SMU drives stalled just about every time. It was 24-7 in favor of Tulsa at the half, but having seen two similar leads dissipate in recent games at Rutgers and at Princeton, I sensed this game was far from over. While the SMU band played *"She'll Be Comin' Round the Mountain"*, not the most stirring of fight songs, at the end of the half, I went to check out SMU's Heritage

Hall. There are tributes to the late Heisman winner Doak Walker and to the 11-0-1 1982 team's 7-3 Cotton Bowl win over Pitt, four years before the NCAA sanctioned the Mustangs with its first *death penalty.* Two more wins this year would end many years of bowl-less frustration for my new, fellow Pony Club members. Our hopes were already fading though after one half of play against Tulsa.

SMU followers dispersed in the second half. Many fans deemed the Ponies done. But a pair of field goals and a TD, sans PAT, brought SMU within reach, 24-19. With off tackle play action, SMU QB Justin Willis faked a hand-off and carried around the right side for a six-yard TD run. Perfectly set-up, Willis ran the QB draw to perfection on the two-point conversion, and SMU took a 27-24 lead with 12:46 left. The Mustang defense stuffed the Tulsa offense in the second half allowing only 80 yards. They forced another punt. SMU drove to the Golden Hurricane 14. Willis fired a long lateral to WR Blake Warren on his left. He picked up two beautiful blocks and went into the end zone to extend SMU's lead, 34-24. A little over four minutes remained. The Ponies held on, and I listened to the public address and the final cheers of the remaining SMU faithful as I approached my rental car to start my search for Highway 35. Great game! On to the next!

One new team down and *two* to go!

Extra point: As for my Pony Club brethren, SMU lost the following week to the Rice Owls to finish the season at 6-6. The 7-6 Owls earned the bid to the New Orleans Bowl. Pony Club bowl frustration continued on The Boulevard until 2009. June Jones was hired from Hawaii to take over the program and returned with his new team to Honolulu for the Hawaii Bowl where the 'Stangs drubbed Nevada, 45-10. It wasn't quite the Cotton Bowl win of 1982, but after a long, dry spell in Dallas, the Pony Club could celebrate a post-season win. It couldn't be better for a nicer bunch of guys.

Dancing under the stars

(113) Florida Atlantic at (114) North Texas State
November 18, 2006

Denton, Texas - Not exactly sure of where I was going from Dallas, I got to Fouts Field mid-way through the first period just as the Mean Green, in black uniforms with green helmets, scored on a three-yard TD run by freshman Evan Robertson. Walking into NTSU's stadium and seeing rows of empty, aluminum bleacher seats, the scene reminded me of my trip to see Ohio U. play at Buffalo. My second impression was what the SMU guys had warned me about—the screeching eagle cry over the loudspeaker is *annoying*! They played it after TDs, on defensive third downs, on offensive third downs, after big plays, whatever—the screech and the two bell gongs can be put to rest, especially with such the small crowd of 9,806 to get any kind of reaction from.

Things got interesting, but not on the field. As the first quarter expired, some real head-knocking was going on along the sideline. FAU's Owl mascot mixed it up with NTSU's Eagle mascot. The Owl literally knocked the Eagle's head off, revealing the small head of some pissed-off college kid. The headless Eagle eventually had to retaliate where at first the best he could do was twist the Owl's head around 180 degrees. He eventually knocked it off, and before the cockfight escalated, "cooler," non-detachable heads intervened. In other sidelines news, I moved to another seat to get a better view of Mean Green's *Dance Team* performing in front of the band. It was a great move on my part for a much better view of the prime action along the sideline!

As for the action on the field, the annoying sound effects continued until cannon fire ended the half. FAU enjoyed a 17-10 lead. Mean Green? Black uniforms? Eagle mascot? Eagle screeches? Bells? Cannons? I'm not sure what North Texas wanted to be. North Texas mustered two field goals by Denis Hopovac in the second half to get within one point. FAU Free safety Taheem Acevedo picked off a Mean Green pass in the end zone in the first half. He then sealed the victory with another in his own territory to thwart NTSU's final drive of the game. Schnellenberger's Owls spoiled all that noisemaking to hold on to a 17-16 win.

Extra point: I was satisfied after a long day, but I wanted to catch the Ohio State-Michigan highlights back at the local hotel. On a day when most of football nation witnessed No. 1 Ohio State's exciting 41-38 victory over No. 2 Michigan, I was thrilled to have attended two close, hard-fought football games not particularly played by the best, but played by athletes giving their best. That's what college football is supposed to be about. Some day, I hope to get to an Ohio State–Michigan game where there's something big at stake! However, these two venues in Texas on a November afternoon and evening offered two competitive games to add three to The Goal to "see 'em all!" Seeing good competition on the playing field and meeting other college football fans in another part of the country made it all very worthwhile. Watching that Mean Green Dance Team made it very worthwhile, too! Best I'd ever seen. My much-anticipated excursion lived up to expectations and beyond. I attended two close, competitive games with extra helpings of atmosphere on the side. I couldn't have asked for much more.

Final Countdown!
(115) Kansas State at Auburn
September 1, 2007

Auburn - Kansas State remained one of five teams left to achieve The Goal! The Wildcats initially fell on Fresno State's schedule as the season home opener for the Bulldogs. I contemplated flying out to the nut farm again with or without Frank Lorito. Later, the game got rescheduled to November 24, Thanksgiving weekend! That wouldn't work. My Goal came down to seeing five remaining teams, but the original schedules announced worked against me. The other four teams pared off against one another on October 27—Oklahoma State at Oklahoma and Idaho at Nevada-Reno. How could I see games in Oklahoma and Nevada on the same day? I sought alternative plans. On October 13, Fresno would play at Idaho. For TV scheduling, Nevada would play at Boise on Sunday night, October 14. I'd never traveled to Idaho before, and the trip would entail two unique venues. I looked forward to the possibility. The IU Vandals play in their 16,000-seat indoor arena, the Kibble Dome. Boise's Bronco Stadium is famous for its blue "Smurf" turf. I always wanted to go there. The Saturday-Sunday schedule gave me time to drive the 300-mile difference. I booked a flight. Several weeks later, Oklahoma and Oklahoma State announced they would start their new Thanksgiving weekend rivalry a year earlier than originally planned. The price to fly to Oklahoma on the big holiday weekend was unfathomable. Plus it wouldn't be appreciated by certain family members that I may miss the traditional Thanksgiving weekend together. I catch enough grief for taking in a local playoff game somewhere in New England on the following Saturday afternoon. I had to re-plan. The airline added a change fee for my formerly free tickets. I rescheduled my Idaho plans to head to Reno to see Idaho play Nevada on October 27. Luckily, the latest TV schedules offered an unexpected opportunity to reschedule the two teams in Oklahoma. I learned through the years that imagination, patience, persistence, and luck allowed me to pursue this dream quicker than I ever thought possible taking into consideration my financial and personal limitations.

What about Kansas State? Should I consider a trip to see them play at Oklahoma State? That would mean an additional trip on another weekend to Oklahoma, but between work, personal plans, and other games on my slate, I couldn't be sure if 2007 could be the year I could finally finish this off. Then, the luck set in. Of all the teams Kansas State chose to open at - Auburn! "Hello, Charlie? If you can get us four tickets, St. Laurie and I would like to come down and visit the Plain at Auburn!" Who better to start the final year of achieving this crazy Goal with? Charlie had been there since the beginning when he invited me down to see Auburn play Georgia. We attended games at The Meadowlands, Richmond, and even saw Rutgers at Princeton! On top of those, there were the games in recent years down at Auburn. We had a done deal.

After a nice visit with our usual Auburn host and hostess, Lynda, we watched the home team enjoy a 6-3 halftime lead. The Auburn Marching Band performed while we got to wander the Nelson Club Level of Jordan-Hare that hosted 86,439 college football fans this evening.

In the third period, KSU played with a different, albeit unexpected, offensive strategy. Four reverse options eventually brought K-State to the Tigers' 25. Chicanery paid off finally on a reverse end-around pass from WR Jordy Nelson to a wide-open James Patton in the right corner of the end zone for the first TD of the game - Wildcats up, 10-6. On K-State's subsequent drive, the deception stopped, but a Brooks Rossman field goal made the score, 13-6, in favor of the visitors. Later in the period, Auburn's Robert Dunn took advantage of poor K-State punt coverage speeding up the middle about twenty yards and breaking a few tackles for a 57-yard return to the Wildcats' 15. Wes Bynum kicked in a 31-yard FG to cut the Kansas State lead to 13-9 heading into the final period.

Auburn trailed with 2:01 left in the game. A play-action move paid off. Wide open TE Gabe McKenzie caught Brandon Cox's pass deep in the left corner of the end zone. The Tigers now led, 16-13. State came out throwing. Auburn rushed hard and on second down, Quentin Groves sacked Josh Freeman from behind, forcing a fumble. Antonio Coleman picked up the ball and ran 34 yards into the end zone untouched to put the game away, 23-13, with 1:09 left. Auburn celebrated a tough but sloppy win. Only four teams remained to be seen.

Extra point: Thanks to Charlie and Lynda, the 115th team toward the Goal was the seventh I added over the years on trips when I visited them.

It would have been tough to do without my Auburn connection. Now I focused on my personal "Final Four".

Will-Call
(116) Oklahoma at Tulsa
September 21, 2007

Tulsa - So how did my plans work out to see Oklahoma and Oklahoma State without seeing their game against one another on Thanksgiving weekend or without taking two trips to see them play somewhere in Big Twelve territory? As luck would have it, TV moved the Oklahoma at Tulsa game to a Friday night. The next day, 70 miles west of Tulsa, the OSU Cowboys would play the pass-happy Red Raiders of Texas Tech in Stillwater! A couple of years back, my brother Chris out in Long Beach told me that if I ever wanted to see a game played at Tulsa, he had a good friend who played for them back in the '60s and had season tickets! "Hello, Chris?" He put me in touch with his friend Joe Pistoia, a former Brooklynite who played for Tulsa as a wide receiver a few years after Howard Twilley back in the 60s. Now his son, Tyler, would be on the squad this season as a red-shirt freshman for the Hurricane. Joe had a ticket for me to be at Skelly Stadium in Tulsa. My "Final Four" came down to Oklahoma (1) at Tulsa, Texas Tech at Oklahoma State (2), and Idaho (3) at Nevada (4).

Before the OU-Tulsa game, I got to experience some local culture at *Ed's Hurricane Lounge* on 11th Street right across the street from Chapman Stadium. Beer cost $2 a bottle, ESPN graced two TV screens, and the ceiling was adorned with more styles of women's brassieres than a *Victoria Secret's* store. I assume paying customers donated them. The smoke cloud was heavy which you rarely find in the northeast any more. Picking up some beer before meeting up with Joe and his wife Joyce and some of Joe's Tulsa acquaintances for a little tailgating, I learned that the state of Oklahoma has some different laws regarding alcohol as well. You can't buy *cold* beer in a liquor store unless it's "*3.2 beer*"! I hadn't even heard the term used since 1975 in Maryland. You can't buy ice at the store either! Despite ads all over the store for Rolling Rock beer, they couldn't sell it because it recently became an Anheuser-Busch product. I didn't understand the laws. I bought two twelve-packs of warm beer.

Joe and Joyce Pistoia met me outside the stadium parking lot and we walked to meet their friends at a pre-arranged tailgate spot. Joyce, Tyler's step-mom, bought wine from a local liquor store, but she found out that she couldn't even buy a cork-screw. They had to buy one elsewhere - culture shock for visitors from both coasts! I showed up to tailgate with my warm beer, and bought bags of ice from some guys who sold them from the back of a golf cart on an afternoon when the temperature soared into the 90s. Joe introduced me to John Dobbs, our host for the pregame get-together. He played ball with Joe at Tulsa. John's father was Glen Dobbs, star TU tailback in the 40's who returned to become one of Tulsa's most successful head coaches. Glen was elected to the College Football Hall of Fame in 1980. He was the main reason Joe came to play at Tulsa for his wide-open passing attack. However, Coach Dobbs stayed only one more year before a successor took over and de-emphasized the passing attack, much to Joe's chagrin.

Joe, Joyce, and I stopped for a burger at the Tulsa Alumni Association tent. From there, Joe left us to take part in a Tulsa tradition where former players go into the locker room to seek out the player wearing the same jersey number each donned for the Hurricane. Joe confided that they look each other in the eye, shake hands, and the former player wishes the current player luck before the game. Joe met up with his number 25, starting RB Tarrion Adams. Joe also mentioned that he played for the 1968 Tulsa team that trailed Houston at the half in the Astrodome, 21-6. Because the entire Hurricane team was hit by a bad flu bug, his coach offered to forfeit at the half because his team was too sick to play. The NCAA said that there would be severe consequences if TU didn't come back out, so they did. Tulsa lost the game 100-6! One hundred points in a game or 79 in one half is hard to imagine.

As a guest of Tyler's, a ticket awaited me at the will-call window with his parents'. We walked together to pick them up. On line, we were met by another blonde woman. Joe took me aside and mentioned that he and Joyce would be sitting below while I'd be sitting in seats farther up with this other woman, Janet. I was a little confused as to what was going on. Janet knew them and kind of showed up out of the blue. She had no idea who I was either. Finally in a somewhat uncomfortable conversation, it became clearer to both of us when I said I was "Joe's friend's brother." She asked, "What's your brother's name?"

"Chris Koreivo," I replied.

"Oh!" she said. "Emily's Dad!" Her daughter attended Wilson High in Long Beach with my niece. Now we both got it! I can be thick at times, but I finally realized that Janet was Tyler's mother. She had just flown into

Tulsa to see the game on her way back from Pittsburgh on business. She's president of a printing business that happened to do a lot of business with the University of Southern California, I learned. Of course, my first thought turned to seeing the Trojans play at the L.A. Coliseum some day.

Janet, like Joe and Joyce, was very concerned about Tyler. He rested in bed all day with a bad sore throat and swollen glands. He felt very weak. They advised him to see a doctor, but he wanted to see how he felt before the game. With three parents in from California to see him suit up in his Tulsa uniform, I couldn't imagine him not making some kind of effort to get out on that playing field, even just to warm up! Janet and I saw him run on the field with the Golden Hurricane. She felt relieved, but still a little concerned.

Paul Smith's 15-yard scoring strike to Jesse Meyer gave Tulsa an early lead, and the home crowd chanted "Tulsa" and "Hurricane" back and forth across Skelly Field during this unusual Friday night game. When the Sooners got to the Tulsa 29, the 'Cane defense stacked up the middle and RB Allen Patrick took advantage, running around right end for OU's first TD and the 7-7 tie. Sam Bradford's TD pass to Juaquin Iglesias and DeMarco Murray's four-yard TD run quieted the home crowd at that point. Tulsa came back to make it 21-14 on Smith's second TD pass, this time to Brannon Marion from the 48. The stout OU defense figured out the Hurricane offense for the rest of the game. If Smith rolled one direction, he always reversed field and threw from the other side. They learned to "stay at home", got the ball back quickly, and set up two more scores on another Bradford TD pass and another Allen rushing TD for a 35-14 halftime lead.

Tulsa scored early in the third, but eleven seconds later, OU's DeMarco Murray returned the ensuing kickoff 81 yards to extend the lead, 42-21. Things didn't improve for Tulsa offensively or defensively, and OU romped, 66-21.

Extra point: After the game, I finally got to meet my real "Tulsa connection". Talk about swollen glands! Tyler had to be hurting. He was cordial through our introduction, but he could barely speak. He didn't disappoint any of us despite not feeling well. I had hoped to get to see him play again, but during his four years of eligibility, he only saw action in a couple of games. Give him credit though, as a walk-on he stuck it out for four years and earned his degree. While there, the Golden Hurricane won the GMAC Bowl in both his redshirt freshman and sophomore years. His team won the Hawaii Bowl against Hawaii at the end of his senior season. Tulsa's record was 36-17 during Tyler's career. I was honored to be able to get a ticket from an actual squad member of a D1 team at the Will-call window! Hey Janet, how about that USC game at the Coliseum? UCLA or Notre Dame will do. Maybe even Stanford.

Shoot-out at OK State

Texas Tech at (117) Oklahoma State
September 22, 2007

Stillwater, Oklahoma – Oklahoma State's pre-game, radio show featured Cowboy fans questioning QB Bobby Reid's fortitude for not playing. Preseason reports rated him highly. I initially anticipated a high-scoring, competitive game when I booked it to see State host Texas Tech, but the Cowboy loss to Troy State the previous week indicated a lesser game than expected. The loss of starting QB Bobby Reid replaced by one-time starter, Zac Robinson, combined with a porous defense against Mike Leach's pass-happy, offensive, scoring machine disappointed me. I may have traveled all the way to Stillwater to watch a blow-out. Aside from that, the OSU ticket I purchased in advance through the ticket office assured me my ticket cost the most I had ever paid anywhere in the country. At $80 a ticket, I'd better see something special.

T. Boone Pickens Stadium was still under construction. Plans called for expansion to 60,000 seats. To fill it, they'll evidently have to start selling tickets at lower prices. This game didn't sell out like I was led to believe. I'll say this though; the seats and aisles offer more room and comfort than many other college stadiums I've visited.

Before the game, I stopped for beers, shade, and scores at the Stonewall Tavern, just a stone's throw from T.B.P. Stadium. Once in the stadium, my ticket thankfully placed me in the shade of the south stands. Four rows from the top, refreshing shade provided a cooling effect. OSU parents sitting next to me received cell phone calls about the agonizingly hot sun from their kids sitting across from us. Hand fan give-aways could be seen flapping vigorously throughout the student section where kids sat in the sun-drenched, 90 degree temperatures. The action on the field got so hot, however, that fans would eventually forget the sweltering heat in Stillwater!

Like rodeo cowboys, a chute opened and the OSU Cowboys burst out on to the field before the game. The first half turned out to be an offensive free-for-all. The two teams combined for nine touchdowns. Tech QB Graham Harrell threw three of his first half TD passes to Mike Crabtree. The other found Eric Morris. Shannon Woods scored on a 6-yard run. State kept up with three running TDs – Dantrell Savage on a 4-yarder, Kendall Hunter on a 42-yard run, and the QB Robinson from 48 yards away. Robinson also tossed a short TD pass to Dez Bryant. *Bullet,* the beautiful black Stallion that carries a Cowpoke with the OSU flag, races out over the Pro-turf after every Cowboy score. The Red Raiders led, 35-28, at the half.

After combining for 63 points in the first half, it looked as if neither would score again until the Cowboys tied it with 1:15 left in the third. With a backfield overloaded to the left, Robinson faked a dive left to his tailback, reverse-rolled to the right, and finished a 68-yard scoring drive with an 11-yard TD run to tie the score, 35-35. The announcer informed the crowd that both teams had already combined for over 1,000 yards before the final period. The Cowboys and Raiders reloaded for a grand finale.

Surprisingly, early fourth-quarter drives stalled. Would the defenses dominate the balance of the game to force this score game into OT? Answer: a 33-yard TD pass from Robinson to Jeremy Broadway gave the Cowboys the lead, but Tech came right back to tie it up again when Harrell hooked up with Danny Amendola for a 41-yard score. Could anyone here play defense now? Trlica put up the first field goal of the game to put Tech on top by three. OSU retaliated with seven points on a 55-yard pass play from Robinson to Brandon Pettigrew for another tenuous Cowboy lead, 49-45. Tech needed another TD.

Tenuous, you ask? Before the first half ended, the Raiders needed only 15 seconds to drive 86 yards for a TD! Not only did 1:28 now remain with the ball on their 28, but Texas Tech had two time-outs left. A 40-yard pass took them almost instantly to Oklahoma State's 18. After a short run and two incomplete passes, the Cowboy defense held the Raiders to a fourth down at the fifteen. With one bullet left in the chamber, Harrell dropped back in the pocket and fired toward his favorite target, Crabtree, over the middle in the end zone. The ball may have slightly been touched by FS Ricky Price, but either way, the ball glanced off the freshman receiver's shoulder pad to end Tech's final offensive threat! The Raiders used their two time-outs over the last :19 while Robinson took a knee three times to run out the clock. Bullet had finished his laps for the day. The Cowboys successfully defended T.B.P. Stadium and reversed their early season struggles against the well-armed Raiders. The combined total of the 49-45 Cowboy victory stood as the third highest I'd seen among all my FBS games over the years.

Extra point: The two offenses combined for 94 points and 1,328 total yards. Robinson aptly replaced Bobby Reid in only his second start completing 16 of 32 for 211 yards and 2 TDs. He ran for 116 yards and two TDs. Harrell performed better than expected in Mike Leach's offense with 46 completions among 67 attempts for 646 yards and 5 TDs. The total yardage amounted to the fourth highest ever in Bowl Division game history! For me, the most expensive game ticket I ever purchased paid off in a thrilling shoot-out that went down to the last minute of play! Not a member of the press, I missed Coach Mike Gundy's well-documented, tirade about being "a man" after the game in defense of his now *former* QB Bobby Reid. I'll never forget this shoot-out for what it was! I'm glad I could be there. It turned out to be worth paying the full price for *this* ticket.

Perfect Ending!
(118) Idaho at (119) Nevada
October 27, 2007

Reno, Nevada – At this time, 119 teams made up the Football Bowl Subdivision (FBS – initials for a dumb name). Well, here I was! Today, my last two of the 119 played each other, and I was able to make it out to Reno, Nevada. I couldn't believe that this crazy Goal could ever be achieved as quickly as it was. Several months earlier through my website, I had been contacted by a Nevada Wolfpack fan, Paul Andrew. Paul invited me to tailgate with him and a bunch of dedicated Nevada fans. He informed me that the Pack didn't have a huge football following, so they would be easy to find. He gave me his cell number, and we talked several times before I headed out. I looked forward to partying with his fellow tailgaters since none of my stalwarts over the years could make it out for my grand finale.

On the flight into Reno on Friday, I noticed a few strange things. First, the heavy, smoky haze from ongoing forest fires in California covered the area. I hoped all my acquaintances back in California were fine, especially my San Diego State friend Tom Ables. I heard back from him that thankfully he had no major problems in his neighborhood. Secondly, I noticed no typical activity taking place around schools on a Friday morning. Parking lots were empty and a school bus depot looked full. I took the shuttle to stay at the *Sands Hotel and Casino* which the locals consider part of "old Reno." Once settled, I checked out the sports lines for the college games I'd be interested in. It's my primary gambling entertainment I enjoy while in Nevada.

That afternoon, I toured the University of Nevada campus. Few people were there. The basketball team scrimmaged in the main arena on campus. The school bookstore was closed. On a Friday before a game day, little on campus stirred. No students walked to classes. Nobody hung out at the student center. No vehicles rolled in or out for the weekend. I know Paul told me that the Wolfpack didn't have a great fan following, but I wondered if Nevada-Reno even had any students! Heading off campus, I stopped by *The Ritz Bar and Grill* on the edge. Chloe, a nice-looking bartender who served me and her one other customer, filled me in. I happened to show up on *Nevada Day*! Schools, state government, the university, and some businesses all closed for the annual holiday to celebrate Nevada's statehood. We hoisted a few shots along with Mike the cook to celebrate. He made great burgers. Chloe gave me information about some of the local celebrations and on some of the casinos. She even checked out my website while I was there. At least I had found the right place for beer and burgers near campus.

I watched *Game Day* Saturday morning at 7 a.m. I watched games played in the east starting at 9 a.m. while drinking Bloody Marys at the *Silver Legacy Casino*. I played several game tickets, but I left at the half of most games already started - doing pretty well - to meet Paul at the tailgate party hosted by his buddy, Steve. I picked up cold beer on the way up Virginia Avenue for my first tailgate party at Nevada. There, I met a great bunch of Wolfpack fans.

Paul introduced me to a couple of dozen people. They grilled, we drank, we ate, and we shared a lot of football stories. Paul's Dad played for Cal back in the early '50s. In the Homecoming edition of Nevada's game magazine, Pack Edge, Paul had written an article entitled, "*The Battle Born Rivalry.*" It highlighted some interesting games in the Nevada-UNLV rivalry played since 1969. He insisted that when I return to Reno, that's the game to go to. With a capacity of 29,964, Mackay Stadium sells out for the "*Battle of the Fremont Cannon*" when UNLV comes to town every other year. Winner takes home the cannon. Reno probably has plenty of UNLV alum managing the growing Casino business downtown. Boise and Fresno in the top-heavy Western Athletic Conference bring in the other big crowds at Mackay.

I noted Nevada had lot of construction under way on campus. Paul told me much of the funding comes through state gambling taxes. Tuition is free for in-state students who maintain good grades. He told me, "Don't worry! Whatever you lose in Reno, just remember that you're helping my kids through school!" That's funny, with Atlantic City and all the lotteries in Jersey, someone in our state government has to explain to me why NJ kids don't get the same benefit. We headed over to Mackay. I bought an extra ticket from some women on the way in. I sat with Paul and his buddies, Todd and Phil, on the 20-yard line right next to the Nevada band. Paul's son played in the Wolfpack band.

For Halloween week game, it seemed appropriate that a team of *Vandals* kicked off to the *Wolfpack*! The Pack took an early, commanding, comfortable, 17-0 lead. It looked like Nevada was on the verge of a big win in the first period, but their faithful remained pessimistic. They'd seen the Pack do this too often before. They enjoyed the lead at halftime, 17-7, holding the Vandals to only 79 yards. The Wolfpack Marching Band celebrated Halloween with local kids in costumes at the intermission.

On a third and nine at Nevada's 18, Idaho QB Nathan Enderle fired a TD pass to Eric Greenwood to cut the score early in the third period, 17-14. Nevada extended the lead, 24-14, when Luke Lippincott took it in from the two. Nevada forced a Vandal punt and took over on its own 15. Frosh QB Colin Kaepernick's 23-yard pass to Kyle Sammons followed by his 18-yard scramble put Nevada at the Idaho 28-yard line. His next pass fluttered into the end zone, but Marko Mitchell came back to get it with a diving catch for the TD and widened the margin, 31-14. The Pack fans cheered, but it disappointed me since I had taken Idaho and the 16 1/2 points at the casino! Hey, I figured I may have to make this game interesting. Besides, what else are you supposed to do when you visit Reno?

Idaho's Deonte Jackson, who came into this game as the nation's eleventh leading rusher, scored from the two to close the gap back to ten, 31-21. I was ahead again. Lippincott's run from deep in the Pistol for 11 yards around the right side gave the Pack a 37-21 lead. The Pack fans were ecstatic as I cringed awaiting a 17-point Nevada win. Brett Jaekle missed the extra point! I was happy – for a while! I found later that another team on that ticket lost. Oh, well! That's why I never bet – unless I visit Nevada!

That was the final score . . . 37-21. The final score of the final game of my Goal! I had seen all 119 teams, but another opportunity loomed on the horizon. Western Kentucky planned to join the FBS in 2009. I planned to see them play as Team #120 when they became an official FBS team. I had to keep up so I could be sure that I could always say that I'd seen 'em all. For now, I was on top of college football fandom!

Extra point: My new-found friend in Nevada came up with a perfect ending to this story to see all 119. Talking about this being my final game to finish The Goal, several people at the tailgate party asked me why I "saved" this game for last. Sarcastically, I told them that I saved the best game for last. They chuckled. They shook their heads knowing the two teams we were about to watch. I mentioned though that I had opted out of the possibility of attending Penn State-Ohio State today for Nevada and Idaho instead - been there, done that! More importantly, I *needed* to see these two teams play. I could have gone to State College, but I didn't want to wait to go to Idaho next year or to wait two years to get back to Reno. Astounded, Paul responded, "You gave up going to see Penn State play Ohio State to come to this game? YOU ARE THE FAN!"

He summed up The Goal perfectly. It took some effort to see them all. I enjoyed every minute, every mile, every game, and every memory of this endeavor. Perfect ending thanks to Paul!

Hilltoppers *rocky-topped! Whew!*

Western Kentucky (120) at Tennessee
September 5, 2009

Knoxville, Tennessee – Western Kentucky shed its transitional status and now joined FBS membership as a full-fledged member of the struggling Sun Belt Conference. If I still wanted to say that I'd seen 'em all, I figured I'd catch them early and take advantage to watch a game at a new venue. My plan was in place when I saw the chance to get a ticket to an opener at Neyland Stadium. Of course with the Labor Day weekend, I made the most of it, so I headed down to Raleigh to catch up with Joe Massimilla and attended the Thursday night game between the NC State Wolfpack and Steve Spurrier's South Carolina Gamecocks. USC prevailed in a surprising defensive struggle, 7-3. I headed west to Knoxville from there. I'm sure the scenery was beautiful, but driving up and down through a curvy, mountainous I-40 West doesn't leave one much pause to enjoy the sights. You have to focus on who's driving slowly ahead of you and who's barreling down behind you. That was my first time through the Appalachians in western North Carolina. I was glad to get to Knoxville. I was even happier to find *Woodruff's Bar and Grill* on Gay Street for Happy Hour that night. It lasted until 10 pm. Brown Nut Ale turned out to be my favorite of all their brews.

The next morning, I walked streets named Phil Fulmer Avenue, Johnny Majors Way, and Peyton Manning Pass. The Vol Walk near Neyland was packed. The Volunteer marching band entertained on the Silverstein

Building steps and then belted out *"Rocky Top Tennessee"* as the team strolled down the path surrounded by a sea of orange. It wasn't until later on that day I could appreciate that the UT band knew more than just one song. The debut of Lane Kiffin brought 98,761 to UT's opener. It was difficult to maneuver near Neyland to hunt for a ticket. I eventually bought an extra from a nice family of Tennessee fans. We sat 17 rows up from the 15-yard line on the WKU sideline. The two grandparents were taking their 8-year old grandson, David, *and me* to our first Tennessee home game.

WKU's defense competed with UT in the first quarter thwarting the first two drives with an interception and a fumble recovery, but the Hilltopper offense was anemic against the quick, hard-hitting Tennessee defense. Western Kentucky played the Tennessee Volunteers to a 0-0 stalemate by the end of the first quarter. You just knew that Tennessee could not be held down by the newest team in D1, and once they scored, the floodgate would open. An 81-yard, ten-play drive resulted in a two-yard TD run by true freshman Bryce Brown to start the second period. After the Vols drew first blood, they scored touchdowns on nine of their remaining twelve possessions. A WKU fumble on the next series put UT at the Topper's 17. QB Jonathan Crompton connected with TE Luke Stocker on a crossing pattern from there for a sudden, 14-0 lead. On the next two Tennessee possessions, Quinton Hancock and Brandon Warren were recipients of Crompton TD passes from nine and four yards respectively. Every first down, every score, every turnover, and every WKU punt was celebrated to the tune of *"Good ol' Rocky Top!"* The Vols raced to 28-0 lead by the end of the second. The band entertained at halftime and finished its performance with their fight song, of course!

In the third, Kiffin challenged his offense on a fourth and four from its 46. WKU took over on downs. On the next possession, Thomas Majors intercepted for WKU. That was the last time that the Hilltoppers would stop a touchdown drive. Montario Hardesty scored on a one-play drive from the WKU 43 to extend the lead. *"Good ol' Rocky Top!"* When UT removed MLB Nick Reveiz for a rest when the defense took the field, the visitors finally scored on a 66-yard drive capped by Bobby Rainey's 19-yard TD run to put Western on the board to trail now, 35-7.

It was all Tennessee in the fourth though as Crompton connected again with Stocker from the six and then with freshman Marsalis Teague from the five. On first downs – *"Good ol' Rocky Top!"* David Oku, another frosh, ran it in from the two and from the one to finish the next two Tennessee drives and make the final score, 63-7. I was *Rocky-Topped out!* Tennessee out-gained WKU 657 to 83 yards and never punted. WKU's Jeremy Moore did an excellent job on his nine punts averaging 44.8 and allowing only 35 return yards. That's the best I could say about the Hilltoppers' inauguration into FBS football.

Extra Point: The Hilltoppers won no games all season. UT finished 6-6 and Lane Kiffen fled town back to Southern California leaving teams of NCAA investigators in his jet stream. He replaced his former mentor Pete Carroll who left L.A. for the pros leaving behind some questions about his program as well.

"Rocky Top" made me appreciate the fact that Penn State's Blue Band has a repertoire of at least ten different school songs. One tune, especially after nine touchdowns, first downs, time-outs, second downs, official time-outs, etc, etc, can get monotonous. Enough with the *"Whews!"* Even David's Grandmother, a UT season ticket holder, leaned over to me at one point and asked, "Are you sick of *'Rocky Top"* yet?" I told her I had been warned and that I was trying to tune it out. They need to learn a few other tunes down in Knoxville. It's not exactly Nashville.

Epilogue: Four new teams will be joining the FBS during the next few years. South Alabama joins first and is already on several schedules of teams looking to welcome them into the big-time. Texas State and UT-San Antonio follow and have veteran FBS coaches Dennis Franchione and Larry Coker respectively running their programs. I'm hoping to see the two of them play against one another so there will be some semblance of competition for both of them. By then, both my kids will be in college somewhere, so I figure I'll save up the mileage and get St. Laurie to come down to Texas with me. I hope to see the game in San Antonio. I think she'll like the River Walk. As I finish editing my adventure, UMass announced that they will join the ranks of the FBS in the Mid-American Conference. Seen them as a 1AA in the past four times – piece of cake to see them play once again!

I love this game, its traditions, its fun, its excitement, the intensity, the teamwork, the efforts, the dedicated coaches, and all the people who root so hard for their respective teams! In recent years, corruption, crime, and scandals have marred this great game. I think and hope that solutions will be found to correct most of those problems. It is truly a great and unique American tradition. I'm glad and fortunate to have lived to enjoy this surreal adventure and to write about this fun and memorable experience to share with so many others. I look forward to continue doing this for many years to come.

--- S.J.K.

BIBLIOGRAPHY

Anonymous." Todd Marinovich." Biographicon: all the people of the world. Jan. 4-23, 2008. <www.biographicon.com/history/lpdc4/Todd_Marinovich>

Fiutak, Pete. "100 Greatest College Football Finishes." CollegeFootballNews.com. 9 July 2007. <http://cfn.scout.com/2/657471.html>

Hutchens, Terry. "Indiana football coach Terry Hoeppner dies." USAToday.com. 20 June 2007 < http://www.usatoday.com/sports/college/football/bigten/2007-06-19-in-hoeppner-obit_N.htm >

McGrath, John. "College Football's Superfan," *Lindy's 2005 Pre-season* (2005): p. 18-20.

Papanek, John (editor-in-chief). "25 Words (or less)," *ESPN The Magazine* (29 October 2001): p 32.

University Archives' Student Life and Culture Archival Program. "Origin of the University of Illinois Homecoming." Admin.illinois.edu 2005 <http://www.library.csi.cuny.edu/dept/history/lavender/footnote.hmtl,>

Wolff, Ted (ed.). "Six years and a flip!" *Texas vs. Penn State Official Game Program*, 29 September 1985: p. 25.